William Rushto

Rules and Cautions in English Grammar

Salzwasser

William Rushton

Rules and Cautions in English Grammar

1. Auflage | ISBN: 978-3-84605-598-4

Erscheinungsort: Frankfurt, Deutschland

Erscheinungsjahr: 2020

Salzwasser Verlag GmbH

Reprint of the original, first published in 1869.

RULES AND CAUTIONS

IN

ENGLISH GRAMMAR

FOUNDED ON THE

ANALYSIS OF SENTENCES.

BY WILLIAM RUSHTON, M.A.

PROFESSOR OF HISTORY AND ENGLISH LITERATURE,

QUEEN'S COLLEGE, CORK.

LONDON:

LONGMANS, GREEN, AND CO.

1869.

RULES AND CAUTIONS

IN

ENGLISH GRAMMAR

FOUNDED ON THE

ANALYSIS OF SENTENCES.

BY WILLIAM RUSHTON, M.A.

PROFESSOR OF HISTORY AND ENGLISH LITERATURE,

QUEEN'S COLLEGE, CORK.

LONDON:

LONGMANS, GREEN, AND CO.

1869.

RULES AND CAUTIONS

IN

ENGLISH GRAMMAR

FOUNDED ON THE

ANALYSIS OF SENTENCES.

BY WILLIAM RUSHTON, M.A.

PROFESSOR OF HISTORY AND ENGLISH LITERATURE,

QUEEN'S COLLEGE, CORK.

LONDON:

LONGMANS, GREEN, AND CO.

1869.

CONTENTS.

A 2

WORKS USED*, OR OCCASIONALLY CONSULTED†.

* ADAMS, Dr. ERNEST, 'Elements of the English Language.' *Bell & Daldy*, 1862.

* ANGUS, Dr. JOSEPH, 'Handbook of the English Tongue.' *Religious Tract Society*, 1862.

† ARNOLD, THOMAS KERCHEVER, M.A., 'An English Grammar for Classical Schools.' *Rivingtons*, 1860.

† BAIN, Professor ALEXANDER, 'English Grammar.' *Longmans*, 1863.

† BECKER, Dr. KARL FERDINAND, 'Schulgrammatik der deutschen Sprache.' *Frankfort*, 1862.

† ——————————— 'Grammar of the German Language, adapted to the use of English Students,' by Dr. J. W. FRAEDERS-DORF. *Williams & Norgate*, 1855.

† CAMPBELL, Dr. GEORGE, 'Philosophy of Rhetoric.' *Wm. Tegg & Co.*, 1850.

† COBBETT, WILLIAM, 'Grammar of the English Language.' *London*, 1833.

† DALGLEISH, WILLIAM SCOTT, M.A., 'Grammatical Analysis.' *Simpkin, Marshall & Co.*, 1866.

† FOWLER, WILLIAM C., 'The English Language.' *Cassell, Petter and Galpin*, 1860.

† GARNETT, Rev. RICHARD, 'Philological Essays.' *Williams & Norgate*, 1859.

† HEAD, Sir EDMUND W., Bart., 'Shall' and 'Will.' *Murray*, 1858.

† KEY, Professor THOMAS HEWITT, 'Latin Grammar.' *Bell & Daldy*, 1858.

† LATHAM, Dr. ROBERT GORDON, 'The English Language.' 1862.

† ——————————— 'Elementary English Grammar.' 1860.

† ——————————— 'Logic in its Application to Language.' *Walton & Maberly*, 1856.

* LOWTH, Dr. ROBERT, 'A Short Introduction to English Grammar.' *London*, 1784.

* MASON, CHARLES PETER, B.A., 'English Grammar, including the Principles of Grammatical Analysis.' *Walton & Maberly*, 1858.

* MORELL, Dr. J. D., 'Grammar of the English Language, together with an Exposition of the Analysis of Sentences.' *Longmans*, 1860.

† MURRAY, LINDLEY, 'English Grammar.' *York*, 1824.

† ROWLAND, Rev. THOMAS, 'A Grammar of the Welsh Language.' *Hughes & Butler*, 1857.

† STODDART, Sir JOHN, 'Universal Grammar,' Encyclopædia Metropolitana. *Griffin & Co.*, 1847.

† TOOKE, JOHN HORNE, 'Diversions of Purley,' edited by RICHARD TAYLOR. *Tegg*, 1829.

† WEDGWOOD, HENSLEIGH, M.A., 'Dictionary of English Etymology.' *Trübner & Co.*, 1859.

INTRODUCTION.

WE WILL SUPPOSE that two persons are about to dispute, and that they lay down a certain book upon the table. One says, 'The book is good;' the other says, 'The book is not good;' and they proceed to argue the question.

- The book is the *subject*, that which is *laid down* for discussion; and the term is derived from the Latin *subjectum*, literally meaning, 'that which is laid down.'

Concerning this subject, the quality of goodness is affirmed by one disputant, and denied by the other; and this quality of goodness is said to be *predicated*, that is 'stated' (either affirmed or denied) of the subject.

The word *predicate* is derived from the Latin *prae-dĭcāre*, 'to show forth, proclaim, declare,' a word not to be confounded by young pupils with *prae-dīcĕre*, 'to foretell, prophesy.' Hence the *predicate* means 'that which is stated,' 'the thing or notion affirmed or denied.'

. Now the book and the quality of goodness are the things signified. One disputant says, that the book belongs to the class of things called good; the other says, that the book does not so belong. But the *word* 'book,' and the *word* 'good,' are signs or sounds, which, in our language, represent the thing or notion in question.

The *written* word is a 'sign;' the *spoken* word is a 'sound;' but both the sign and the sound are marks or tokens of the things signified.

In Metaphysics, this distinction is most important. For our purpose, it will be sufficient merely to indicate the distinction, and to observe that the terms *subject* and *predicate* are, in Grammar, applied to the words themselves as they stand in a proposition.

. In this sentence, 'The book is good,' we have a 'proposition,' that is 'an indicative or declaratory sentence;' and it is also called an 'affirmative proposition,' because it affirms or 'says yes.'

But in the sentence, 'The book is not good,' we have a 'negative proposition;' that is, a declaratory sentence which denies, or 'says no.'

In both these sentences, Logicians call 'the book' the *subject* of the proposition, and 'good' the *predicate*; and they term 'is' the *copula*, that is the 'link' or 'tie' which joins the subject and the predicate together. In negative sentences, they attach the negation to the copula; thus, in the sentence 'The book *is not* good,' they make *is not* the copula.

In such propositions as, 'The sun shines,' the Logicians say that both predicate and copula are contained in the word 'shines;' for 'shines' is equivalent to 'is shining;' and so they analyse

Subject.	*Copula.*	*Predicate.*
The sun	is	shining.

Of those writers who have applied logical analysis to the grammar of a modern language, one of the most distinguished is Dr. Karl Ferdinand Becker, whose Grammar of the German Language enjoys a high reputation. In our own country, Dr. Latham has written on 'Logic in its application to Language;' but his treatise on that subject is not so extensively known as his works on the 'English Language.'

The principal followers of Becker, in England, are Dr. Morell and Mr. Mason; to each of whom I have to acknowledge many obligations, though I am often at variance with both, in theory and in detail. Where I am obliged to differ from them, I have endeavoured to state my views with moderation and candour.

More recently, Professor Bain, of Aberdeen, has published an English Grammar founded upon the Analysis of Sentences. This work I have consulted with advantage from time to time.

Now the application of Logic to Grammar is attended with considerable difficulty. If, indeed, the logical subject and predicate were always represented, each by a single word, the application of logical terms to Grammar would be comparatively easy. But in Logic, the subject and the predicate may each be represented by several words; thus

Subject.	Copula.	Predicate.
The early sun	is	brightly shining.
The royal army	is	utterly defeated.

Those writers who apply Logic to Grammar have generally retained the terms *subject* and *predicate*, but with a distinction. Thus, in the sentences just given, ' sun ' (the old-fashioned ' nominative to the verb ') is called the *grammatical subject*; the words ' the early ' are then an *enlargement* of the grammatical subject; and so ' the early sun ' is termed the *enlarged subject*. Hence it follows that ' the early sun,' which is the *logical subject*, is the *enlarged grammatical subject*. In like manner, ' army ' is the *grammatical subject*; and ' the royal army ' (the *subject* in Logic) is the *enlarged subject* in Grammar.

First, they restrict the term, and then they enlarge it; with the additional disadvantage of employing the same term (*subject*), in one sense in Logic, and in another in Grammar.

Similarly the grammatical predicate does not always coincide with the logical predicate; for, in some instances, the logical predicate is, in a grammatical point of view, the ' extended predicate.' Dr. Morell says (*Grammar*, p. 66), ' In grammatical analysis, it is more convenient to regard the copula as belonging to the predicate; so that, instead of having three essential elements to every sentence, as is the case in Logic, we shall have only two, namely (1) the Subject, which expresses the thing about which we are speaking; and (2) the Predicate, which contains what we affirm of the subject.' According to this view, we have, in the examples given, ' is shining,' and ' is defeated,' for the *grammatical predicates*; but we are further informed that the adverbs ' brightly ' and ' utterly ' are *extensions of the predicate*; whence ' is brightly shining ' and ' is utterly defeated ' are *extended predicates*.

Here, again, we observe a restriction followed by an extension.

But the difficulties presented by the Copula are not so easily surmounted. According to the more recent works on Logic, the copula is explained as merely indicating the agreement or disagreement of two terms. But in the system hitherto received, Logicians reduce every proposition to the form 'A is B' or 'A is not B;' and accordingly the verb of the predicate (or the predicate-verb, as we shall term it) is resolved into *is* with a participle; for example, 'The sun shines' is resolved, 'The sun is shining.'

Further, as they maintain that an adjective or participle is not significant by itself, they tell us that some substantive must be supplied to complete the sense. Thus, 'Thomas is wise' is explained to be 'Thomas is a wise man.' So, 'The sun is shining' is 'The sun is a shining body,' or 'a shining substance.' Hence the sentence 'John walks' is resolved into 'John is walking,' and this is explained 'John is a walking man.'

They are not, however, all agreed as to the exact form of the copula. Some of them say, that any finite part of the verb *be* may be so used; others restrict the copula to the present tense indicative of that verb. According to the view taken by the latter, this sentence, 'The way of the wicked shall be darkness,' must be resolved,

The way of the wicked
       is   a way which shall be darkness,
or   is   a way tending to darkness.
                 (See *Hill's Aldrich*, p. 18.)

All this seems very artificial. But further, it gives rise to numerous ambiguities; and we shall see that the word *is*, innocent as it looks, is one of the most deceptive little words in the language.

First of all, the word *is*, apart from its use as a copula, may be employed by itself as a predicate-verb, denoting existence; for example, 'God is,' that is, 'God exists.' And so here :—

My thought, whose murder yet is but fantastical,
Shakes so my single state of man, that function
Is smothered in surmise; and nothing *is*,
But what *is not*.

Macbeth, i. 3.

We find an emphatic use of *is* in a remarkable passage in
the *Winter's Tale*, iv. 3, touching upon the relation of art to
nature :—

This is an art
Which does *mend* nature, *change* it rather; but
The art itself *is* nature.

Shakespeare often dwells upon the distinction between
'being' and 'seeming;' as in the dialogue between the Queen
and Hamlet :—

Queen. Good Hamlet, cast thy nighted colour off,
And let thine eye look like a friend on Denmark.
Do not, for ever, with thy vailed lids
Seek for thy noble father in the dust:
Thou know'st, 'tis common; all that live must die,
Passing through nature to eternity.
Hamlet. Ay, madam, it is common.
Queen.   If it be,
Why seems.it so particular with thee ?
Hamlet. Seems, madam ! nay it *is* : I know not
'seems.'
'Tis not alone my inky cloak, good mother,
Nor customary suits of solemn black,
Nor windy suspiration of forced breath,
No, nor the fruitful river in the eye,
Nor the dejected haviour of the visage,
Together with all forms, modes, *shows* of grief,
That can denote me truly ; these, indeed, *seem*,
For they are actions that a man might play :
But I have *that within* which passeth *show* ;
These but the trappings, and the suits of woe.

Hamlet, i. 2.

Compare the assertion of Iago :

For, sir,
It is as sure as you are Roderigo,
Were I the Moor, I would not be Iago :
In following him, I follow but myself;

Heaven is my judge, not I for love and duty
But *seeming* so, for my peculiar end:
For when my outward action doth demonstrate
The native act and figure of my heart
In compliment extern, 'tis not long after
But I will wear my heart upon my sleeve
For daws to peck at: I *am not* what I *am*.

Othello, i. 1.

Now contrast the following passage:

Sir Toby. Jove bless thee, master Parson.

Clown (personating Sir Topas the Curate). *Bonos dies*, Sir Toby: for, as the old hermit of Prague, that never saw pen and ink, very wittily said to a niece of King Gorboduc, ' That that is is'; so, I *being* master Parson, *am* master Parson; for what is 'that' but *that*, and 'is' but *is*?

This is the very point. No doubt, ' whatever is, is,' in the sense that ' whatever exists, exists.' But let us consider the various significations which may be implied in the word *is*, used as a copula, in the simple sentence ' A is B.'

' A is B ' may mean,

1. A is co-extensive with B :   Man is a rational animal.
2. A is of the same meaning with B :   Fidelity is faithfulness.
3. A is in the condition implied by B :   The sailor is saved.
4. A is included in the class of B :   Man is an animal.
5. A is possessed of attributes common to the class of B :   Man is an animal.
6. A is possessed of attributes implied in the term B :   God is a Spirit.
7. A is the cause of B :   Intemperance is the death of thousands.
8. A is like B :   The hero is a lion in the fight.
9. A is analogous to B :   Athens is the eye of Greece.

In fact, it is difficult to fix a limit to the various meanings which may be assigned to the word *is* in the simple sentence ' A is B.'

In Mathematics we find nothing of this laxity in the statement of propositions. There everything is judged by measure, number, or proportion. Things are said to be equal, or not equal, to one another; in exact ratio, or not in exact ratio: so that there is no room for any play of meaning.

But in ordinary conversation, or argument, the latitude is so great, that it is no wonder if misunderstandings arise. The only wonder is, that disputants can ever come to issue at all.

For example, we hear it said that 'Knowledge *is* power.' But what does this mean? It may signify that knowledge is identical with power, or as good as power, or a kind of power, or a source of power, or the way to power, &c. &c. Practically, it is generally understood to imply that knowledge gives or confers power; so that a man who possesses knowledge has more power than another who does not possess such knowledge. But the proposition says ' Knowledge *is* power;' and this rhetorical phrase conveys to the mind an indefinite notion of grandeur.

Again, Napoleon proclaims that ' The empire *is* peace.' No one supposes this to mean ' peace at any price,' or that France will not go to war under any circumstances. It may mean that Napoleon will not make war for the wanton love of it, or unless he is obliged. But while this proposition has no definite meaning, it carries an imposing sound, and has actually produced the effect of tranquillising the apprehensions of neighbouring states. This, no doubt, was the object intended.

Hence, when a man says that anything *is* anything, or that anything *is* something else, we cannot tell whether he is right or wrong until we know what he means by *is*.

And we may well doubt whether this word is not one of the most unsuitable that could be chosen as the Copula or Tie to join other words together. Still more strange does it seem that every other verb must be resolved into a participle coupled with this ambiguous word *is*.

On these discrepancies in the Logical system, Mr. Mason remarks (*Grammar*, § 847, *note*):—' In Logic, the terms *predicate* and *copula* involve a little difficulty. In the proposition " The earth is a globe," it would be said that the predicate (*prædicatum* or *thing asserted*) is *a globe*; that is, *what we assert* of the earth is, *a globe*. This mode of speaking requires a technical meaning to be put upon it, before it has any sense. More strictly in accordance with the meaning of the language, it should be said that *what we assert*, or the *thing asserted* about the earth, is its *being a globe*. Again, the so-called *copula* in Logic is really more than a copula or *link* by which two ideas are connected. If we have a finite form of the verb *be* (and without a finite form there can be no predication), we may ignore, but we cannot eliminate, either the root-meaning of the verb, or the *idea of time*. *Is* and *are* involve the notion of present time as essentially as *was* and *were* that of past time. This little difficulty however is quietly swallowed by the logicians, who tell us that the copula, as such, has no relation to time. The fact is, that technical logic ought to have some abstract sign for the copula, something like = in mathematics, and not the verb *be* at all. Now if we put together the two facts that there may be a perfect proposition without the verb *be*, and that when that verb is used there is no proposition unless the verb *be* is in a finite form, the inference is plain that the real copula consists of those inflections by which a verb assumes a finite form.'

Hence Mr. Mason considers that ' the grammatical copula in every sentence consists of the *personal inflections* of the verb; that is, the inflections by which number and person are marked, and by which the verb is made a *finite* verb. In the sentence " Time flies," the subject is *Time*; that which is predicated or asserted of *time* is *flying*; the personal termination of the verb *flies* unites this idea to the subject.'

The same doctrine is laid down by Mill, *Logic*, I. iv. He says:—' A predicate and a subject are all that is necessarily required to make up a proposition; but as we cannot conclude, from merely seeing two names put together, that they are a predicate and a subject, that is, that one of them is intended to be affirmed or denied of the other, it is necessary that there should be some mode or form of indicating that such is the intention; some sign to distinguish a predication from any other sign of discourse. This is sometimes done by a slight alteration of one of the words, called an *inflection*; as when we say "Fire burns," the change of the second word from *burn* to *burns* showing that we mean to affirm the predicate "burn" of the subject "fire."'

But let us inquire whether any *link* or *tie* is absolutely necessary to unite words in a sentence; whether the mere juxtaposition is not enough; and whether there may not be predication without a finite verb.

In Latin we frequently find such forms as these:—*Numen lumen*; *Victrix fortunæ virtus*; *Salus populi lex suprema*; *Vex populi vox Dei*, and many similar sentences.

Grammarians assert that the copula is omitted here, and that *est*, 'is,' must be 'understood,' as they phrase it. But that is the very point at issue. What they mean is that they think it ought to be there, and they tell us to supply it. We contend that it is not there; and that, if the Latin does not want it, neither do we.

In Hebrew, the union of Subject and Predicate is most commonly expressed by simply writing them together, without any copula; as 'Jehovah mighty,' for 'Jehovah *is* mighty;' so, 'The gold of that land good' (*Genesis* ii. 12), for 'The gold of that land *is* good.' In *Zechariah* xiii. 9, our version reads:—'I will say, It *is* my people; and they shall say, The Lord *is* my God;' but the original has it, 'I will say, My people he; and he shall say, Jehovah my God.'

Less frequently the copula is expressed by the verb *hayah*, 'be.' See Gesenius, *Hebrew Grammar*, § 141.

In Chinese there are no parts of speech in the sense recognised by us; but difference of meaning depends upon the order of words. Thus, *ta fu* means 'a great man;' but *fu ta* signifies 'the man is great.' See Max Müller, *Science of Language*, Second Series, p. 85.

There is room to doubt whether any copula, link, or tie is absolutely necessary in a sentence. We are accustomed to expect it in English and other languages; and we are ready to infer that where it is not found, we must supply some connecting link. Here we may perhaps do well to revise our judgment.

We should also beware of rashness in applying logical terms to Grammar. We have reason to fear that nothing but confusion must result from an attempt to strain the logical terms beyond the purposes for which they were originally designed. It is always more or less dangerous to transfer the nomenclature of one science to another; and if we can do so at all, we should endeavour to alter the signification of the terms as little as possible. This, however, we may do: if we wish to adapt the logical method, or any part of it, to grammatical purposes, we may modify the terms to suit the requirements of Grammar.

A valuable suggestion is offered by Professor Key in his *Latin Grammar*, § 847. He says:—' Some grammarians are in the habit of treating those sentences which have the verb *be* as the forms to which all others are to be reduced. Hence they divide a sentence into three parts:—

The Subject, that of which you speak;

The Predicate, that which you say of the subject; and

The Copula, or verb *be*, which unites the subject and predicate.

' Thus, for instance, in the sentence or proposition " Man is an animal," *man* is the subject, *animal* the predicate, *is* the copula.

' The subject according to this system is the nominative case. When, instead of the verb *be*, another verb is used, they resolve it into some part of the verb *be* and a participle. Thus, *Cicero writes a letter*, is resolved into *Cicero is writing a letter*; where *Cicero* is the subject, *writing a letter* the predicate, *is* the copula.

' The substantive, adjective, or participle that accompanies the verb *be* as a predicate, is in Latin made to agree in case with the subject nominative, and is called the nominative of the predicate.'

So far we have two distinct terms: the *subject-nominative*, corresponding to '*the* nominative' of the old grammars; and the *predicate-nominative*, of which the old grammars took no special notice. Hence, in 'The sun is shining,' *sun* is the 'subject-nominative,' and *shining* is the 'predicate-nominative;' while in the sentence, 'The early sun is brightly shining,' *sun* is still the 'subject-nominative,' and *shining* is still the 'predicate-nominative;' while the words, 'the early,' and 'brightly,' are qualifications of the subject-nominative and the predicative-nominative respectively.

By this method, we have the great advantage of obtaining distinct terms for the grammatical subject, and for certain forms of the grammatical predicate. But the difficulty of the copula is untouched. In all verbs, except the verb *be*, the copula and predicate are blended together; and the artifice of resolving a verb into some part of the verb *be* and a participle is open to many objections. Besides, as Mr. Mason observes (*English Grammar, Preface,* p. x.), 'If in the sentence, "He is rich," *rich* is the predicate and *is* the copula, why, in the sentence, "He becomes rich," should we not call *becomes* the copula? The notion of *becoming* has quite as good a right to be considered copulative as the notion of *being.*'

This is the most knotty point of the whole question; and various solutions have been proposed. Dr. Morell, as we have seen, thinks it more convenient to regard the copula as belonging to the predicate. Mr. Kerchever Arnold proposes to make different kinds of copulas; for example, he calls 'become,' 'seem,' &c. *strengthened copulas.* Mr. Mason says, 'the difficulty is removed, and the anomaly obviated, when we regard neither *be* nor *become* as a copula, but treat them as verbs of *incomplete predication.*'

The truth is, that the Logical and the Grammatical systems have been drawn up at various times, and with different views; so that when we bring them together we find a discrepancy.

The Logical arrangement is threefold:

Subject.	*Copula,*	*Predicate.*
Man	is	mortal.

The Grammatical arrangement is twofold :

Nominative.	*Verb.*
Time	flies.

In Grammar, we must take the grammatical arrangement as the basis, but with a modification of the terms : we call the nominative of the subject the *subject-nominative*, and the verb of the predicate the *predicate-verb*. We discard the copula, and make no distinction whatever between the verb *be*, and any other intransitive verb. We analyse these sentences in the following manner, taking the second as the model :—

I. Time	*Subject-nominative*
flies.	*Predicate-verb.*
II. Man	*Subject-nominative*
is	*Predicate-verb*
mortal.	*Predicate-nominative.*

By the term *Predicate-verb* we understand the ' verb of the predicate,' or ' the verb in the predicate.' According to this method we are able to point out the chief word in the logical subject, namely the *subject-nominative*; and the chief word or words in the logical predicate, whether it be a *predicate-verb*, or a *predicate-nominative* accompanying a *predicate-verb*.

It follows that we make no distinction between such sentences as these :—

1. Thomas is wise.
2. Thomas seems wise.

We analyse:

I. Thomas	*Subject-nominative*
is	*Predicate-verb*
wise.	*Predicate-nominative.*
II. Thomas	*Subject-nominative*
seems	*Predicate-verb*
wise.	*Predicate-nominative.*

It may be objected, that after all this circumlocution, we have come back very nearly to the old-fashioned doctrine of 'the nominative and the verb.' So we have; but with this difference, that we have explained what is meant by '*the* nominative,' and '*the* verb.'

Under the old system, it is common to say that a verb must agree with its nominative case; whereas, more strictly, the verb agrees with a 'substantive in the nominative case;' and further, the *nominative* is often used as synonymous with the *subject* of the sentence.

But although, no doubt, there is inaccuracy under the old system, there may be some danger of confusion under the new systems which are propounded. If, on the one hand, the term 'nominative' is loosely employed to denote the 'subject,' it is no less true, on the other hand, that many pupils of the new school bandy about the terms 'subject' and 'predicate' without any definite notion of the meaning implied in those terms. Sometimes, in examination, when a boy has written down 'enlargement of the subject,' or 'extension of the predicate,' he fancies that he has said a good thing, no matter whether the phrase be appropriate or not. We must try to avoid error on both sides. Where the old school talked of '*the* nominative,' we speak of the '*subject*-nominative;' and where the new school employs an ambiguous term 'subject,' we use the more precise 'subject-*nominative*.'

ANALYSIS OF SENTENCES.

CHAPTER I.

SIMPLE SENTENCES, INDICATIVE.

1. A Sentence is a collection of words expressing a complete thought : as ' The bird sings ; ' ' Summer is charming.'

A collection of words, not expressing a complete thought, is sometimes termed a *Phrase* : as ' The poems of Homer ; ' ' Quietly waiting ; ' ' Now and then.'

Sentences have been divided into Simple and Compound. Simple sentences, again, have been subdivided into Indicative, Interrogative, Imperative, and Optative. We shall, in the first instance, confine our attention to Simple Indicative (i. e. declaratory) Sentences, which may be either Affirmative or Negative : as,

> Mirth is good . . . . . (*affirmative*).
> Folly is not good . . . . (*negative*).

SIMPLE INDICATIVE SENTENCES.

2. A Simple Sentence contains one subject-nominative, and one predicate-verb : as ' Time flies.' Or it may contain one subject-nominative, one predicate-verb, and one predicate-nominative : as ' Mirth is good.'

We shall, first of all, consider the subject-nominative and the predicate-nominative, and then proceed to the use of verbs. A remark, however, is necessary in reference to terms which will repeatedly occur, namely, *qualification* and *substantive*.

By a *qualification* we understand any word or phrase which explains, modifies, or limits any other word or phrase. Thus, as an adjective qualifies a noun, so an adverb qualifies a verb.

A *substantive* is a word which, by itself and single-handed,

B

can form either a subject or a predicate.* The term comprehends nouns, certain of the pronouns, and the infinitive mood of a verb used substantively.† In employing the word *noun* we shall always understand a *noun-substantive*.

THE SUBJECT-NOMINATIVE.

3. The subject-nominative answers to the question *who?* or *what?* and must be a substantive, as,

    1. A *noun* . . . . . . *Alfred* is king.

    2. A *pronoun* . . . . . *He* speaks well.

    3. An *adjective* used substantively; more commonly in the plural, but sometimes in the singular: as, ' The *wicked* flee when no man pursueth; but the *righteous* is as bold as a lion.'

      Obs.—The adjective used substantively is most commonly found in connection with the definite article. I do not hold, however, that the adjective and the article are together equal to a substantive; but that the adjective being used substantively is capable of receiving the article.

    4. The *infinitive mood* of a verb, used substantively: as,

      To err is human.

      Seeing is believing.

      Obs.—The infinitive in *-ing* is termed by some grammarians the *gerund*. The form in *-ing* will demand special consideration. See §§ 31–35.

With impersonal verbs, as they are termed, the subject is indefinite, and the pronoun *it* takes the place of a subject-nominative: as ' It rains,' ' It freezes.'

There is another use of the pronoun *it*, which must be carefully observed. In English we often place the subject last, and the predicate first. In such cases we may use the pronoun *it* as the representative or forerunner of the subject, to show that the subject is coming. Thus, instead of saying ' To ride is pleasant,' we may say ' *It* is pleasant to ride;' but in both instances *to ride* is the logical subject, and *pleasant* is the predicate. See Whately, *Logic*, II. 1, 3.

The adverb *there* is used in a manner somewhat similar: as, ' *There* came a philosopher from India.'

---

* Latham, *Logic in its Application to Language*, p. 254.

† Mason, *English Grammar*, § 352 and § 131.

QUALIFICATIONS OF THE SUBJECT-NOMINATIVE.

4. The subject-nominative may be qualified by an *attribute*, that is, by an adjective, or by any word or phrase having the force of an adjective: as,

1. By an adjective:
   A *merry* heart goes all the day.

2. By a demonstrative pronoun:
   These things are true.

3. By the definite article:
   The die is cast.

> *Obs.*—Some grammarians consider the article so closely connected with the noun as to form one notion. But, strictly speaking, the definite article is a qualification; indeed, in Greek and German, as well as in English, the definite article is a modified form of the demonstrative pronoun.

4. By a noun standing in apposition with the subject-nominative: as,
   Cicero, *the orator*, made a speech;
   where the additional words, 'the orator,' inform us that it was Marcus Cicero, and not brother Quintus, or any other Cicero.

5. A substantive in the possessive case has the force of an adjective: thus the *royal army* means the 'King's army,' or the 'Queen's army.' Hence a noun or pronoun in the possessive case may be used to qualify the subject-nominative: as,
   Buckingham's end was unfortunate.
   His work was done.

6. The English possessive may be otherwise expressed by means of the preposition *of*: 'the *King's* army' is 'the army *of the King*;' and both forms are equivalent to a genitive case in Latin. Hence the prepositional phrase *of the King* may be employed to qualify a subject-nominative: as,
   The army *of the King* was defeated.
   A man *of virtue* is respected.
   The point *of honour* is debated.

Other prepositions are used in the same way: as,
   The desire *for fame* is natural.

7. Passive participles are equivalent to adjectives, and may qualify a subject-nominative: as,

> *Born* to command, he ruled with firmness.
> *Adorned* with amiable qualities, she was an agreeable woman.

But the case of active participles is not so clear. In the sentence 'William, *having conquered Harold,* ascended the throne,' Dr. Morell considers the phrase 'having conquered Harold' as an 'enlargement of the subject,' or, as we term it, a 'qualification of the subject-nominative.' It would seem, however, that the phrase in question qualifies the predicate rather than the subject : for the meaning is that 'William ascended the throne when he had conquered Harold,' or, 'after having conquered Harold.' In fact, we might turn the participle into a verb, coupled with the conjunction *and,* thus throwing the phrase into the predicate : 'William *conquered* Harold, *and* ascended the throne.' On the other hand, if we expressed the sentence thus, 'William, the conqueror of Harold, ascended the throne,' the phrase 'the conqueror of Harold' would be a manifest qualification of the subject-nominative.

THE PREDICATE-NOMINATIVE.

5. The predicate-nominative answers the question, *Of what kind ? Of what nature ?* or, *Of what class ?*

It may be :

1. An *adjective* : . . . . Heaven is *high.*
2. A *noun* : . . . . . Arthur is *king.*
3. A *pronoun* : . . . . I am *he.*
4. The *infinitive mood* of a verb used substantively: To hear is *to obey.*
        Seeing is *believing.*

> *Obs.*—This form in *-ing* is called by some grammarians the *gerund.*

An apparent difficulty occurs where an adverb, or a prepositional phrase, occupies the place of the predicate : as,

> Thomas is *here.*
> He is *of sound mind.*

Three explanations of this construction might be offered :

1. That these sentences are elliptical ; in other words, that the predicate-ncminative is omitted. For, it is argued, we might supply its place in the following way :

Thomas is (present) here.

He is (a man) of sound mind.

In some instances we are obliged to supply a word. For example, we cannot say 'He is of great ability,' but ' He is *a man* of great ability.' So also, 'It is *a matter* of difficulty : ' ' That was *an affair* of honour;' where the words *man, matter,* and *affair* are the predicate-nominatives of the sentences; while the prepositional phrases, ' of great ability,' ' of difficulty,' ' of honour,' are used to qualify the predicate-nominatives. We learn what sort of a man he is, what kind of an affair it was, and so forth. According to this view, in the sentence ' Thomas is here,' the predicate-nominative is understood, and the adverb *here* qualifies the predicate-nominative understood. But this artifice of ' understanding' and ' supplying' is always open to suspicion.

2. That the verb *is,* here employed to assert ' existence' or ' presence,' stands as a predicate-verb; and that the adverb *here,* or the adverbial phrase *of sound mind,* is a qualification of the predicate-verb ' is.'

3. That the adverb or adverbial phrase is used as a predicate-nominative, or in the place of a predicate-nominative. Professor Key is guarded in dealing with this construction. He says (*Latin Grammar,* § 876, 1), ' although a noun substantive or adjective with ĕs—*be,* usually constitutes the predicate, *the place may be supplied* by a descriptive word or phrase of a different form : as (*a*) a genitive or ablative of quality ; (*b*) dative of the light in which a thing is regarded ; (*c*) a prepositional phrase ; or (*d*) an adverb.' And again, § 1401 : ' Adverbs are used in some phrases with the verb ĕs—*be,* when an adjective or participle *might have been expected.'*

6. The truth is, that in practical composition, the distinction between the parts of speech is not so absolute as etymology would lead us to suppose. The function, or power in a sentence, seems to determine the character of the word ; and on this principle, perhaps, we may venture to call the adverb a predicate. If so, of course we may extend the same principle to the adverbial phrase.

In Fraedersdorf's translation of Becker (*German Grammar,*

§ 195), we read : ' The predicate is expressed, in German as in English, by

    a. A verb.

    b. An adjective (not inflected).

    c. A substantive in the nominative case.

    d. A substantive in the genitive case.

    e. A substantive with a preposition.

    f. An adverb.'

Here Becker says distinctly that the predicate may be expressed by an *adverb*.

QUALIFICATIONS OF THE PREDICATE-NOMINATIVE.

7. Of course, these qualifications will depend upon the nature of the predicate-nominative itself. Hence,

    I. An adjective used as a predicate-nominative may be qualified,

      1. By an adverb : as,

          Heaven is *very* high.

          Charles is *exceedingly* foolish.

      2. By an adverbial phrase : as,

          Harry is praiseworthy *in some respects.*

    II. A noun used as a predicate-nominative may be qualified,

      1. By an adjective : as,

          Arthur is a *good* king :

      and this, in turn, may be further qualified by an adverb, as,

          Arthur is a *very good* king.

      2. By a noun or pronoun in the possessive case : as,

          Bolingbroke was the *poet's* friend.

          That was *his* fault.

      3. By a prepositional phrase : as,

          Buckingham was the servant *of the king.*

          He is a man *of ability.*

      4. By a noun used in apposition : as,

          The greatest Roman orator was Cicero, *the consul.*

In this sentence, analysed grammatically, the subject-nominative is ' orator ; ' the adjectives ' greatest ' and ' Roman ' are qualifications of the subject-nominative ; the predicate-nominative is ' Cicero ;' and *the consul* (used in apposition with ' Cicero,' and therefore in the nominative case) is a qualification of the predicate-nominative.

 III. An infinitive mood in *-ing*, otherwise termed the gerund, used substantively as a predicate-nominative, may be qualified by an adjective : as,

   That was *good* hearing :

And this may be further qualified by an adverb,

   That was *very good* hearing.

THE PREDICATE-VERB.

8. The older grammarians divided verbs into active, passive, and neuter; but this arrangement sometimes led to perplexity. It was easy to understand that ' to kill' was an active verb, and that ' to sleep' was neuter. But the verb ' to run,' which implies lively action, in the sense of bodily motion, was termed a *neuter* verb, because the action does not pass over to any other person or thing, but remains with the agent.

To meet this objection, later grammarians proposed a new classification. They termed Transitives (from the Latin *transire*, ' to go over') all those verbs in which the action could be supposed to ' pass over' to any object; while those to which such a supposition could not apply were called Intransitives. In this view, *to kill* was considered Active and Transitive ; whereas *to run* was Active but Intransitive.

But we should beware of confounding the meaning of the verb as a word, with its grammatical power in a sentence. We should keep to one principle ; and if any verbs possess a certain grammatical power in a sentence, while others do not, this alone seems to be a fair basis of classification. Now some verbs can govern an objective case, while others cannot ; practically the former correspond to Transitives, and the latter to Intransitives ; nor is there any necessity to alter these terms ; but we must modify their signification, and we propose a definition which refers exclusively to the power of verbs in a sentence.

 Transitives :—Those verbs which can govern an objective case ; as, *love, hate, kill, flatter*, &c.
 Intransitives :—Those verbs which can *not* govern an objective case ; as, *run, walk, sit, sleep*, &c.

The term ' neuter,' as applied to verbs, should be altogether discarded; and the terms ' active' and ' passive' should be strictly confined to the *forms*, or, as they are commonly called, the *voices*.

Hence we would not speak of ' active verbs' or ' passive verbs,' but we say that Transitives are used in two voices, the Active and the Passive; whereas Intransitives are used in one form alone, which (in point of *form*) corresponds with the Active voice of verbs Transitive.

9. As a general rule, though one liable to many exceptions, Intransitives are capable of furnishing a complete sense (or of making a complete predication); while Transitives almost always require some word or words to complete the predicate.

For example, in these sentences, *He sleeps, She sits, They run*, the verbs are Intransitive, and the meaning in each sentence is complete. But when we say *John beats*, the question naturally arises ' *Whom* does he beat?' and if we answer ' *John beats Thomas*,' the inquiry is satisfied. It is not that ' John beats' tells us *less* than ' John sleeps;' but it raises a new question, and until this is answered there is a sense of incompleteness.

There are, indeed, exceptions both ways. Some Intransitives, as *become, seem*, and many others, are not by themselves capable of forming a complete predication; and on the other hand, a Transitive verb is sometimes used *absolutely*, as the phrase is: for example, *William conquers*, that is, *William is victorious*; but in such sentences the meaning is, ' William conquers all his enemies,' or ' every obstacle,' or words to the same effect.

INTRANSITIVES.

10. As a general rule Intransitive verbs are capable of giving a complete sense, or, in other words, of making a complete predication: as *He comes, She goes, Time flies*. Here the subject-nominative and the predicate-verb are quite sufficient to constitute a perfect sentence; and we analyse,

subject-nominative	*predicate-verb*
Time	flies.

It will be remembered that by the term *predicate-verb* we mean the leading verb of the predicate. The Intransitive (used as a predicate-verb) may be qualified in various ways by adverbs and adverbial phrases: as, 'Time flies *swiftly*,' 'Time flies *with great rapidity*;' but it will be better to postpone these considerations until we come to discuss, generally, the qualifications of predicate-verbs.

But some intransitives do not form a complete predication. To say 'Thomas becomes,' or 'Harry seems,' would have no meaning; but 'Thomas becomes *rich*,' 'Harry seems *wise*,' are intelligible sentences.

Here the adjectives *rich* and *wise* complete the predication: they tell us what it is that Thomas and Harry 'become' and 'seem,' and they agree in case with the subject-nominatives. They are, in fact, predicate-nominatives. As for example: 'Thomas becomes rich.'

Thomas . . . . *Subject-nominative*.
becomes . . . . . . *Predicate-verb*.
rich . . . . *Predicate-nominative*.

11. As before remarked, we treat all parts of the verb *be* as parts of an ordinary Intransitive verb; and therefore we analyse 'Harry *was* first,' 'Edward *will be* successful,' thus:

Harry . . . . . . *Subject-nominative*.
was . . . . *Predicate-verb*.
first . . . . *Predicate-nominative*.
Edward . . . . . . *Subject-nominative*.
will be . . . . . . *Predicate-verb*.
successful . . . . . *Predicate-nominative*.

The use of the predicate-nominative accompanying a predicate-verb is not confined to verbs of incomplete predication. We may say 'The grass grows,' and this gives a complete sense; but we may also say 'Thomas grows tall,' where we have,

Thomas . . . . . . *Subject-nominative*.
grows . . . . . . *Predicate-verb*.
tall . . . . *Predicate-nominative*.

But very great care is necessary to determine this use of the adjective, from the fact that many of our old Saxon adjectives appear to be used adverbially. For example, in these sentences,

The rose smells *sweet*,
The wine tastes *sour*,

the adjectives 'sweet' and 'sour' are not predicate-nominatives, or nominatives at all, but what are called in Latin grammar *neuter accusatives*. See § 23.

TRANSITIVES.

12. The Predicate-verb Transitive does not, as a general rule, furnish a complete meaning, inasmuch as it raises a new question, demanding an answer; and the word or words which, after a Transitive verb, help to complete the predicate, are usually termed the *object*.

But as we distinguished between the logical 'subject' and the grammatical 'subject-nominative,' so we must make a difference between the *object* and the *objective*, by which we mean 'a substantive in the objective case.'

For example, in the sentence 'Thomas reads books,' the word *books* completing the predicate is the 'object' of the verb *reads*, and is also the 'objective' governed by the verb. But when we say 'Thomas reads many good books,' the *object* is the phrase 'many good books;' but the *objective* is 'books;' while 'many' and 'good' are *qualifications of the objective*.

> *Obs.*—The term 'objective' is equivalent to 'object-accusa-tive,' 'object-dative,' or 'object-genitive.' We shall hereafter distinguish between the 'object-accusative' and the 'subject-accusative,' commonly called the 'ac-cusative before the infinitive.'

13. Whenever we have occasion to discriminate between the objective immediately dependent upon a Transitive verb, and other objectives in a sentence, we shall call the former the Primary Objective.

The Primary Objective.

We have said that the objective must be a substantive: and it may be,

1. A *noun*: Scipio loved *honour*.
2. A *pronoun*: The people saw *him*.
3. An *adjective* used substantively:
    The Lord loveth the *righteous*.

> *Obs.*—As far as the mere form is concerned, 'the righteous' may be either singular or plural.

4. A verb in the *infinitive mood*, used substantively:
    He desires *to study*.
    He practises *writing*.

Qualifications of the Objective.

14. These are very much the same as the qualifications of the subject-nominative. We may have,

1. An *adjective*: as,
   The baker makes *good* bread.

2. A demonstrative *pronoun*:
   We know *these* things.

3. The definite *article*:
   Wellington pursued *the* enemy.

4. A *noun* in apposition with the objective:
   They applauded Cicero *the consul*.

5. A *noun* or *pronoun* in the possessive case:
   Falkland beheld the *king's* army.
   Cromwell knew *his* weakness.

6. A *prepositional phrase*:
   Cromwell defeated the army *of the king*.

The Complement-Objective.

15. It is clear that there is a difference between the sentences 'They applauded Cicero the consul' and 'They made Cicero consul:' for in the first instance, the term 'consul' is merely added by way of explanation, to qualify the objective 'Cicero;' but in the latter case it is essential to the meaning; it tells us what they made him. Here, as the objective stands in close connection with the predicate-verb and helps to complete the predication, we shall term it the *complement-objective*. We analyse the sentence thus:

They . . . . *Subject-nominative.*
made . . . . . . *Predicate-verb.*
Cicero . . . . . . *Objective (primary).*
consul . . . . . . *Complement-objective.*

This 'complement-objective' is sometimes termed the 'factitive accusative,' from the Latin verb *facere*, ' to make,' which is taken as a type of the whole class of verbs admitting this construction. But we must guard against supposing that the construction is in any way peculiar to verbs of ' making;' on the contrary, a general principle is involved.

The complement-objective may be,

1. A *noun*: as
   The citizens made Whittington *mayor*.

2. An *adjective*: as
   Alfred made his people *happy*.

Analysing these sentences, we have

1. The . . . *Article, qualifying the subject-nominative.*
   citizens . . *Subject-nominative.*
   made . . *Predicate-verb.*
   Whittington *Objective (primary).*
   mayor . . *Complement-objective.*

2. Alfred . . *Subject-nominative.*
   made . . . *Predicate-verb.*
   his . . . *Pronoun, in the possessive case, qualifying the primary objective.*
   people . . *Objective (primary).*
   happy . . *Complement-objective.*

And observe, that when these verbs are employed in the passive voice, just as the primary objective is turned into the subject-nominative, so the complement-objective is turned into a 'complement-nominative:' thus,

'Whittington was made *mayor* by the citizens;' and the analysis will be

Whittington *Subject-nominative.*
was . . . *Predicate-verb.*
made . . . *Predicate-nominative.*
mayor . . *Complement-nominative.*
by the citizens *Adverbial* (or *prepositional*) *phrase, qualifying the predicate-nominative.*

16. As we have said, this construction is by no means confined to verbs of 'making.' It is found:

1. With verbs of 'choosing, electing, appointing,' as,
   The Romans elected Cicero *consul.*
   The people chose Arteveldt *burgomaster.*

2. With verbs of 'calling' and 'naming:' as,
   They called him *John.*
   The English named Edward *Longshanks.*

Some difficulty arises with 'to think, deem, consider, regard, &c.,' in such sentences as:

They think him *happy.*
He deemed them *foolish.*
They considered him *a philosopher.*

It might be argued: if, in these sentences,

They *make* him *happy,*
They *call* him *happy,*

'happy' is a complement-objective, the same explanation must surely apply to the sentence:

They *think* him *happy*.

But in 'make him' and 'call him,' *him* is the immediate object of the verbs. They do 'make him' and 'call him;' but they do not 'think him.' In 'make . . . happy' and 'call . . . happy,' the adjective is so bound up with the verb, that the idea might be expressed in each case by a single word, 'beatify' and 'felicitate.'

On the other hand, when we say 'They think him happy,' we mean

They think that he is happy, or,
They think him (to be) happy.

If this view be correct, the construction must be explained upon another principle, which we shall discuss when we consider the doctrine of the 'subject-accusative.'

In support of this view we may remark the tendency to insert after these verbs a conjunction or some other particle before the second objective: as,

They regarded him *as* a philosopher.
They took him *for* a judge.

The Secondary Objective.

17. Quite apart from the Complement-objective, many Transitive verbs can govern two cases. In Latin, where there is great variety of inflection, these are readily distinguished: thus, some verbs are said to govern two accusatives; others an accusative and a dative; others an accusative and a genitive.

Grammarians have classified these instances under the headings of the 'direct' and 'indirect' object; or, as others prefer to say, the 'immediate' and the 'remote' object. But as we wish to keep the terms *object* and *objective* quite distinct, we employ the terms Primary and Secondary Objective.

Let us take the sentence, 'Socrates taught the Athenians philosophy.' In Latin this would be *Socrates Athenienses philosophiam docuit;* where the Latin grammarians say that *philosophiam* is the 'immediate' object, and *Athenienses* the 'remote' object. On the same principle, in 'Socrates taught the Athenians philosophy,' we might call *philosophy* the primary objective, and the *Athenians* the secondary objective.

But we ought to observe that much depends upon the way

in which we look at a sentence of this kind. It may be said, with truth, that what Socrates taught was 'philosophy,' and that the persons affected by his teaching were the 'Athenians;' in fact, that

Socrates taught philosophy *to* the Athenians; and that therefore 'philosophy' is the primary objective.

But it is equally true that

Socrates taught (i. e., instructed) the Athenians *in* philosophy :

and according to this view, the *Athenians* take the place of the primary objective.

The former aspect of the case appears to have generally occurred to the writers upon Greek and Latin grammar; and we shall adhere to it; but where two interpretations are possible, neither should be passed over in total silence.

18. After verbs of 'giving, granting,' &c., the secondary objective is generally preceded by the preposition *to*, corresponding to a substantive in the dative case in Latin : as,

Augustus gave power *to Tiberius.*
William granted land *to Fitzroy.*

The pronouns *me, thee, him, her, them*, represent datives in Anglo-Saxon; accordingly they are used as secondary objectives without the preposition *to* :

The master gave *me* a book.
The citizens granted *him* a triumph.
The prince gave *her* a crown.

It is evident that the terms 'primary' and 'secondary' have nothing to do with the *position* of the objective in a sentence. Nor can any general rule be laid down to determine the application of the terms. It frequently happens that the primary objective is used in speaking of *things*, and the secondary objective in speaking of *persons*; but not always, as may be seen from the next example.

19. After verbs of 'accusing, charging,' &c., the secondary objective, denoting the ground of accusation (and corresponding to a substantive in the genitive case in Latin), is preceded by the preposition *of* or *with* : as,

Bradshaw accused Cromwell *of ambition.*
Cromwell charged the members *with sedition.*

Here the primary objective refers to persons; and yet by a turn of the sentence we may say,

> Bradshaw charged ambition *upon Cromwell.*
> Cromwell charged sedition *upon the members.*

The infinitive mood of a verb used substantively is often employed as a primary or secondary objective : thus,

> The general forced him *to serve.*
> I counsel you *to wait.*

And which objective shall be here considered primary or secondary will depend upon the way of looking at the sentence : whether, for example, we understand ' The general forced him *to service,*' or, ' The general forced service *upon him.*'

20. When any Transitive verb (which in the active voice governs two objectives) is employed in the passive voice, one of the objectives is turned into the subject-nominative, and the other remains attached to the verb : thus,

> Mr. Thomson taught *Henry arithmetic*

may be expressed

> *Henry* was taught *arithmetic* by Mr. Thomson,

or,

> *Arithmetic* was taught *to Henry* by Mr. Thomson.

Where, in construction with the active voice, the secondary objective is preceded by the preposition *to,* there is a little awkwardness in converting that objective into a subject-nominative : thus, in place of the *active* construction,

> The Council awarded a prize *to Robinson,*

it is, no doubt, grammatically correct to say, in the *passive,*

> *Robinson* was awarded a prize by the Council ;

where ' Robinson ' is made the subject-nominative, and ' prize ' is the primary objective remaining attached to the verb, in the passive voice ; but it is more usual to say

> A prize was awarded *to Robinson* by the Council.

QUALIFICATIONS OF THE PREDICATE-VERB.

21. The general term *adverb* is employed to denote a word which qualifies a verb ; and appears to signify, literally, ' that which is *at* or *bye* the verb,' or, ' that which is attached to the verb.'

This term is confined, strictly speaking, to a single word ; when two or more words, taken together, are used adverbially, we call the whole an 'adverbial phrase.' It sometimes happens that a preposition and the noun it governs are thus used; and though such a combination is often termed a 'prepositional phrase,' inasmuch as it involves a preposition, yet it may, when qualifying a verb, be called an 'adverbial phrase,' because it has the force of an 'adverb.'

As a general rule, then, the predicate-verb may be qualified by an adverb : thus,

Socrates spoke *wisely*.
Cicero wrote *well*.

On this subject, however, many cautions are necessary. If we wish to 'qualify' a verb, we employ an *adverb*; but if we want to 'complete the predicate,' we use an *adjective* as a predicate-nominative : thus,

Henry grows *tall*.
They appear *wise*.

Hence 'He stood firm,' and 'He stood firmly,' are both correct, but with different significations : the first means 'He stood, and *he was firm* as he stood;' the second asserts that 'He stood in a firm manner :' that 'his *standing* was firm.'

22. But this is not all. Some adjectives appear to be used as adverbs, in such sentences as 'He hits *hard*,' 'The horse runs *fast*;' where the words 'hard' and 'fast' evidently qualify the verbs, or tell the character of the 'hitting' and the 'running.'

For an explanation of this we must refer to the older forms of the language. In Anglo-Saxon *e* is the usual termination by which adverbs are formed from adjectives : as

Adjective.		Adverb.	
riht	'right'	*rihte*	'right,' 'rightly.'
			(Lat. *recte*.)
wíd	'wide'	*wíde*	'widely.'
lang	'long'	*lange*	'long.'

Rask, *Anglo-Saxon Grammar*, § 335.

Dr. Adams thinks that this *e* is the suffix (or case-ending) of the dative case, used to express manner : and this termination, he says, is retained in Old English, as, *softe, brighte, swifte*, 'softly, brightly, swiftly;' but when, in process of time, the *e* was lost, these adverbs assumed the appearance of adjectives.—Adams, *Elements*, § 396.

Some persons are offended at the apparent irregularity of the phrase 'He hits *hard*,' and prefer to say 'He hits *hardly*,' which would imply, if it means anything, that ‘he scarcely hits at all.’

The termination *-ly* is derived from the Anglo-Saxon *-lice,* which is formed by adding the termination *e* to adjectives ending in *-lic* (-like).

In later English the case-ending *-e* was lost, so that the adverb and the adjective assume the same form. Thus, for example, *early* may be either an adjective or an adverb. So, too, in the phrase ‘a godly man,’ *godly* is an adjective; but in the phrase ‘to live soberly, righteously, and *godly*,’ it is an adverb meaning ‘in a godly manner.’

In course of time the termination *-ly* came to be regarded as the mark of an adverb; but where the adjective has already the termination *-ly*, the same should not be added to form an adverb. We cannot say *godlily* or *manlily*, though we might say *holily*, because the *l* of ‘hol-y’ belongs to the root of the word, and does not form part of an adjective termination.

23. Now let us take these examples:

> The rose smells *sweet*.
> The wine tastes *sour*.

Some critics condemn these sentences altogether; they say that the use of the adjective is incorrect; and they would alter thus:

> The rose smells *sweetly*.
> The wine tastes *sourly*.

Other grammarians defend the sentence ‘The rose smells *sweet*,’ on the ground that *sweet* forms part of the predicate, and agrees with the subject, meaning that ‘the rose *is* sweet of smell,’ or ‘with respect to smell.’

In English, adjectives do not vary their terminations to mark the changes of gender, number, and case; hence we might argue for ever upon the word ‘sweet’ without being able to arrive at a definite conclusion. But in Latin the adjectives do vary; and if we turned this sentence into Latin prose, it would be ‘Rosa *suave* olet,’ where *suave* is a neuter accusative attached to the verb *olet*.*

Hence, arguing from the analogy of the Latin language, we say that in the ‘Rose smells sweet,’ *sweet* is a neuter accusative, used as equivalent to an adverb. Accordingly, the use of an

---

* Compare ‘anser plebeium sapit.’—Petronius (poet.), § 93.
  ‘Goose tastes vulgar,’ *i e.* ‘has a vulgar taste.’ And so
    ‘ *Dulce* ridentem Lalagen amabo,
      Dulce loquentem.’—Horace, Odes, I. xxii. 23.

actual adverb in ' The rose smells *sweetly* ' is strictly correct ;
and ' The rose smells *sweet* ' may also be defended on the
ground we have taken.

24. A similar distinction must be observed in the use of
participles. Let us consider this sentence .

> The messenger came *running*.

Here, if *running* be taken adverbially, the meaning is, that
' the messenger came *at a running pace*.' But if it be taken
as a participle, it means ' the messenger came, *and he ran* as
he came.'

Take these lines :

> The church of the village
> Stood *gleaming white* in the morning sheen.

The words *gleaming white* express the notion of the Latin
candidus ; * they do not tell us the manner in which the
church stood, but the colour and appearance of the church
itself. We may consider that *gleaming* qualifies the adjective
white, and that the term *gleaming white* is a predicate-nominative.

It is difficult to decide whether the perfect participle active
should be taken adverbially as qualifying the predicate-verb,
or be regarded as completing or filling up the predicate. No
doubt, in the sentence ' William, *having conquered* Harold,
ascended the throne,' the participle explains at what time, and
after what action, William ascended the throne. But, as before remarked, we might turn the sentence thus : ' William
conquered Harold, *and* ascended the throne.' On the whole,
I am inclined to consider ' having conquered ' as a kind of
predicate-nominative. See § 4.

25. We have next to discuss *adverbial phrases*, as qualifying predicate-verbs.

1. A preposition, with the substantive which it governs,
may be used adverbially : as,

> The enemy advanced *with boldness*.

Here the phrase ' with boldness ' is equivalent to the adverb
' boldly.'

This will furnish us with a rule for the use of that unfortunate adverb *otherwise*, which is very unfairly treated by careless writers. The word means ' in another manner,' and ought
never to be employed except as an adverb, and in phrases

---

* Compare *candidus*, ' brilliant white,' with *albus*, ' dead white ;' and *niger*,
' jet black,' with *ater*, ' dull black.'

where ' in another manner,' ' in another way,' or words to
that effect, might stand in its room. ' Whoever is found in
this domain, breaking fences, stealing nuts, or *otherwise*, will
be prosecuted with the utmost rigour of the law.' Here
' otherwise ' is used as the equivalent of a participle ; and it
is evident that ' stealing nuts or in another manner ' makes
absolute nonsense. If the caution had been worded ' stealing
nuts or otherwise trespassing,' it would have signified ' stealing
nuts, or trespassing in any other way,' which is intelligible
enough ; for there may be many other acts of trespass beside
breaking fences and stealing nuts.

26.—2. Substantives are often used adverbially to denote
the time *when*, the manner *how*, or the attendant circumstances.

Since we have lost the dative (or ablative) cases of our
noun-substantives, there is no *form* left to distinguish constructions of this kind ; so that a knowledge of syntax is our
only guide.

> The letters came *every day*.
> The vessels sailed *every week*.
> They fought *hand to hand*.

But the construction is explained by observing that, in similar
instances, prepositions are employed :

> They travel *by day*.
> We fly *by night*.

In ordinary English, *yesterday*, *last night*, &c., are used adverbially ; but in Cork we constantly hear *on yesterday*, *on
last night*, and even *on to-morrow*, where there is a needless
accumulation of prepositions.

In the phrases ' once *a* week,' ' sixpence *a* pound,' it is a
doubtful point whether the word *a* is the indefinite article, or
a remnant of the Anglo-Saxon preposition *an*, which signifies
' in,' ' on.' See § 304.

27.—3. Under the head of adverbial phrases, we may mention the construction whereby a substantive (noun or pronoun)
and a participle are used *absolutely*, to mark the time, the
circumstances, &c. : as,

> *This said*, they both betook them several ways.
> > Milton, *Paradise Lost*, x. 610.

> With that she fell distract,
> And, *her attendants absent*, swallowed fire.
> > *Julius Cæsar*, iv. 3.

This construction has been called the 'nominative absolute,'
or by others the 'case absolute.'   Dr. Adams prefers to call it
the 'dative absolute.'   He says, after citing the instances just
quoted, that the words marked in italics 'have no grammatical
connection with the rest of the sentence: i. e., are not governed
by any word or words in the sentence to which they are attached, and are therefore called *Datives Absolute*, or *Detached
Datives*.   In Latin, the ablative is employed in these detached
or absolute phrases; in Greek, the genitive; and in Anglo-
Saxon, the dative.   This A.-S. dative was the origin of the
absolute construction in English.   Most grammarians, since the
case-endings are lost, prefer to call these words *nominatives*.
But the loss of a suffix cannot convert one case into another.
The *meaning* conveyed by these absolute words cannot be expressed by a true nominative.'—Adams, *Elements*, § 493.

In support of this view, we may take the instance quoted
by Dr. Adams from Milton:

> And, *him destroyed*,
> Or won to what may work his utter loss,
> For whom all this was made, all this will soon
> Follow, as to him linked in weal or woe.
> > *Paradise Lost*, ix. 130–3

To which we may add, from the same poet,

> ———by whose aid
> This inaccessible high strength, the seat
> Of Deity supreme, *us dispossessed*,
> He trusted to have seized.—*Ibid.* vii. 140–3.

This proves that Milton, at all events, thought the construction demanded an oblique case, that is, some case other than
the nominative.   But Milton was a learned poet, and here, as
elsewhere, he may have been imitating the Latin or Greek.

As the point is doubtful in English, we may be content to
employ the term Case Absolute in reference to these constructions, leaving the particular case an open question.   But in
practice we should be very careful in using this construction,
especially at the beginning of a sentence.   For the reader may
mistake the noun used absolutely, thinking it a subject-nominative; and presently, when the true subject-nominative is
introduced, like the true Amphitryon in the play, it appears
that another has usurped his place.

28. The following classification of adverbs and adverbial
phrases may be useful:—

Adverbs are frequently classed in accordance with their meaning—

1. *Time* . . . . once, always, daily, before.
2. *Place* . . . . here, aloft, around.
3. *Degree* . . . much, very, greatly, almost.
4. *Manner* . . . well, thus, truly, so.
5. *Cause* and *Inference* } . . therefore, wherefore, hence.

Many of the adverbs may have their places supplied by an adverbial or prepositional phrase—

1. *Time* . . . always = at all times.
             daily = every day.
2. *Place* . . . here = in this place.
             aloft = on high.
3. *Degree*. . . greatly = in a great measure.
4. *Manner* . . thus = in this way,
             truly = in truth.
5. *Cause* and *Inference* } . therefore = for this cause.
              = for this reason.
              . wherefore = for which cause.
              = for which reason.

THE INFINITIVE MOOD OF A VERB USED AS A SUBSTANTIVE.

29. 'Sometimes the Infinitive is the Nominative case to the Verb,' said the old rule. In truth, the Infinitive is a Verbal Substantive, and is used sometimes as a nominative, sometimes as an objective.

But in the English language this point is attended with peculiar difficulties, arising from the fact that our grammatical forms have been subject to various changes, and that the origin of those forms has sometimes been forgotten or obscured.

The first thing, therefore, is to inquire, what is the English infinitive?

If we are asked what is the infinitive of the verb *love*, we answer *to love*, and we call *to* the 'sign' of the infinitive.

But here, at the very outset, we must make a distinction, which is of great importance. Sometimes, indeed, *to* is a mere sign of the infinitive, and may be omitted in certain instances. For example, we say ' He dares *to go*,' and 'He dares not *go*.' After many auxiliaries it is usual to omit the sign *to*; and so also after other verbs, as *bid*, *make*. ' They *bid* him *ccme*,' ' They *make* him *leap*;' where *come* and *leap* are infinitives dependent upon the governing verbs ' bid ' and ' make.'

In older English there are variations both ways; our fore-fathers sometimes emitted the sign where we use it, and used the sign where we omit it.

So Shakespeare :

You *ought* not *walk*.

Julius Cæsar, i. 1.

and on the other hand,

I *durst*, my lord, *to wager* she is honest.

Othello, iv. 2.

There are also many varieties in provincial dialects; in some counties we may hear ' They *helped* him *mow* the grass,' for ' *to mow*.'

30. But, in many other instances, the word *to*, so far from being a mere sign, is a true preposition, meaning *in order to*; as, ' He came *to see* me,' that is, ' in order to see me,' or ' for the purpose of seeing me.' This distinction is to be carefully remembered when we are translating from English into other languages. When *to* is a mere sign, we may gene-rally render the verb by the Latin infinitive. But it is a gross error to do so where *to* signifies *in order to*; in such instances we must employ the preposition *ad* with a gerund, or with a noun coupled with the participle in -*dus*, or we must use *ut* with a verb in the subjunctive mood.

At one period in the history of the language our forefathers forgot the original force of the preposition *to* in these con-structions, and inserted an additional preposition *for*; as,

What went ye out *for to see?*

Matthew, xi. 8.

In some parts of the country similar phrases are even yet occasionally heard; and sometimes *for* is employed before the sign *to*, where there is not even the shadow of an excuse to justify it; as, ' He told me *for to do it*.'

31. But in English we have another form of the infinitive in -*ing*, the same in sound and spelling as the present par-ticiple. Thus instead of saying ' *to see* is *to believe*,' we gene-rally say ' *seeing* is *believing*.' In like manner 'it is healthful *to rise* early,' may be expressed ' *rising* early is healthful.'

In the sentence '*riding* is pleasant,' or ' he loves *riding*,' the form *riding* is used substantively, and is really an infinitive, or, as some prefer to call it, a gerund. But in the sentence ' he came *riding* at full speed,' *riding* is a participle, and has the force of an adjective.

Grammarians have produced much needless perplexity by confounding the two forms, and by supposing that a participle or a participial phrase can ever be used substantively. The very employment of these forms must convince us that they are infinitives, and not participles ; for the participle partakes of the nature of an adjective, and not of a substantive.—See Whately, *Logic*, II. 1. 3.

32. The forms in -*ing* demand very careful attention. For the English termination -*ing* represents no less than three distinct endings in Anglo-Saxon—namely, those of the infinitive, the present participle, and the verbal substantive. The Anglo-Saxon verb *writan*, ' to write,' gives us the following forms :—

Infinitive :	*writan*,	' to write,'	' writing.'
Gerund :	*to writanne*,	' to write,'	' for writing.'
Present Participle :	*writende*,	' writing.'	

It so happens that the Verbal Substantive derived from this verb ends in -*ing, writing*; but the more usual termination of verbal substantives is -*ung*, as *mearcung*, ' a marking,' *clænsung*, ' a cleansing.'

33. The so-called Gerund in Anglo-Saxon appears to be nothing more than the Dative case of the infinitive governed by the preposition *to*. When the infinitive was used substantively, the form *writan* was employed for the nominative and accusative cases ; *to writanne* was used as the dative.

In process of time,

writan became *write, writing* ;
to writanne became *to write* :

and the following confusion took place :—The infinitive form *writing* was confounded with the participle present, and its true origin was forgotten. The form *to write* was not confined to phrases denoting a purpose, where a dative case is proper, but was used generally for an infinitive, even in phrases requiring a nominative or an accusative case.

For example, we say

To err is human.

But etymologically, this is as great a violation of the principles of Anglo-Saxon grammar, as *Ad errandum est humanum*.

would be a violation of Latin grammar. No doubt, custom
sanctions our present usage; but, etymologically, *to err* represents the dative of the infinitive used substantively, and not
the nominative.

34. Thus the nominative and accusative *writ-an* assumed
the forms *writ-en, writ-in,* and finally *writ-ing.* This form of
the infinitive is also known to modern grammarians as the
Gerund, a term borrowed from the Latin Grammar, and one
which might, in the opinion of Dr. Adams, be advantageously
excluded from the grammar of the English language.—See
Adams, *Elements,* § 287.

However, since the term *Gerund* has obtained admission
into many schools, some teachers may wish to retain it, as applicable to the form in -*ing.* But if so, they should carefully
distinguish between,

1. The Gerund in -*ing,* as *writing.*
2. The Gerund with *to,* as *to write* ; where *to* signifies *in
order to,* and must not be confounded with *to* the
ordinary sign of the infinitive : thus,

He loves *to ride* . . . . *Infinitive.*
He came *to see* me . . . . . *Gerund.*

The termination of the present participle in Anglo-Saxon
was -*ende,* which we have converted into -*ing.* But in Old
English and Old Scottish the participial termination -*and* was
preserved :

> Pointes and sleeves be well *sittand,*
> Right and streight on the hand.
> Chaucer, *Romaunt of the Rose,* 2264.

> Before them all there came *ridand*
> With helm on heid and spear in hand,
> Sir Henry the Boon, the worthy,
> That was a wicht knicht, and a hardy.
> Barbour, *Bruce.*

> His *glitterand* armour shined far away,
> Like glauncing light of Phoebus' brightest ray.
> Spenser, *Faerie Queene,* I. vii.

The Anglo-Saxon verbal substantive *writing* is the same
in termination and meaning with our own 'writing.'—See
Adams, *Elements of the English Language,* §§ 286, 287 ; and
compare Max Müller, *Science of Language,* Second Series,
pp. 15—18.

35. It is very necessary, in English, to discriminate between these three different words, infinitive, present participle, and verbal substantive, which in form appear to be the same—*writing.*

The infinitive can be distinguished from the participle by this test, that the infinitive may be used substantively; whereas the participle can be employed as an adjective only, and never as a substantive.

It is not always easy to distinguish between the infinitive (*writing*) and the verbal substantive (*writing*). For example, in this sentence, 'the breaking of the waves upon the shore is harmonious,' some persons might contend that *breaking* is an infinitive used substantively; and others that it is a verbal substantive. But in phrases where the infinitive governs an objective case, there can be no doubt whatever; for the infinitive, though used substantively, may retain its powers as a verb; whereas the verbal substantive never has any such powers. Thus in the sentence, 'Honestly *meeting* difficulties is wiser than *shunning* them,' *meeting* and *shunning* are manifestly infinitives (or gerunds, if that term be preferred).

36. In the preceding pages we have remarked the several constructions in which the infinitive is used substantively. We shall now recapitulate them, in order to obtain a clear view of the whole question, making some additional observations upon points of interest.

The infinitive is used,

1. As a subject-nominative :
> *To walk* is healthy.
> *Walking* is agreeable.

2. As a predicate-nominative :
> To hear is *to obey.*
> Seeing is *believing.*

3. As a primary objective :
> John loves to *study.*
> He enjoys *walking* in the fields.

4. As a secondary objective :
> The general forced him *to serve.*
> I counsel you *to wait* patiently.

37. Particular care must be taken in analysing sentences which contain an infinitive dependent upon verbs of perception or sensation, 'seeing,' 'hearing,' 'knowing,' &c. In reference to this construction, we shall examine the doctrine of the *subject-accusative.*

Suppose we take the sentence,

I know him to be eloquent.

We shall endeavour, first of all, to prove that *him* is not, strictly speaking, an objective; but that the whole phrase 'him to be eloquent' is the *object* of the verb 'know.'

Another form of the sentence would be,

I know that [he is eloquent,]

and since, by the idiom of the English language, we are allowed in such constructions to omit *that*, we may say,

I know [he is eloquent.]

Now this clause 'he is eloquent' is really a subordinate clause, which may be analysed separately; thus—

he	*Subject-nominative.*
is	*Predicate-verb.*
eloquent . .	*Predicate-nominative.*

If, however, we wish to throw this clause into a form immediately dependent upon the governing verb, to make it, in fact, the object of the verb 'know,' we turn the subject-*nominative* into the subject-*accusative*; the indicative *is* into the infinitive *to be*; and the predicate-*nominative* into the predicate-*accusative*; and we say,

I know [him to be eloquent.]

Obs.—The Latin language shows the *form* of the predicate-accusative.

Ille est facund*us* : 'He is eloquent.'

Scio illum esse facund*um* : 'I know him to be eloquent.'

That the word *him* is not an objective dependent upon *know*, must be clear from the following consideration. We do not mean to assert that we know *him* absolutely; we may be ignorant of his character, or of his general capabilities. We merely assert that we are acquainted with his merit as a speaker. But as the whole clause is the *object* of the verb 'know,' and stands *in the position of an objective case*, the *subject* of the clause is attracted into the *accusative*, and the *indicative* is turned into that part of the verb which is not modified by number and person, namely the *infinitive*. Finally, the predicate of the clause, ' eloquent,' must agree in case with the subject, and is therefore in the accusative; hence we term it the *predicate-accusative.*

38. We have, in this enquiry, adopted the term *accusative* in preference to *objective*, in order to avoid the harshness of talking about the 'subject-objective.' Although, when properly explained, that term is correct enough: it means 'the subject in an objective clause.'

Practically, however, I have observed that in constructions where a subject-accusative stands before an infinitive, we may distinguish two different relations.

1. Sometimes, as we have just seen, the subjective-accusative stands to the infinitive in the relation of a subject-nominative to a finite verb:

I know [him to be eloquent]

is equivalent to

I know [he is eloquent.]

2. At other times, the subject-accusative stands to the infinitive in the relation of a substantive in the possessive (or genitive) case to another substantive:

I wish [him to stay]

is equivalent to

I wish [his staying]:

for what I want, with respect to him, is ' his staying.'

Thus the sentences

We heard the thunder *roll*,
They saw the ship *sink*,
I never knew him *to fail*,

might be paraphrased

We heard the *thunder's roll*,
They saw the *ship's sinking*,
I never knew *failure on his part*.

CHAPTER II.

SIMPLE SENTENCES OTHER THAN INDICATIVE.

39. Hitherto we have considered Simple Indicative Sentences, otherwise called *propositions* or *statements*. We have now to deal with other Simple Sentences, namely :

    Interrogative Sentences or Questions.
    Imperative Sentences or Commands.
    Optative Sentences or Wishes.

First of all, we have to remark a variety of form ; a change in the order of words : as for example :

Indicative : The messenger speaks.

Interrogative : Speaks the messenger ?
           more commonly,
               Does the messenger speak ?
      or,
               Is the messenger speaking ?

Imperative : Messenger ! speak.

Optative : May the messenger speak !

Now the method of analysis, which we have discussed, is founded upon Indicative Sentences or *statements*; and a very important part of the sentence was termed the *predicate* or ' thing *stated*.' We can therefore easily understand that there will be a difficulty in applying this form of analysis to sentences wherein there is *no statement at all*, but where a question, a command, or a wish is expressed.

40. Mr. Mason endeavours to meet the difficulty, by distinguishing between the *word* (or *sign*), and the *thing signified* ; between the *subject of a sentence*, and the *subject of discourse*. He says :

The subject of a sentence stands for some object of thought: the predicate denotes some fact or idea which we connect with that object, and the union between the two is effected by the copula.

But this union may be viewed in more ways than one.

1. When it is our intention to declare that the connexion, which is indicated between the subject of discourse and the idea denoted by the predicate, does exist, the sentence is *affirmative*; as, 'Thomas left the room.'

Note.—A *negative* sentence is only a particular variety of affirmative sentence. If we deny that John is here by saying, 'John is not here,' *we affirm* that John *is not here*.

2. When it is our wish to know whether the connexion referred to subsists, the sentence is interrogative; as, 'Did Thomas leave the room?'

3. When we express our *will* that the connexion, between the object of thought described by the subject and that which is expressed by the predicate, should subsist, the sentence that results is called an imperative sentence; as, 'Thomas, leave the room.'

4. When we express a *wish* that the connexion may subsist, the sentence that results is called an optative sentence; as, 'May you speedily recover!'

In some imperative sentences, the *will* is so weakened as to become simply a *wish*; as, 'Defend us, O Lord;' 'Sing, heavenly muse.' The *grammatical* force of the sentence, however, is not altered by this.

In all the above-named kinds of sentences, the *grammatical* connexion between the subject and the verb is the same. It is sufficient, therefore, to take one as a type of all. The affirmative sentence is the most convenient for this purpose.—*English Grammar*, § 356.

41. No doubt, the affirmative sentence is the most convenient. It is the form upon which the system is based. But we must consider, whether it be true that the grammatical connexion is the same in all these cases, and that the grammatical force is not altered.

In Interrogative sentences the order of words is changed; no statement is made, but a question is asked.

In Imperative sentences the nominative becomes vocative, and the indicative mood is changed to the imperative. We surely cannot say that a noun in the vocative case forms the *subject* of a verb in the imperative mood. For the expression ' Thomas, leave the room,' means this : ' Thomas, I address you, and my command to you is to leave the room.' This may, probably, furnish a reason why, in many languages, the infinitive sometimes takes the place of an imperative. Even if the vocative be termed the ' nominative of address,' that does not obviate the difficulty, unless it can be shown that the vocative becomes a ' *subject*-nominative.'

There is, no doubt, a certain analogy running through the ideas expressed in these various forms of sentence; but I think we shall find that an attempt to apply the terms *subject* and *predicate* to Imperative sentences, or even to Interrogatives and Optatives, is encumbered with difficulty.

42. Dr. Latham, in dealing with this question, is more guarded. He says: ·

All statements, assertions, or declarations are propositions.
Is the converse of this true?
Are all propositions statements, assertions, or declarations?
Up to the present stage of our enquiries, the three parts, members,

or constituent elements of a proposition—the two *somethings* and the *link* that joins them—the *subject, predicate,* and *copula*—have been considered from one point of view only.

Let us now, however, instead of saying

Bread is dear,

say,

Is bread dear?

Does this latter combination of words constitute a proposition?

It certainly has some of the elements of one, and those very important ones.

It contains the two words significant of the two 'somethings'—*bread, dear.* It contains the word which connects them—*is.*

It contains all this, and it contains nothing else. A chemist would say that a sentence, like the one in question, gave us the same elements as the other, with a different arrangement.

Nevertheless, there is no assertion, no statement, no declaration: none, at least, of a direct and straightforward kind.

Instead of this, there is a *question.*

Now, at the first view, few things can be more unlike each other than a question and an assertion. The latter implies knowledge, the former the want of it. The latter contains a certain amount of information, real or supposed; the former seeks for such information; and for this reason, the chief works on logic have, formally and by name, excluded *Questions* from the class of *Propositions.* All, however, that the grammarian says is, that a question is not an assertion, a declaration, or a statement. All that the grammarian says is, that whenever there is an assertion, a declaration, or a statement, there is also a proposition. He never says that wherever there is a proposition there is also a statement.

The fact is, that in grammar a Question is neither more nor less than a variety of the ordinary proposition, implying that the subject is something concerning which the speaker requires information; something unexplained, but not incapable of explanation; explanation that may possibly be supplied by the person spoken to.

The sentence—What is this?—This is what?

What=something upon which information is requested.

It may be objected, however, that it is not the habit of language to use such expressions as *this is what?* but, on the contrary, to prefer the form, *what is this?*

All that need be said upon this point is, that it is not the *general* custom of the *English,* and *certain other languages,* to do so. The English, and certain other languages, transpose the predicate and subject when the proposition is a question; but there is no necessity for their doing so. It is merely a particular practice, and no general law of language.

A question, then, or interrogation, is only an ordinary assertional, or declaratory proposition, with its parts transposed.—*Logic in its Application to Language,* § 17.

43. Now in comparing an Indicative with an Interrogative sentence we may, indeed, find the *same words,* with a different arrangement; but whether we have the *same elements* is quite another question, the truth of which Dr. Latham assumes.

In the indicative sentence we have the 'subject of a *statement*,' and a *predicate* or *thing stated*.   But in the interrogative sentence we find 'the subject of an *enquiry*,' and *something interrogated*.

And even though we might allow the term 'subject' or 'subject-nominative' to be used in both cases, it is only by a violent extension of meaning that we can call a 'thing interrogated' a *predicate*, when in fact nothing is predicated.

Doubtless, from the imperfection of all human language, we are often obliged to admit extensions of meaning; but this should be allowed only in cases of strong necessity, when no ingenuity can devise another term.   Poverty of language should never be made an excuse for want of precision; and certainly no kind of education can be worse, than to acquire the habit of using terms without a clear perception of their meaning.   But if a pupil is taught to employ the term *predicate* where there is no predication, he is in danger of falling into habits of inaccuracy.

44. Thus we find that there are difficulties about the so-called 'predicates' of interrogative sentences.   But in imperative sentences there are difficulties about 'subject' as well as 'predicate.'

Dr. Morell says, (*Grammar*, p. 71): 'In an imperative sentence the 'subject' *thou* or *ye* is often omitted, though it is still *involved* in the use of the verb; as 'go (*thou*) home;' 'hasten (*ye*) into the town.'

According to this, a noun or pronoun in the vocative case may be the subject of a sentence.

Mr. Mason tells us, (*English Grammar*, § 380) that 'the subject of a verb in English is always put in the nominative case;' and yet in § 505, he analyses thus:

'Give me that large book.'

Subject	'thou' (understood).
Predicate	'give.'
Object of verb	'book.'
&c.	&c.

Here *give* does not express a predication but a command; and *thou*, which is supplied to do duty for a 'subject,' is certainly not a *subject-nominative*.

45. Dr. Latham admits the greater difficulty in this instance. He says, (*Logic in its Application to Language*, §19):

At the first view, few things can be more unlike each other than an assertion and a command; indeed, it may be admitted that the propositional character of commands is less clear than that of questions. Words like *walk, stand*, &c., convey neither an affirmation, nor a denial, as a matter of direct assertion. Nevertheless, they are essentially affirmative, and, by attaching to them the word *not*, can be made negative; *walk not, stand not, fear not, eat not, drink not, do not.*
Again:—

> Walk = thou be walking.
> Stand = thou be standing.
> Eat = thou be eating, &c.

And what is *thou* but a subject, *be* but a copula, and *walking* but a predicate?

46. In the first place, I object to the resolution of *walk* into *thou be walking*. But if we let that pass, for the sake of argument, *be* is not a copula in the logical sense. If we wish to reduce the expression *walk* to the form of subject, copula, predicate, we must say, 'My command to you is that you should walk,' or 'My command to you is to walk.'

To take a form applicable to indicative sentences, and to force it upon imperative sentences, must inevitably lead to confusion.

The case of Optative sentences is somewhat similar to that of Interrogatives; so that no further remark is necessary upon that part of the subject.

47. The whole system must be revised. Even in dealing with simple indicative sentences, the youthful student is often quite bewildered with logical subjects and grammatical subjects, logical predicates and grammatical predicates, enlargements of the subject, and extensions of the predicate. But when he has to apply the same principles of analysis to interrogative, imperative, or optative sentences, where, to say the least, the application is very dubious, it is not surprising if he despairs of the whole business.

I believe that, in some of our Middle Class Examinations, the terms 'subject' and 'predicate' are used at random; while very few of the candidates have a clear notion of the principles upon which the system of analysis depends.

Before schoolmasters adopt this method, they would do well to consider, (1) whether the system itself is sound; (2) whether the books which profess to teach it are free from serious error.

In the present work an attempt is made to explain Indicative Sentences, Simple and Compound. And until the method of analysis is more fully developed, I venture to suggest that Interrogative, Imperative, and Optative sentences should be treated on the old-fashioned parsing system.

Certainly, nothing can be worse than the habit of straining terms, and forcing their application in cases for which they were not designed.

CHAPTER III.

COMPOUND SENTENCES.

48. We have seen that a Simple Sentence contains one subject-nominative, and one predicate-verb. Any sentence containing more than one subject-nominative, or more than one predicate-verb, is called a *Compound Sentence.*

A Compound Sentence may contain two or more independent sentences, either coupled by conjunctions, or standing side by side; as,

    1. Hannibal crossed the Alps, and the Romans marched to meet him.

    2. He came, he saw, he conquered.

In the first of these examples, the two independent sentences are joined together by the conjunction *and*; in the second, three sentences stand side by side. And since, in each example, the sentences are of *equal rank*, they are called *co-ordinate sentences,* from the Latin *con-,* ' together,' and *ordo,* ' a rank.' In the first example we have two co-ordinate sentences in one compound sentence; and in the second, we have three co-ordinate sentences in one compound sentence. Thus:

    First Co-ordinate : Hannibal crossed the Alps.

    Second Co-ordinate : The Romans marched to meet him.

So too:

    First Co-ordinate . . . . He came.
    Second Co-ordinate. . . . He saw.
    Third Co-ordinate . . . . He conquered.

49. But, as language progresses, there is a tendency to pass from the Co-ordinate to the Cor-relative form.

In the older stages of a language, we often find Co-ordinate sentences, where the later stage would exhibit Correlative forms. In the Greek of Homer and Pindar, for instance, we observe independent sentences introduced by demonstrative pronouns or adverbs, where, in later Greek, one of the sentences would be thrown into the relative form, introduced by a relative pronoun or adverb. Even in later authors we meet with occasional examples of similar construction, as, '*And* it was now late . . . *and* the Corinthians suddenly began to back water,' for, '*when* it was now late . . . the Corinthians,' &c.: 'Ἤδη δὲ ἦν ὀψὲ . . . καὶ οἱ Κορίνθιοι ἐξαπίνης πρύμναν ἐκρούοντο.—Thuc. i. 50. So too, '*And* it was now about forenoon, *and* the station, where he intended to halt, was near at hand:' καὶ ἤδη τε ἦν ἀμφὶ ἀγορὰν πλήθουσαν, καὶ πλήσιον ἦν ὁ σταθμὸς ἔνθα ἔμελλε καταλύειν.—Xen. *Anab.* i. viii. 1.

In Anglo-Saxon this form is very common: so, ða* Herodes ðæt gehyrde, tha wearð he gedrefed: '*then* Herod heard that, *then* became he troubled.' (*Matth.* ii. 3.) Sometimes the particle is doubled in the first sentence; as, tha ða men slepon, tha com his feonda sum, '*then then* men slept, *then* came one of his foes.'—*Matth.* xiii. 25.

Observe that, in this form, a demonstrative particle stands at the beginning of each sentence. But when, in course of time, one sentence was made relative, and was introduced by a relative particle, the other, employed as a principal sentence, no longer needed an introductory particle.

We may suppose the process to have been of the following kind:—

1. *Then* Herod heard this, *then* was he troubled.
2. *When* Herod heard this, *then* he was troubled.
3. When Herod heard this, he was troubled.

Even in modern composition, after several sentences commencing with *when* or *if*, the conclusion sometimes receives additional emphasis by the introduction of *then*, or *then indeed*.

50. Now, the view commonly taken by grammarians is somewhat to this effect: that in passing from the Co-ordinate to the Correlative form, one of the co-ordinate sentences retains its rank, while the other falls into a subordinate position.

The sentence which retains its rank is usually termed the Principal Sentence; and that which takes an inferior rank is called the Subordinate Sentence, or the Dependent Sentence.

I am inclined to think that the terms Subordinate and Dependent do not exactly represent the state of the case; and in this connexion I prefer the term *clause* to *sentence*.

In point of fact, the Correlative clauses are, respectively, relative and demonstrative. For example, in the compound sentence, 'When Herod heard this, he was troubled,' we have:

When Herod heard this, . *Relative Clause.*

he was troubled, ... *Demonstrative Clause.*

---

* ð equivalent to *dh*, is pronounced like our *th* in '*that*,' '*thine*,' '*those*.' The modern English *th* does double duty, for *th* as in '*thin*,' and for *dh* as in '*thine*.'

However, not to multiply terms, we may accept, in this connexion, the terms suggested by Becker; Principal Clause, and Accessory Clause, thus:

When Herod heard this, . *Accessory Clause.*

he was troubled, ... *Principal Clause.*

51. We shall consider Compound Sentences under three divisions:—

    I. COMPOUND SENTENCES CONTAINING CO-ORDINATE SENTENCES.

    II. COMPOUND SENTENCES CONTAINING CORRELATIVE CLAUSES.

    III. COMPOUND SENTENCES COMPRISING SUBORDINATE CLAUSES.

We have then,

52.—I. COMPOUND SENTENCES CONTAINING CO-ORDINATE SENTENCES.

The Co-ordinate sentences which form a Compound Sentence may, with regard to signification, stand in various relations to one another. The second may add something to the meaning of the first; or choice may be implied between them; or the one may stand in opposition to the other. Accordingly we may divide them into three classes: (1) Copulative, (2) Alternative, (3) Adversative.

1. *Copulative.*

53. Here the first sentence makes a statement, while the second or following sentences furnish an addition to the meaning: as,

Sunk are thy bowers in shapeless ruin all,
And the long grass o'ertops the mouldering wall;
And, trembling, shrinking from the spoiler's hand,
Far, far away, thy children leave the land.
             Goldsmith, *Deserted Village.*

2. *Alternative.*

54. Sometimes two or more sentences joined together imply the notion of choice: as,

He must pay the money, *or* he must go to prison.
He must work hard, *or* he will not succeed.

In the full form, both the co-ordinate sentences have intro-

ductory particles; in the affirmative, *either* . . . *or*; in the
negative, *neither* . . . *nor*: as,

> *Either* you must come, *or* your friend must write.
> *Neither* the letter came, *nor* was the money paid.
>
> *Obs.*—When 'nor' signifies 'and not' it has a copulative, and
> not an alternative force: as,
>
> My ventures are not in one bottom trusted,
> Nor to one place; *nor* is my whole estate
> Upon the fortune of this present year.
> *Merchant of Venice*, i. 1.

8. *Adversative.*

55. Here the co-ordinate sentences are in opposition to one
another; either absolutely, in the way of negation, or by way
of limitation and contrast.

> Men may come, and men may go;
> *But* I go on for ever.   Tennyson.

These were thy charms, *but* all these charms are fled.
Goldsmith, *Deserted Village.*

56.—II. COMPOUND SENTENCES CONTAINING CORRELATIVE CLAUSES.

> *Obs.*—This section comprehends the cases where the Accessory
> Clause is otherwise termed the Adverbial Sentence, or
> the Adverbial Clause.

In this division we shall observe some remains of old Co-
ordinate forms; and we shall find some Compound Sentences
exhibiting a change more or less complete from the Co-ordinate to the Correlative form.

We have remarked that, as language progresses, there is a
tendency to pass from the co-ordinate to the correlative form
of sentence. The co-ordinate sentences are resolved into what
we call the Principal Clause and the Accessory Clause.

We observed too, that in many cases each co-ordinate sentence originally had an introductory particle (Adverb or Conjunction).

As a general rule the Principal Clause no longer needs this
introduction; but the particle, sometimes in a modified form,
remains with the Accessory clause.

When the second of two co-ordinate sentences becomes the
principal it frequently takes the first place, and the accessory
clause is transferred to the second place.

We shall consider the various relations of (1) Time, (2)
Place, (3) Manner, (4) Degree, (5) Cause and Effect, (6)

Reason and Conclusion, (7) Action (or State) and Result, (8) Purpose and End, (9) Condition and Consequence, (10) Concession and Declaration.

If we arrange these, as they would stand, if each clause were introduced by an appropriate particle, we have :—

	I.	II.
1. Time	*When*	*then.*
2. Place	*Where*	*there.*
,,	*Whence*	*thence.*
,,	*Whither*	*thither.*
3. Manner	*As*	*so.*
4. Degree (equality)	*As*	*so.*
,, ,,	*The*	*the.*
,, (inequality)		*than.*
5. Cause and Effect	*Because*	*therefore.*
6. Reason and Conclusion	*Because*	*therefore.*
7. Action (or State) and Result	*(So)*	*that.*
8. Purpose and End	*So*	*that.*
9. Condition and Consequence	*If*	*then.*
10. Concession and Declaration	*Though*	*yet.*

1. *Time.*

57. In the older forms, we find *when* answered by *then*; as,

> *When* Israel was a child, *then* I loved him.
> *Hosea*, xi. 1.

When I would have healed Israel, *then* the iniquity of Ephraim was discovered.   *Id.* vii. 1.

The second co-ordinate has a tendency to become the Principal Clause, and the particle *then* is omitted; as,

> *When* Ephraim spake trembling, he exalted himself in Israel.   *Hosea*, xiii. 1.

The next step is, that the Principal Clause takes the first place; as,

> Every one listens, *when he speaks.*
> I was glad *when he had finished.*
> He read *while I wrote.*
> He punished the boy, *whenever he did wrong.*

The particle 'when,' which introduces the Accessory Clause, is variously termed a 'relative adverb,' a 'conjunctive adverb,' an 'adverbial conjunction,' or a 'continuative conjunction.'

58. The clauses introduced by these particles are commonly termed *adverbial clauses,* because they are supposed to stand in the place of single adverbs, and to be used in qualifying verbs, adjectives, or adverbs.

Mr. Mason maintains (*English Grammar,* § 424), that the relative adverbs have a double force. He says : ' It must be observed that the relative adverbs, which introduce such clauses, not only connect the adverbial clause with the principal clause, but themselves qualify the verb of the clause, which they introduce.'

For example, in the sentence, 'Every one listens, *when he speaks,*' the adverbial clause ' when he speaks ' is said to qualify the verb ' listens '; the particle ' when ' connects the adverbial clause with the principal clause ' every one listens,' and itself qualifies the verb ' speaks ' in the subordinate sentence ' when he speaks.'

This explanation is far from satisfactory, and it seems laboured. It is more simple to deduce the sentence from the co-ordinate form :

> When he speaks, then every one listens.
> When he speaks, every one listens.
> Every one listens, when he speaks.

59. Other connective particles used in reference to time are, *whenever, as, as soon as, now that, ere, while, whilst, until, as often as.*

> *As* he came, they went away.
> *Now that* you have come, we will go.
> He stood there, *whilst* the house was on fire.
> He remained, *until* the work was done.
> He writes, *as often as* he wants money.

The words *before* and *after* are originally prepositions; but they were used as connective particles in the phrases ' before that,' and ' after that.'

> *Before that* certain came from James, he did eat with
> the Gentiles.   *Galatians,* ii. 12.
> Surely, *after that* I was turned, I repented; and
> *after that* I was instructed, I smote upon my
> thigh.   *Jeremiah,* xxxi. 19.

In reading such a passage, it is a mistake to lay any emphasis upon *that*; the accent should fall upon 'befóre,' 'áfter;' and ' that' should be lightly passed over as an enclitic.

2. *Place.*

60. We find examples of the old form *where* . . . *there* : as, *Where* your treasure is, *there* will your heart be also.
Matthew vi. 21.

If we compare the Anglo-Saxon version of this passage, we observe that the clauses are both introduced by *thær*, ' *there* ':

thær thin gold-hord ys, *thær* ys thin heorte,
there thy gold-hoard is, *there* is thine heart,
where thy treasure is, *there* is thy heart.

In modern English ' there ' is generally omitted. The second sentence becomes the Principal Clause, frequently taking the first place ; and the first sentence becomes an Accessory Clause, introduced by *where, wherever, whither, whence* : as,

I will remain, *where you are.*
Whither thou goest, I will go.
He returned, *whence he came.*

> *Obs.*—Instead of *whence*, some writers say *from whence*; to which an objection has been raised, that ' whence' means 'from which place;' and that therefore in ' from whence' the word *from* is superfluous.

3. *Manner.*

61. Co-ordinate sentences indicating manner or resemblance are introduced by the particles *as* . . . *so*, respectively : thus,

As the hart panteth after the water brooks,
So panteth my soul after thee, O God.
Psalm xlii. 1.

This is the true explanation of such a Compound Sentence ; namely, that it comprises two co-ordinate sentences. An attempt to regard one of the clauses as a Principal Sentence, and the other as a Subordinate Sentence, is to introduce needless perplexity. We may also remark, both here and elsewhere, that in the second clause, there is a tendency to invert the order of words ; to put the predicate-verb before the subject-nominative.

The introductory particle *so* is often omitted ; then the sentence, before which it stood, is regarded as a Principal Clause, and frequently occupies the first place ; thus,

He succeeds, *as his father succeeded before him.*

He did *as he was told.*
It turned out *as I expected.*
As I hear, I judge.

62. Mr. Mason remarks, (*English Grammar,* § 429,) ' Here the dependent clauses qualify the verbs of the main sentence, while the adverb *as* refers to the manner of the action spoken of in the dependent clauses themselves. It must be remembered, however, that clauses beginning with *as* are generally elliptical. At full length the above would be,

He did as he was told *to do,*

where *as* indicates the idea of manner with relation to the verb *to do.*

It turned out as I expected *it to turn out,*

where *as* indicates the idea of manner with relation to the verb *to turn out.*'

With all deference to Mr. Mason, this seems to be laboured. A comparison of the co-ordinate forms would furnish a simpler explanation :

As he was told, *so* he did.
As I expected, *so* it turned out.

We do not find co-ordinate sentences in the form *as . . . as.* But it frequently happens that, in a Principal Clause, some word or phrase is qualified by *as* ; and then the Accessory Clause follows, introduced by *as* : for example,

He is *as* merciful, *as he is strong.*

The particle *so* is likewise used to qualify a word or phrase : thus,

He is not *so* wise, *as he seems.*

The words *such* and *same* are answered by *as* ; for example,

She wrote *such* a letter, *as might have been expected from her.*

They are the *same, as ever they were.*

Hence some have contended that *as,* in these constructions, is a pronoun ; but this has probably arisen from confounding relative adverbs with relative pronouns. A relative is not necessarily a pronoun.

4. *Degree.*

63. In sentences indicating Degree or Proportion, we must distinguish the relations of equality and inequality.

In the relation of equality, the co-ordinate forms are expressed by

as . . . . . . so.
the . . . . . . the.

The use of *as* . . . *so* corresponds with the usage in sentences relating to Manner, and need not be discussed further.

The particle *the*, which must not be confounded with the definite article, has come down to us from the Anglo-Saxon *thy*, the ablative case of the demonstrative pronoun, *se, seo, thæt.*

The sentences introduced by *the* are pure co-ordinates, and are a remnant of the old language : for example,

The more you learn, *the* wiser you will become.

This means, ' in proportion as you learn more, in that proportion you will become wiser.'

In § 270 of his *English Grammar,* Mr. Mason suspects the truth ; but in § 433, he gives the following exposition :—

' " The more I learn, the more I wish to learn." Here the adverbial sentence, " *the more I learn,*" qualifies the demonstrative adverb *the*, which in its turn qualifies the adverb *more* in the principal clause ; the word *more* in the adverbial clause, being itself qualified by the relative adverb *the*.'

The explanation that the sentences are co-ordinate is simpler, and more in accordance with the older forms of the language.

64. In the relation of inequality, accessory clauses are introduced by *than.*

In older English, down to the time of Shakespeare, *then* was constantly used in these constructions, where we now employ *than.* Both the words are derived from the Anglo-Saxon *thonne* or *thænne* ; but in our modern language we restrict *than* to the purposes of comparison.

In *King Lear,* i. 4, the First Folio reads thus :

Marke, nuncle ;
Haue more then thou showest,
Speak less then thou knowest,
Lend less then thou owest,
Ride more then thou goest,
Learn more then thou trowest.

The modern copies read *than* for *then.*

Dr. Bosworth, in his *Anglo-Saxon Dictionary,* distinguishes *thonne* (adverb) ' then,' from *thonne* (conjunction) ' than ' ; but this distinction appears to be quite arbitrary.

We shall compare a few instances of the use of *thonne* in Anglo-Saxon, translating it by the word ' then ':

> fortham Fæder is mara thonne ic.
> *for-that Father is more then I.*

> ' for my Father is greater than I.'
>   *John* xiv. 28.

> thes ys mærra thonne thæt templ.
> *this is more then the temple.*

' in this place is (one) greater than the temple.'
>   *Matthew* xii. 6.

> thes ys mara thonne Salomon.
> *this is more then Solomon.*

' a greater than Solomon is here.'—*Id.* xii. 42.

> Se the lufað fæder oððe modor ma
> *he that loveth father or mother more*
> thonne me, nys he me wyrthe.
> *then me, ne-is he of-me worthy.*

' he that loveth father or mother more than me, is not worthy of me.'—*Id.* x. 37.

The construction seems to have arisen from the order of succession : for example :

> this (one) is greater;
> then Solomon [is great].

In like manner :

> he that loveth father or mother more; then [he loveth] me.

This appears to have been the origin of the construction; but afterwards the use of *then* may have been extended to cases where this explanation is not obvious.

65. *Caution.*   In using ' than,' it is very necessary to bear in mind the construction of both clauses, otherwise errors or confusion may ensue.

For example, both these sentences are correct :

> 1. She loves him more than *I* :
> 2. She loves him more than *me* :

but they bear very different significations.   The first means, ' she loves him more than I love him;' the second, 'she loves him more than she loves me.'

5. *Cause and Effect.*

66. Co-ordinate Sentences, denoting cause and effect, are introduced respectively by the words *because* and *therefore.* These are originally 'by-cause' and 'there-for,' namely, 'for that (cause).' The prepositions *for* and *fore* are constantly confounded.

In the full form, then, we have,

> *Cause.* Because—it froze last night.
> *Effect.* Therefore—the pools are covered with ice.

But, on this subject, a seeming inconsistency is observable. When 'because' is omitted, and we say,

> It froze last night; therefore, the pools are covered with ice;

the grammarians maintain that the two clauses are still co-ordinate sentences, connected by the *adverb* 'therefore.' But when 'therefore' is omitted, and we say,

> The pools are covered with ice, because it froze last night,

we are told that 'The pools are covered with ice' is now a Principal Sentence; and that the words 'it froze last night,' constitute a Subordinate Sentence, attached by the *conjunction* 'because.'

At first sight, the distinction is not obvious, nor is the difference between *adverb* and *conjunction* very clear. Still the distinction may exist, and the following point deserves notice:

In the sentence 'It froze last night; therefore the pools are covered with ice,' we may insert the conjunction *and* between the clauses; thus,

> It froze last night, *and* therefore the pools are covered with ice.

Now here we have two co-ordinate sentences coupled by the conjunction *and.*

But in the sentence, 'The pools are covered with ice, because it froze last night,' the two clauses are so intimately bound up together, that we cannot insert a conjunction between them. If the two clauses are *not* co-ordinates, we must expound one as the Principal, and the other as the Accessory Clause.

At all events, it is objectionable to discuss these forms in different parts of the grammar; the one under the head of Co-ordinate Sentences, the other under the head of Principal and Accessory. It is very important that the pupil should acquire precise notions upon the relation of Cause and Effect. For this purpose, the whole subject should be brought under one view. Younger pupils should remember, that we may first assign the cause, and then state the effect; or we may first state the effect, and then assign the cause. For example, we may say,

> The season was dry, *therefore* the crops failed,

or,　The crops failed, *because* the season was dry.

Again, The string is pulled too tight, *therefore* it breaks,

or,　The string breaks, *because* it is pulled too tight.

6. *Reason and Conclusion.*

67. Sentences which express reason and conclusion are called *illative,* that is, 'inferential,' because they are used in drawing ' inferences.'

It is often a source of perplexity that the ' illative conjunctions' *because* and *therefore* are employed to denote reason and conclusion, as well as cause and effect.

1. *Cause and Effect* :

> The ground is rich, and *therefore* the trees flourish,

or,

> The trees flourish, *because* the ground is rich.

2. *Reason and Conclusion* :

> The trees are flourishing, and *therefore* the ground is rich,

or,

> The ground is rich, *because* the trees are flourishing.
>
> See Whately, *Logic,* I. 2.

The difficulty vanishes, if, in stating the Reason and Conclusion, we substitute ' by-reason ' for *because,* and ' thereby (we know that)' for *therefore.*

We shall state the sentences as co-ordinates.

1. *Cause and Effect* :

> Because . . . . the ground is rich,
> Therefore . . . the trees flourish.

2. *Reason and Conclusion* :

> By-reason . . . the trees are flourishing,
> Thereby (we know that) . . . the ground is rich.

Some writers have used the phrase ' by reason ' instead of ' because,' where a reason or motive is signified. Thus we read of Sir Roger de Coverley :

> It is said, he keeps himself a bachelor, *by reason* he was crossed in love by a perverse beautiful widow of the next county to him.　　*Spectator,* No. 2

However, this form is not usual; and no substitute has been provided in corresponding cases for ' therefore.'

In ordinary argument it is very common to state the conclusion first, and then to assign the reason or reasons: thus,

>Emulation is useful, *because* it promotes diligence.

>Emulation is injurious, *because* it excites envy.

Instead of *because*, other particles are often used to introduce the reason : *for, as, since*, or the more formal *whereas*.

7. *Action (or State) and Result.*

68. A sentence expressing Action and Result differs from one denoting Cause and Effect, just as a mere narrative differs from an argumentative statement.

The simplest form exhibits two co-ordinate sentences: as,

>He ran fast, and he was out of breath.

If we say,

>He ran fast, and *so* he was out of breath,

the word *so* occupies a place analogous to *therefore* in a formal argument. But, in our view, the sentences are still co-ordinate.

If, however, we proceed a step further, and say,

>He ran *so* fast, *that* he was out of breath,

we must consider the first clause as a Principal, and the second as an Accessory Clause.

In analysing such a sentence, the followers of Becker would regard *so* as an 'adverb' qualifying the adverb 'fast;' and ' that he was out of breath,' as an *adverb-clause* modifying the adverb *so*.

The following method, however, may be worthy of consideration :—

>He ran . . . fast, . . *Principal Clause.*
>so , . . that . . . . *Adverbial (or Conjunctional) phrase introducing the Accessory Clause.*
>he was out of breath, . *Accessory Clause.*

8. *Purpose and End.*

69. The sentences denoting this relation had passed in Anglo-Saxon into the advanced stage; and the Accessory Clause was introduced by *thæt* alone : as,

ðas thing ic eow sæde, þæt ge habbon sibbe on me.
these things I to-you said, that ye may-have peace in me.

John xvi. 33.

The Vulgate reads, 'Hæc locutus sum vobis, ut in me pacem
habeatis.' The Anglo-Saxon made no distinction between the
past tense 'said' and the present-perfect 'have said.' But
our English version is wrong: 'These things I *have spoken*
unto you, that in me ye *might* have peace.' We may read
'I spoke . . . that ye might,' or 'I have spoken . . . that ye
may;' but we must not mix the two constructions.

Instead of an Accessory Clause introduced by *that*, we may
have a gerund with *to*: thus, for

> He labours, that he may become rich:
> He studies, that he may improve:

we may say

> He labours to become rich:
> He studies to improve:

where *to* denotes 'in order to,' 'for the purpose to;' and
therefore 'to become,' 'to improve,' are not simple infinitives,
but what we call 'the gerund with *to*.' The Latin scholar
will see at once, that 'to become,' 'to improve,' could not be
rendered in Latin by infinitives.

Where the subordinate sentence involves a negative, we
often find *lest* as equivalent to *that . . . not*: as,

> He labours, *lest* he should be dependent,

or,

> He labours, *that* he may *not* be dependent.

9. Condition and Consequence.

70. Grammarians have dwelt at considerable length on this
relation; and some of the terms which they employ present
difficulty to the learner.

Mr. Mason says, (*English Grammar,* § 440,) 'In adverbial
clauses of *condition*, the principal sentence is called the *consequent clause (i. e.* the clause which expresses the *consequence*);
the subordinate sentence is called the *hypothetical clause (i. e.*
the clause which expresses the *hypothesis, supposition* or *concession*).'

The Greek *hypothesis* is equivalent to the Latin *suppositio,*
and literally means the 'groundwork' or 'foundation,' hence

'that which is laid down as the basis of an argument.' By the Greek grammarians, the hypothetical (or supposing) clause is termed the *protasis* (*i. e.* the 'putting forward'); while the consequent clause is named the *apodosis*, (*i. e.* the 'paying back,' the 'rejoinder').

With younger pupils, I have found it simpler to call these clauses respectively the 'if-clause,' and the 'then-clause;' for although, in modern English, *then* is not very often found introducing the consequent clause, it sometimes held such a position in the older stages of the language.

We have then the following comparison of terms:

if-clause . . . . *then*-clause.
hypothetical clause . . . . consequent clause.
protasis . . . . apodosis.

By some writers, the hypothetical clause is termed the *conditional* clause.

Although the general tendency of philological opinion is now rather against Horne Tooke's derivation of 'if,' I still think the word is derived from *gif*, 'give,' the imperative mood of the Anglo-Saxon verb *gifan*. In many instances, we find two co-ordinate sentences, with an imperative mood in each clause; and this may have been the original form: as,

Gyf thu hyt eart, hat me cuman to the.
Give thou it art, bid me come to thee.
'If it be thou, bid me come to thee.'
Matthew xiv. 28.

Here *gyf* means 'give that,' 'grant that,' or 'suppose that.' Sometimes we find a question in the second clause: as,

Gyf Dauid hyne Dryhten clepað, hu ys he hys sunu?
Give David him Lord calleth, how is he his son?
'If David call him Lord, how is he his son?'
Matthew xxii. 45.

71. At other times, we find an indicative in the second clause, introduced by the particle *thonne* 'then:' as,

Gif ge forgyfað mannum heora synna, thonne forgyfð
Give ye forgive to-men their sins, then forgiveth
eower se heofenlica Fæder eow eowre gyltas.
your the heavenly Father to-you your guilts.
'If ye forgive men their trespasses, your heavenly Father will also forgive you.'—*Matthew* vi. 14.

We find similar constructions in early English, as,

> Forgiff me, Virgill, gif I thee offend.
>> Douglas, *Preface*, p. 11.

> Gif luf be verteu, than it is leful thing :
> Gif it be vice, it is your undoing,

that is,

> If love be virtue, then it is lawful thing :
> If it be vice, it is your undoing.
>> *Id. Prol. to 4th boke.*

If is often followed by *that* : as,

> Ne I wol non reherse, *if that* I may.
>> Chaucer, *Man of Lawes Prologue.*

> She wolde weepe, *yf that* she saw a mous.
>> *Id. Prologue to Canterbury Tales.*

72. The form *if . . . then* may throw some light upon the reading or pointing of *Macbeth* iii. 4. Horne Tooke quotes from the First Folio :

> Approach thou like the rugged Russian beare,
> The arm'd rhinoceros, or th' Hirean tiger,
> Take any shape but that, and my firme nerues
> Shall neuer tremble. Or be aliue againe
> And dare me to the desart with thy sworde,
> If trembling I *Inhabit* then, protest mee
> The baby of a girle.

He then remarks : 'Pope here changed *Inhabit* to *Inhibit*. Upon this correction Steevens builds another, and changes *then* to *thee.* Both which insipid corrections Malone, with his usual judgment, inserts in his text. And there it stands,

> ' " If trembling I inhibit thee."

' But for these tasteless commentators, one can hardly suppose that any reader of Shakspeare could have found a difficulty ; the original text is so plain, easy and clear, and so much in the author's accustomed manner.

> ' " Dare me to the desart with thy sworde,"

' " If I inhabit then "—*i.e.* If then I do not meet thee there ; if trembling I stay at home, or within doors, or under any roof, or within any habitation : If when you call me to the desart, I then HOUSE me, or through fear, hide myself from thee in any dwelling :

> ' " If trembling I do *House me then*—Protest me, &c." '
>> *Diversions of Purley,* ii. 54.

The Second, Third, and Fourth Folios read :—

> If trembling I inhabit, then, &c.

And although the reading of the First Folio may be more energetic, the pointing of the other folios is more in accordance with grammatical form ; *if—then, i.e.,* ' *If* trembling I keep the house (or " keep at home "), *then* protest me the baby of a girl.'

73. It may be useful to point out the relation of affirmative and negative clauses in sentences of this kind : as,

1. If . . . . then (*affirmative-affirmative*).
2. If not . . then not (*negative-negative*).
3. If . . . . then not (*affirmative-negative*).
4. If not . . then (*negative-affirmative*).

As for example :

1. If he comes, (then) I will go.
2. If he does not come, (then) I will not go.
3. If he writes, (then) I will not go.
4. If he does not write, (then) I will go.

As before remarked, *then* is generally omitted. And observe, that *if . . . not* may be represented by *unless,* or by any word, or words, to the same effect: as, *except, save that.* Thus, instead of sentences marked 2 and 4, we might say,

2. *Unless* he comes, I will not go.
4. *Unless* he writes, I will go.

So,

Except these abide in the ship, ye cannot be saved.

Acts xxvii. 31.

74. In these sentences involving condition and consequence, the use of the subjunctive mood demands particular attention. Theories derived from the doctrine of the Latin subjunctive have affected English composition ; and in many cases, where the English subjunctive is used, it is possible that the employment of the mood has been introduced by classical scholars, who laboured under a false impression that the Latin required a subjunctive. Professor Key has shown, (*Latin Grammar,* § 1153,) that in suppositions, which may be the fact or not, so far as the speaker professes to know, conditional sentences have nearly always the *indicative* in Latin in both clauses, and not the subjunctive.

75. Dr. Webster, in the Introduction to his *English Dictionary,* states his opinion, that the subjunctive form of the verb *if he be, if he have, if he go, if he say, if thou write, whether thou see, though he fall,* which was generally used by the writers of the sixteenth century, was in a great measure discarded before the time of Addison.

Whether this change resulted from the prevalence of colloquial usage over grammar rules, or because discerning men perceived the impropriety and inconsistency of the language of books, Dr. Webster does not pretend to determine. But he

observes that Locke, Watts, Addison, Pope, and other authors
who adorned the close of the seventeenth, and the beginning of
the eighteenth century, generally used the indicative mood to
express condition, uncertainty, and hypothesis in the present
and past tenses.

He then quotes the following examples :—

> If principles *are* innate.—*Locke*.
> If any person *hath* never examined this notion.—*Id*.
> Whether that substance *thinks* or no.—*Id*.
> If the soul *doth* think in sleep.—*Id*.
> If the reader *has* a mind to see a father of the same
> stamp.—*Addison*.
> If exercise *throws* off all superfluities.—*Id*.
> If America *is* not to be conquered.—*Lord Chatham*.
> If we *are* to be satisfied with assertions.—*Fox*.
> If it *gives* blind confidence.—*Id*.
> If my bodily strength *is* equal to the task.—*Pitt*.
> A negro, if he *works* for himself, and not for a master, will
> do double the work.—*Id*.
> If he *finds* his collection too small.—*Johnson*.
> Whether it *leads* to truth.—*Id*.
> If he *warns* others against his own failings.—*Id*.

76. This, according to Dr. Webster, is generally the language
of Johnson.   Except the substantive verb [be], there is in
his *Rambler* but a single instance of the subjunctive form
in conditional sentences.   In all other cases, the use of the
indicative is uniform.

But neither Johnson, nor other authors, are consistent in the
use of moods; thus Johnson writes :—

> If it *is* to be discovered only by experiment.
> If other indications *are* to be found.

But in the next sentence,—

> If to miscarry in an attempt *be* a proof of having mis-
> taken the direction of genius.

The following expressions occur in Pope's Preface to
Homer's Iliad, in the compass of thirteen lines :—

> If he *has* given a regular catalogue of an army.
> If he *has* funeral games for Patroclus.
> If Ulysses *visit* the shades.
> If he *be* detained from his return.
> If Achilles *be* absent.
> If he *gives* his hero a suit of celestial armour.

The verb *be* is often used in the subjunctive form by writers who never use that form in any other verb. Dr. Webster thinks the reason is, that *be* is primarily the indicative as well as the subjunctive mood of that verb. But as the form *be* is, in modern usage, restricted to the subjunctive, and as this is the only verb exhibiting a marked difference of form, writers may have been tempted to avail themselves of this difference. Our grammar presents so few varieties, that when we have one we are apt to use it too freely. As Falstaff says, ' it was always yet the trick of our English nation, if they have a good thing to make it too common.'—*2nd Hen. IV.* i. 2.)

77. The preceding remarks and quotations refer to the present and past tenses. Dr. Webster, in criticising Dr. Lowth, sets up a distinction, which appears to me untenable.

Dr. Lowth remarks (*English Grammar*, p. 61, *note*) that the forms of the subjunctive mood carry with them something of a future sense. Dr. Webster says this is true; but he charges Dr. Lowth with overlooking the distinction between ' an event of uncertain existence in *present* time and a *future* contingent event.' For example :—

Present: If the mail that has arrived *contains* a letter for me, I shall soon receive it.

Future : If the mail arriving to-morrow *contain* a letter for me, I shall be happy to receive it.

78. This distinction is fanciful; nor is it supported by good usage. Dr. Webster appeals to the Anglo-Saxon laws, many of which begin with *gif* followed by a subjunctive. But in other laws an indicative follows. The usage is not uniform, any more than among ourselves. We shall see that the Anglo-Saxon had no distinct form for the future, even in the indicative; or rather, that one form did double duty for the present, and for the future. Even in modern English we constantly say, ' I *go* to London to-morrow,' ' They *come* to see us next week.' No doubt, the present subjunctive has sometimes a future force; but so, sometimes, has the present indicative. And therefore Dr. Webster appears to be in error, when he insists so strongly upon the future sense of the present subjunctive. In the passage, ' If his son *ask* bread, will he give him a stone?' he says the words are unintelligible, unless we take *ask* in the sense of *shall ask*.

I believe that to say ' If his son *shall ask*' is not so idiomatic as ' If his son *asks*.' In Cork people constantly say, ' If it will be,'

for ' if it *is* '; and it is possible that this usage may have crept
in from the Gaelic idiom.   The following sentence appeared
in a Cork newspaper :—

' It appears from the Lord Lieutenant's answer to the peti-
tion in favour of Burke, that not only will he be executed, but
in all probability every man who *will be* found guilty of high
treason.'

79. Therefore, with regard to those suppositions which may
or may not be the actual fact, we have authority, in English,
for using the indicative in both clauses.

With reference to those conditional sentences which put an
imaginary case, the non-existence of which is implied in the
very terms, we must distinguish between present time and
past time.

In sentences relating to time present, we have the past-
imperfect subjunctive in the *if*-clause : as,

If he *were* here, he would tell us.

If he *were* present, I would speak to him.

In sentences relating to past time we have the auxiliary *had*
in the if-clause : as,

If he *had* confessed his fault, I should have forgiven him.

In older English we find *had* in both clauses : as,

I *had* fainted, unless I *had* believed.—*Psalm* xxvii. 13.

80. Observe that, except in the second person singular, we
cannot distinguish, in English, between the past perfect indicative *had fainted*, and the past perfect subjunctive *had fainted*.
The Germans distinguish *hatte* (indicative) and *hätte* (subjunctive).   For instance, the sentence just quoted might be rendered, in German,

Ich hätte verzweifelt, wenn ich nicht geglaubt hätte.

81. In Anglo-Saxon, we sometimes find the past imperfect
subjunctive in such cases : for instance, our version reads,

If thou hadst been here, my brother had not died.—*John*
xi. 21, 32.

but the Anglo-Saxon reads,

Gif thu wære her,   nære   min brothor dead.
If thou wert here, ne-were my brother dead.

10. *Concession and Declaration.*

82. In the older stages of the language, there are many examples of co-ordinate forms used to express this relation.   The

co-ordinate clauses are introduced respectively by *though* . . . yet, or *although* . . . yet. If there is occasion to distinguish them, they may be termed the ' *though*-clause,' and the ' *yet*-clause.'

Sometimes we find the indicative in the *though*-clause, and at other times the subjunctive: as,

Indicative:

> Though ye *have* lien among the pots, yet shall ye be as the wings of a dove covered with silver.—*Psalm* lxviii. 13.
>
> Although affliction *cometh* not forth of the dust . . . yet man is born unto trouble.—*Job* v. 6, 7.
>
> Although thou *sayest* thou shalt not see him, yet judgment is before him.—*Id.* xxxv. 14.

Subjunctive:

> Though he *slay* me, yet will I trust in him.—*Job* xiii. 15.
>
> Though the root thereof *wax* old in the earth . . . yet through the scent of water it will bud.—*Id.* xiv. 8, 9.
>
> Though his excellency *mount* up to the heavens, yet he shall perish for ever.—*Id.* xx. 6, 7.

83. In the following passages the form does not help us to determine whether the verbs are in the indicative or the subjunctive:

> Though I *speak*, my grief is not asswaged.—*Job* xvi. 6.
>
> Though after my skin worms *destroy* this body, yet in my flesh shall I see God.—*Id.* xix. 26.

Sometimes we have the future indicative in the *though*-clause: as,

> Although the fig-tree *shall* not *blossom*, neither *shall* fruit *be* in the vines; the labour of the olive *shall fail*, and the fields *shall yield* no meat; the flock *shall be* cut off from the fold, and there *shall be* no herd in the stalls; yet I will rejoice in the Lord, I will joy in the God of my salvation.—*Habakkuk* iii. 17, 18.

84. When an imaginary case is put, the non-existence of which is implied, we find the past-imperfect subjunctive in the *though*-clause; as,

> Whom, though I *were* righteous, yet would I not answer.   *Job* viii. 15.

Though I *were* perfect, yet would I not know my soul.

                                                  Id. viii. 21.

When the *yet*-clause becomes a Principal Clause, the particle *yet* is omitted, and the *though*-clause becomes accessory; as,

> Though I speak, my grief is not asswaged.—*Job* xvi. 6.
> Vain man would be wise, though man be born like
> a wild ass's colt.   *Id.* xi. 12.

III. COMPOUND SENTENCES COMPRISING SUBORDINATE CLAUSES.

85. That which we term the Subordinate Clause forms an integral part of the Compound Sentence.

The Subordinate Clause may be a Subject or an Object, in the whole Compound Sentence of which it forms a part; or it may take the place of an Adjective.

When the Subordinate Clause is a Subject or an Object, it is termed a *Noun-clause*.

When the Subordinate Clause stands in the place of an Adjective, it is termed an *adjective-clause*.

An attempt is sometimes made to divide sentences of this kind into two parts: (1) Principal Clause, (2) Subordinate Clause. For instance, in the sentence, ' I saw that something was wrong,' Professor Bain (*English Grammar*, p. 157) makes the following division :—

> I saw . . . . . *Principal Clause.*
> that something was wrong . *Subordinate Clause.*

86. But the clause ' that something was wrong' is the object of the verb ' saw.' The clause is comprised within the whole Compound Sentence, like a wheel within a wheel. In fact, the entire sentence, ' I saw that something was wrong,' occupies the position of a Principal *Sentence*, and the Subordinate *clause* ' that something was wrong' forms part of the whole.

In dealing with Correlative Sentences, it was easy to distinguish two separate *clauses*, which we termed the Principal Clause, and the Accessory Clause. But here we recognise no Principal *Clause*. We do not object to call the whole Compound Sentence a Principal *Sentence*; with the understanding, that it comprises, or involves within itself, one or more Subordinate Clauses, whether they be Noun-clauses or Adjective-clauses.

1. *The Noun-clause.*

87. The Noun-clause occupies the place, and follows the construction of a noun, in the whole compound sentence, of which it forms a part.

It may therefore be used :—

1. As a *subject-nominative* :
   That he said so is certain.

2. As a *predicate-nominative* :
   The result was *that they came forward.*

3. As an *objective* :
   His friends expect *that he will succeed.*

4. As a *noun in apposition* :
   The idea *that money alone is wealth,* has been the
   cause of great mistakes.

Sentences of this kind may be easily deduced from two
Co-ordinates :

   That he said so is certain.

   First Co-ordinate : He said so.

   Second Co-ordinate : That is certain.

Hence,—

   That [he said so] is certain.

So,—

   His friends expect that he will succeed.

   First Co-ordinate : He will succeed.

   Second Co-ordinate : His friends expect that.

   His friends expect that [he will succeed.]

See *Diversions of Purley,* i. 83—97.

88. There are two kinds of Noun-clauses :

1. Those that contain a direct statement.
2. Those that involve an indirect question.

1. Those Noun-clauses which contain a direct statement,
are generally introduced by the word *that,* commonly called a
conjunction, though originally it is a demonstrative pronoun.
For example, if my friend intends to visit me, and I am
aware of the fact, I say,

   I know *that* he will come,

where *that* implie the fact,' ' the following truth,' namely,
' his intended coming.' Similarly, ' I know that he is
returned ' may be resolved into two sentences, ' He is
returned,' ' I know that fact.' See Key, *Latin Grammar,*
§ 847, *note.*

And so completely is *that* regarded as introductory of the

following sentence, that we often omit the conjunction, and say, 'I know he will come.'

In Greek and Latin it is customary to give these sentences another turn, by which the subject-nominative of the Subordinate clause is made the subject-accusative, and the verb is thrown into the infinitive mood.

He will come . . . . . Ille veniet.

I know that *he will come* . . Scio *illum venturum esse.*

89. 2. Noun-clauses involving an indirect question. These are introduced by relative pronouns, or by relative adverbs (otherwise termed 'conjunctive adverbs'), as *when, where, how,* and some others. For example :—

I know *who you are.*
I understand *what you want.*
I know *when he will come.*
I see *how he did it.*

2. *The Adjective-clause.*

90. The Adjective-clause follows the construction of an adjective, and may qualify any noun or pronoun in the Compound Sentence. Hence it may be attached to the subject-nominative, to an objective, or to any substantive which occurs in phrases qualifying the predicate-nominative, or the predicate-verb.

1. With the *subject-nominative* :

The man, *who loves his country,* will never speak ill of her to strangers.

He is thrice armed, *that hath his quarrel just.*

The house, *that Jack built,* is wonderful.

The people, *with whom you associate,* are agreeable.

Hard was the hand *that gave the blow.*

Red were those lips *that bled.*

91. 2. With the *predicate-nominative* :

This man was the friend *who promised to help us.*
This is the letter *which he wrote.*
Spring is the time *when blossoms come.*
Ireland is the country *where I dwell.*

3. With an *objective* :

They want a leader *that knows the way.*
He lost all the money *which he had saved.*
I know a bank *whereon the wild thyme blows.*

4. With a *noun* or *pronoun* in *qualifying phrases* :

She came at the moment *when all was over.*

They lived on the estate *that their father left.*

He went with those *who planned the expedition.*

Obs.—Sentences of this kind may be deduced from the Co-ordinate form. Thus, 'The house that Jack built is wonderful.'

First Co-ordinate : That house is wonderful.

Second Co-ordinate : That house Jack built.

Again,—' Hard was the hand that gave the blow.'

First Co-ordinate : Hard was that hand.

Second Co-ordinate : That hand gave the blow.

The Adjective-clause is introduced by the relative pronouns *who, which, that,* or by the relative adverbs *when, where, whither, how,* &c.

92. Professor Bain makes a distinction in the use of the relatives ' that,' ' who,' and ' which.' To some this distinction may seem novel ; but he contends that it is the revival of an old and idiomatic usage. According to his view (*English Grammar, Preface,* p. iv.) the distinction between ' that' on the one hand and ' who' and ' which' on the other, was clearly perceived by our idiomatic writers up to the beginning of the last century ; but owing to an unfortunate misapprehension as to the English idiom of throwing a preposition to the end of a clause, the relative ' that' is now very little employed in book composition, ' who' and ' which' being made to serve in its stead.

Hence, he says (*English Grammar*, p. 159), ' The Adjective Clause, being by its nature restrictive, should be introduced by the restricting relative " that " or its equivalents, rather than by " who " or " which " the relatives more properly adapted for co-ordination. " The man *that* is wise" (meaning the same as " the *wise* man ") is preferable to " the man who is wise."

' This construction (*Grammar*, p. 23) avoids ambiguities that often attend the indiscriminate use of " who" and " which" for co-ordinate and for restrictive clauses. Thus when we say,

> his conduct surprised his English friends, who had not
> known him long,

we may mean, either

> (1) that his English friends generally were surprised (the
> relative being in that case *co-ordinating*) ;

> • or, (2) that only a portion of them—namely, the particular por-
> tion that had not known him long—were surprised.

' In this last case the relative is meant to define or explain the antecedent, and the doubt would be removed by writing thus—

> his English friends *that* had not known him long.'

93. This suggestion is worth considering, and may advantageously be applied in cases where ambiguity is likely to

arise from the employment of 'who' or 'which.' But the
custom of the language has so far sanctioned the indiscriminate
use of the pronouns, that an attempt to revive the distinction
will hardly find general acceptance.

94. The relative is sometimes omitted in English, but only
in constructions where, if expressed, it would stand in the objective case: as,

> The man I met was an old friend,

that is,

> The man *whom* (or *that*) I met was an old friend.

But we must be careful to avoid ambiguity; and if the omission of the relative might possibly throw doubt upon the
meaning of the sentence, we ought to insert it. Thus,

> The man I saw was your friend,

might mean, either

> The man, *whom* I saw, was your friend,

or,

> The man, *as* I saw (i. e., as I observed), was your friend.

Caution.

95. Care must be taken not to confound the noun-clause
with an adjective-clause. They may both be introduced by
the same connective :

I know *when we ought to start*	*Noun-clause.*
I know the time *when we ought to start* .	*Adjective-clause.*
I know *where it is*	*Noun-clause.*
I know the place *where it is*	*Adjective-clause.*

The test is this. When the clause is used to qualify a noun,
it is an adjective-clause. But when the whole clause stands
in the place of a subject or an object, it is a noun-clause.

CHAPTER IV.

CONTRACTED SENTENCES.

96. We have said that any sentence containing more than one subject-nominative, or more than one predicate-verb, is called a Compound Sentence.

But considerable difficulties arise where two or more subject-nominatives have only one predicate-verb, or where one subject-nominative has two or more predicate-verbs.

Take for example sentences of the copulative class :—

1. Where two subject-nominatives have one predicate-verb : as,

Cæsar and Pompey came to Rome,

2. Where one subject-nominative has two predicate-verbs : as,

Cæsar conquered the Gauls, and invaded Britain.

The question is, how we must deal with examples of this kind. But this question, which has been much perplexed, is connected with another enquiry, namely, whether conjunctions can be said to couple words as well as sentences; or whether we ought to hold that conjunctions can couple sentences only, and not individual words.

97. Those grammarians who maintain that conjunctions couple sentences only, explain all these cases upon one principle—that of *contraction*. They say, for example, that 'Cæsar and Pompey came to Rome' is a contraction for two simple sentences, 'Cæsar came to Rome,' and 'Pompey came to Rome.' Similarly, 'Cæsar conquered the Gauls, and invaded Britain' will be a contraction of the two simple sentences, 'Cæsar conquered the Gauls,' and 'Cæsar invaded Britain.'

But, on the other hand, it is objected that the principle will not always hold good. For, if we examine the sentence 'John and Jane are a handsome couple,' we cannot say that 'John is a couple,' and 'Jane is a couple.' Or, if we take 'one and one make two,' we cannot explain it as contracted from 'one makes two,' and 'one makes two.'

98. Those who are moved by this objection have recourse to another explanation. They say, that 'Cæsar and Pompey came to Rome' is a simple sentence with a *compound subject*, the conjunction *and* coupling the words 'Cæsar' and 'Pompey,' as though it were '[Cæsar and Pompey] came to Rome.'

They wish to know why conjunctions may not couple individual words. The answer is, that if conjunctions couple words, grammarians find a difficulty in discriminating between conjunctions and prepositions. But this is met by the rejoinder, that prepositions can govern the cases of nouns, whereas conjunctions cannot. This part of the subject we shall consider hereafter; see §§ 441–445.

99. Similar diversity is found in explaining sentences of the alternative class. We are told, for instance, that, 'Neither Cæsar nor Pompey came to Rome,' is a contracted compound sentence, made up of two simple sentences, 'Neither Cæsar came to Rome,' 'nor Pompey came to Rome.'

But 'All men are black or white,' cannot be contracted from 'all men are black,' or 'all men are white;' for the meaning is 'all men are [either black or white].'

100. It may be, that perplexity has arisen from the confusion of form and meaning which sometimes enters into grammatical investigations. Similar forms are sometimes employed in cases where the meaning is at variance with the form. It does not follow, because the application of the principle will not suit the *meaning* in all instances, that therefore the principle itself did not *originate* from the method of contraction.

101. At the same time we must guard against that love of uniformity which so often leads grammarians astray. We should beware of hastily laying down general rules; and we should rather examine the cases separately as they arise. In instances where two or more subject-nominatives are answered by one predicate-verb, we may distinguish the cases, (1) where the predicate is true of the subjects severally; (2) where the predicate is true of the subjects, not severally, but jointly.

For example, in the sentence 'Cæsar and Pompey came to Rome,' it is true that 'Cæsar came to Rome,' and that 'Pompey came to Rome.' But in 'John and Jane are a handsome couple,' the predicate is not true of 'John and Jane' severally. Here we must analyse thus :—

John and Jane .	Two subject-nominatives, united by the conjunction 'and.'
are	Predicate-verb.
a	Article, qualifying the predicate-nominative, 'couple.'
handsome . . .	Adjective, qualifying the predicate-nominative, 'couple.'
couple	Predicate-nominative.

And if, in such a case, we are obliged to adopt this method of analysis, the same method must be at least optional in other cases. For example :—

Cæsar and Pompey came to Rome.

Cæsar and Pompey . Two subject-nominatives, coupled
by the conjunction 'and.'
came . . . . . Predicate-verb.
to Rome . . . . Adverbial phrase, qualifying the
predicate-verb, 'came.'

102. And similarly, where one subject-nominative has two predicate-verbs; as

Cæsar conquered the Gauls and invaded Britain.

Cæsar . . . Subject-nominative.
conquered . First predicate-verb.
the . . . . Article, qualifying the objective, ' Gauls.'
Gauls . . . Objective, dependent on the first predicate-verb, ' conquered.'
and . . . Conjunction, coupling the two predicate-
verbs, 'conquered' and 'invaded.'
invaded . . Second predicate-verb.
Britain . . Objective, dependent upon the second
predicate-verb, 'invaded.'

Elliptical Sentences.

103. Although grammarians have abused the privilege of 'understanding' and 'supplying' words at pleasure, still we must admit that words are sometimes not found where we expect to see them, or where, according to grammatical theory, such words might find place. Nay, further, words are omitted in one language, which must be expressed in another. For example, we omit the relative pronoun in instances where the omission would be considered barbarous in Latin; as, ' This is the man I saw,' meaning '*whom* I saw.'

We omit the relative in constructions where, if expressed, it would stand in the objective case. The Welsh, however, carry this much further; as

Gwelais y dyn oedd yn-canu,
I saw the man was singing,

for ' I saw the man *who* was singing.' Thus, a Welshman, who has an imperfect acquaintance with English, will say, ' This is the man was driving the horse,' for ' *who* was driving the horse.'

104. Let us take these examples:—

> This is the book I gave you.
> This is the house I live in.
> This is the way I came.
> He left the day I arrived.

In one stage of the English language, the word *that* would have been employed in these sentences:

> This is the book that I gave you.
> This is the house that I live in.
> This is the way that I came.
> He left the day that I arrived.

Here *that* has the force of a relative pronoun. In more modern English, there is a tendency to substitute *who, which,* for *that*; and as a notion has prevailed that sentences should not end with a preposition, many writers say ' in which I live,' rather than ' which I live in.' Accordingly these sentences might stand,

> This is the book which I gave you.
> This is the house in which I live.
> This is the way by which I came.
> He left the day on which I arrived.

105. According to our notions of grammatical construction, founded in a great measure upon the grammar of the Latin language, we cannot analyse sentences of this kind without supplying some word to stand in the place of a relative pronoun; as ' This is the book *that* I gave you.'

This	Subject-nominative.
is	Predicate-verb.
the	Article, qualifying the predicate-nominative, ' book.'
book	Predicate-nominative.
that I gave you	Adjective-clause, qualifying the predicate-nominative, ' book.'

If I might offer a conjecture, the sentence 'This is the book I gave you,' represents the ancient British idiom, answering to the modern Welsh idiom; for I believe that the traces of the old British are much more numerous in our language than is generally surmised. The sentence ' This is the book *that* I gave you,' corresponds to the Anglo-Saxon form; and 'This is the book *which* I gave you,' is the modern English, founded *upon* imitation of the Latin construction.

RULES AND CAUTIONS.

————◦◦————

CHAPTER V

NOUNS.

NOMINATIVE.

RELATIONS OF SUBJECT AND PREDICATE.

The *Nominative and* The *Verb.*

106. ' *The* Verb agrees with *its* Nominative case in number and person,' said the old rule.

But as there may be many verbs and many nominatives in a sentence, the rule was somewhat indefinite, and was learned rather by practical application, than from any precision in the terms employed.

' The nominative *to* the verb ' meant the *subject*-nominative; and ' the nominative *after* the verb ' meant the *predicate*-nominative.

By *the* Verb was understood the *predicate*-verb.

The form of analysis, which we propose for simple sentences, is

1. Time flies.

Time. . . . . . . *Subject-nominative.*
flies . . . . . . *Predicate-verb.*

2. Mirth is good.

Mirth . . . . . *Subject-nominative.*
is . . . . *Predicate-verb.*
good . . . . . . *Predicate-nominative.*

107. We shall first consider the relations of the subject-nominative and the predicate-nominative. Then we shall proceed to the relations of the subject-nominative and the predicate-verb.

Relations of the Subject-nominative and the Predicate-nominative.

As the terms themselves imply, the subject-nominative and the predicate-nominative agree in case; but with regard to gender and number, the agreement depends upon several considerations.

If the predicate-nominative be an *adjective*, it agrees with the subject-nominative in gender and number, as well as in case. And though, in English, adjectives do not vary their ending to show this agreement, the difference must be expressed in translating from English into Latin or any other language, where such variations are necessary. For example,

The boy is *good*	Puer est bon-*us*.
The girl is *good*	Puella est bon-*a*.
The boys are *good*	Pueri sunt bon-*i*.
The girls are *good*	Puellæ sunt bon-*æ*.

108. But if the predicate-nominative be a *noun*, there may be diversity of gender and number. If, indeed, a noun changes its form to denote difference of gender, we generally make the change; we say, for example,

> John Kemble was an act*or*.
> Mrs. Siddons was an act*ress*.

However, we do not always follow the rule exactly. For though, in strictness, we ought to say 'Sims Reeves is a singer' and 'Jenny Lind is a songstress;' still, in ordinary conversation, we commonly call Jenny Lind a 'singer.' And yet, during the height of her popularity, when admiring critics rose into enthusiasm, she was sometimes styled 'this gifted songstress,' 'this divine songstress.'

109. Greater latitude is allowed, with regard to number. We say,

> Dutiful children are great blessings,

or,

> Dutiful children are a great blessing.
> The fine arts are sources of delight,

or,

> The fine arts are a source of delight.

But when the number is not the same on both sides, a difficulty sometimes arises in the use of the verb, which might agree with either, but cannot possibly agree with both.

Very often the verb agrees with the nominative which comes first, as in the examples just given : and so here,

This convention *was* really the two Houses of Parliament.
Kerr's Blackstone, i. 138.

But not always ; as,

His pavilion round about him *were* dark waters and thick clouds of the skies.—*Psalm* xviii. 11.

The wages of sin *is* death. —*Rom*. vi. 23.

A similar question occurs, when the subject-nominative and the predicate-nominative differ in *person*, as we shall see more particularly in considering the use of pronouns. We commonly say, ' It *is* I,' but Chaucer says ' It *am* I ; ' and instead of ' It *is* the sheriff's men,' he has ' It *ben* the sherrefes men.'

Relations of the Subject-nominative and the Predicate-verb.

110. Generally speaking, the form must be our guide ; singular follows singular, and plural follows plural. Sometimes, however, the meaning overrides the form ; and we have to enquire whether the idea of unity, or of plurality is intended.

When the subject-nominative is in the singular, the predicate-verb is in the singular ; as, ' Time flies.'

No matter how many singular or plural nouns, *dependent on prepositions, or under any other government*, may intervene between the subject-nominative and the predicate-verb, they cannot affect this rule.

But even the best writers are liable to trip, in such instances ; as

The right to recall the governor-general and to declare war *are* vested in the court of directors.
Kerr's Blackstone, i. 96.

As when the *excellence* of the Church, of the House of Lords and Commons, of the procedure of law courts, &c., *are* inferred from the mere fact that the country has prospered under them.
Mill, *Logic*, i. 422.

Here the *&c.* must depend on the preposition *of* : and then we have ' the *excellence* . . . *are*.' If it be replied that *&c.* stands in the place of a second subject-nominative, what are we to understand by ' the excellence . . . &c. ? '

I recently observed the following passages in the reviews and magazines :—

> The discovery of gold, however, brought a greatly increased population to the adjacent colony of Victoria, and the superior *richness* of its gold-fields *have* since maintained it at the head of the group.
>
> *Edinburgh Review*, April 1865.　No. 248, p. 357.

> Our *fancy* to speak of books, and their writers, and sellers, *have* led us aside from the area marked out by Mr. Thornbury for his own explorations, so we must return to bounds, within which we find Lincoln's-Inn Fields.
>
> *Dublin University Magazine*, July 1865.

111. These are mere slips of the pen, and without constant care anyone may fall into similar errors. But some persons are guided almost entirely by the ear. In ' the ship *sails*,' and ' the ship*s* sail,' 'the boy *walks*,' and ' the boy*s* walk,' there is an alternation of the letter *s* which catches the ear, and is the chief guide which many people follow. Hence, in examining a written sentence, they will ask *how it reads*, often meaning nothing more than *how it sounds*. And thus, if several dependent nouns, in the plural, occur between the subject-nominative and the predicate-verb, the notion of plurality takes possession of the mind, and the verb follows in the plural. But it is evident that this is a very unsafe method of judging; for we ought to be guided by the sense, and not by the sound alone. Here, therefore, we should always keep the subject-nominative distinctly in view.

112. If the subject-nominative has a plural form, but is still regarded as one thing, the predicate-verb is generally in the singular; as ' The " Pleasures of Hope" was written by Campbell ; ' because we mean to assert that the poem called ' The Pleasures of Hope,' was written by Campbell. And yet, Dr. Johnson, speaking about his 'Lives of the Poets,' says, ' My " Lives" *are* reprinting,' where the Lives are regarded as plural. In these instances, the intention of the writer, and not the form, must be the guide.

113. Some nouns, which have a plural form, are often used as singular ; for example, ' news,' ' pains,' ' means,' ' summons,' and the names of sciences, as, ' mathematics,' ' ethics,' ' optics.'
Older writers vary considerably in the employment of these

words. For example, Shakespeare employs 'news' sometimes in the singular, at other times in the plural : as,

> *Gonzalo.* What *is* the news?
> *Boatswain.* The best news *is*, that we have safely found
> the king and company.
>
> > *Tempest*, v. 1.

> *This* news *is* old enough ; yet it is every day's news.
>
> > *Measure for Measure*, iii. 2.

> Thus answer I in name of Benedick,
> But hear *these* ill news with the ears of Claudio.
>
> > *Much Ado*, ii. 1.

> But wherefore do I tell *these* news to thee.
>
> > *1st Hen. IV.* iii. 2.

> *These* news *are* everywhere; every tongue speaks *them*.
>
> > *Hen. VIII.* ii. 2.

> *Wolsey.* What more?
> *Cromwell.* That Cranmer is returned with welcome,
> > Installed Lord Archbishop of Canterbury.
> *Wolsey.* That's *news*, indeed.
>
> > *Ibid.* iii. 2.

114. So in the use of ' means,' we observe variety. Occasionally we find the singular form ' mean : ' as,

> Yet nature is made better by no *mean*,
> But nature makes *that mean*; so, o'er that art,
> Which, you say, adds to nature, is an art
> That nature makes.—*Winter's Tale*, iv. 3.

But we also find 'means ' used in the singular: as ;

> I am courted now with a double occasion ; gold, and *a
> means* to do the prince my master good.—*Ibid.* iv. 3.

> By *this means* shall we sound what skill she hath.
>
> > *1st Hen. VI.* i. 2.

But it occurs just as often in the plural, and this is the
more usual construction in modern English :

> *Chief Justice.* Your means *are* very slender, and your
> > waste is great.
> *Falstaff.* I would it were otherwise; I would my means
> > were greater, and my waist slenderer.
>
> > *2nd Hen. IV.* i. 2.

> With all appliances and *means* to boot.—*Ibid.* iii. 1.

115. It is more usual to find ' pains ' in the plural ; but
even this word is found in the singular : as,

> Nay, then, thou lov'st it not,
> And all my pains *is* sorted to no proof.
> > *Taming of the Shrew*, iv. 3.
> > . . . . for *this pains*
> Cæsar hath hanged him.
> > *Ant. and Cleop.* iv. 6.

116. A collective noun represents a number of individuals collected in one mass or group; as, *army, government, committee*. It is singular in form, but it may often be regarded as conveying the idea of plurality. In older English, these nouns were frequently considered as singular, where modern writers would use them with a verb in the plural: as,

> Blessed *is* the people that know the joyful sound: they shall walk, O Lord, in the light of thy countenance.— *Psalm* lxxxix. 15.

Here, however, we observe a mixture of two constructions; for 'know' and 'they' imply plurality.

Accordingly, the older grammarians decided that nouns of this kind might be treated as either singular or plural. But modern grammarians hold that, when the idea of unity is prominent, the verb must be used in the singular; when, on the other hand, the idea of plurality is prominent, the verb must be in the plural: as,

> The House *has* decided the question.
> The College of Cardinals *have* elected the Pope.

117. Professor Bain distinguishes between a *collective noun* and a *noun of multitude*, in this way, that a 'collective noun' represents a great number of individuals included in one mass or body. Thus he says, (*English Grammar*, p. 12,) 'when a multitude act together, as a "fleet," or a "parliament," they are spoken of in the singular number and have a singular verb: as "the fleet *was* victorious," "the Parliament *was* opened by the Queen in person." But the designation "noun of multitude" is applied to express collective bodies, whose *action* is not *collective* but *individual*: as "the clergy *were* opposed to the measure."'

According to this view, when the predicate is true of the whole mass in its collective unity, the verb should be in the singular: as 'the fleet *is* under orders to sail.' But when the predicate applies to the individuals of the collection acting separately, the verb should be in the plural: as 'the people of the rude tribes of America *are* remarkable for their artifice and duplicity : ' ' the public *are* often deceived by false appearances.'—See Bain, *English Grammar*, p. 172.

118. Where so much depends upon the intention of the writer, it is difficult to lay down precise rules. We might suppose, however, that consistency was desirable ; that having once made up our minds to prefer the singular or the plural construction, we ought to persevere in the same to the end of the sentence. Yet Dr. Angus says (*Handbook*, § 365), ' Sometimes the two usages are combined in the same sentence with peculiar force : as,

> Behold, the people *is* one, and *they have* all one language.
> —*Gen.* xi. 6.'

And Professor Bain remarks (*English Grammar*, p. 173) :— ' The following sentence sounds awkward, but it is strictly correct: " The Megarean sect *was* founded by Euclid, not the mathematician, and *were* the happy inventors of logical syllogism, or the art of quibbling."—*Tytler*. In the first part, the sect is spoken of in its collective capacity ; and in the second, as individuals.'

But, to say the least, this sudden change of construction within the limits of a sentence, leaves the whole sentence open to cavil. Professor Bain admits that the sound is awkward ; and this very objection is likely to arouse the suspicion of a critic. Besides, if a sentence is somewhat long, and *pronouns* are introduced referring to the collective noun, confusion will almost inevitably ensue ; so that, in careless compositions, we may even find *it* in one clause, and *they* in another.

119. The safest rule is this :

1. *As to mere form* : A collective noun, used as a subject-nominative, may take the verb in the singular, or in the plural.
2. *As to meaning* : Consider whether you intend to give prominence to the idea of unity or of plurality ; and put the verb in the singular, or in the plural, accordingly.
3. But never attempt to combine both constructions in the same sentence.
4. And if pronouns are introduced, referring to the collective noun, be careful to employ them consistently, in the singular, or in the plural, according to the view originally taken.

120. When two or more subject-nominatives are used in the same sentence, some difficult questions are involved. We have to consider the doctrine of contraction, and the vexed question whether conjunctions couple sentences alone, or whether they may be said to couple words also. See §§ 99–102.

We shall discuss the particular cases.

121. I. Cases, where the subject-nominatives are in the *singular*; and where the conjunction *and* is the connective employed.

    (a) When the predicate is true of the subjects, *not severally*, but *jointly*, the verb must be in the plural: as,

> William and Mary *are* a handsome couple.
> Two and three *make* five.
> The bishop, the earl, and the sheriff *hold* the shire-mote.
> Octavian, Antony and Lepidus *constitute* the triumvirate.

    (b) When the predicate is true of the subjects *severally*, the doctrine of contraction may be applied, and the predicate-verb, in the singular, may be understood of each subject-nominative. In some languages, as in Latin and in German, the principle is admitted more freely than with us. Thus, in one of Uhland's ballads, the hostess says,

> Mein Bier und Wein *ist* frisch and klar:
> My   Beer and Wine *is*   fresh and clear.

122. However, there are limitations. If the nouns used as subject-nominatives denote *living beings*, and especially *persons*, the verb is always in the plural: as, ' Cæsar and Pompey go to war.' And in regard to *things without life*, the same rule is observed where distinct objects are signified. But in the case of nouns denoting *abstract ideas*, as ' virtue,' ' piety,' ' vice,' ' folly,' and the like, we find considerable variation. Here the Latin language freely admits a verb in the singular: as, ' Cum tempus necessitasque *postulat*, decertandum manu est : ' ' when occasion and necessity *demands*, we must fight amain.' And those English writers who have formed their style upon the Latin models sometimes employ the same construction : so Hooker speaks of ' the glorious inhabitants of those sacred palaces, where nothing but light and blessed immortality, no shadow of matter for tears, discontentment, griefs, and uncomfortable passions to work upon; but all *joy, tranquillity,* and *peace,* even for ever and ever *doth dwell.'*— *Ecclesiastical Polity,* i. 4.

The Oxford edition of 1807 reads, ' *do* dwell.'

123. But this form does not find general approval with modern critics; and by some it is condemned as a breach of English grammar; on this ground, that nouns in the singular, coupled by the conjunction 'and,' are equivalent to a plural.

As to principle, the form may be defended, if we admit the doctrine of contraction. But in practice the following rules will be found to work well:—

> *Rule I.*—When the two or more nouns, in the singular, mean different things, or represent distinct ideas, put the verb in the plural.

> *Rule II.*—But when the two nouns mean the same thing, or very nearly the same, strike out one of them, put the verb in the singular, and learn to avoid using two words where one is enough.

124. Whenever modifying words are introduced, such as ' every,' ' each,' ' no,' showing that the predicate is asserted of the subjects severally, the predicate-verb must be in the singular. For here, the doctrine of contraction clearly applies; in other words, the predicate-verb is evidently applicable to every one of the subject-nominatives: as,

> Every limb and feature *appears* with its appropriate grace.

When subject-nominatives in the singular are emphatically distinguished, they belong to different propositions, and the verb follows in the singular: as,

> Somewhat, and, in many cases, a great deal *is* put upon us.

The same principle operates when the phrase ' as well as,' or the conjunction ' but ' is used: so,

> Veracity, as well as justice, *is* to be our rule.

125.—II. Cases where the conjunction *or* or *nor* is used.

Where the connective ' or ' or ' nor ' is used, the whole sentence really involves distinct propositions. Hence, if the subject nominatives are in the singular, the verb must be in the singular: as,

The secretary or the treasurer *draws* up the report.

Neither the master nor the scholar *understands* the question.

126.—III. Cases where the subject-nominatives, or some of them, are in the plural.

Where the subject-nominatives are all in the plural, the predicate-verb must be in the plural : as,

> Joys and sorrows follow in succession.

When some of the subject-nominatives are in the singular, and some are in the plural, we have to consider the connection of the whole sentence :

(*a*) Where the conjunction 'and' is used, even one subject-nominative in the plural will require a verb in the plural. For, according to the doctrine of contraction, the verb must apply to each subject-nominative; and upon no supposition can a verb in the singular agree with a noun in the plural, if it be a genuine plural. But it is quite consistent, that one or more nouns in the singular, together with a noun in the plural, should be followed by a verb in the plural.

(*b*) When subject-nominatives of different numbers are separated by 'or' or 'nor,' the verb is generally in the plural; and it is then convenient to place the plural subject-nominative next the verb : as,

> Neither the king nor his ministers were in favour of the change.

When two subject-nominatives of different numbers are found in different clauses of the sentence, there are really two distinct propositions, and the verb had better be repeated; as,

> The voice is Jacob's, but the hands are Esau's.

127. Some peculiarities deserve notice in constructions where the verb precedes the subject-nominatives. In the Welsh language there is a curious rule that when the verb stands first it must be in the singular, even though the subject-nominative following be in the plural. Without going to this extreme, many of our English writers use great license, when the verb stands first. Shakespeare says,—

> There *is* tears for his love ; joy for his fortune ; honour for his valour ; and death for his ambition.
> *Julius Cæsar*, iii. 2.

There 's two or three of us have seen strange sights.
Julius Cæsar, i. 3.

Hence when a predicate-verb is followed by two or more subject-nominatives in the singular, the verb will often be found in the singular, as,

Now *abideth* faith, hope, charity; these three.
1· *Cor.* xiii. 13.

Thine *is* the kingdom, and the power, and the glory.
Matthew vi. 13.

His sceptre shows the force of temporal power,
The attribute to awe and majesty,
Wherein *doth sit* the *dread* and *fear* of kings.
Merchant of Venice, iv. 1.

POSITION.

128. Those languages which have great variety of inflection admit many changes of position in the order of words. Thus in Latin, the sentence ' Cæsar Gallos vicit' will admit six different collocations, each having a different emphasis; as,—

1. Cæsar Gallos vicit.
2. Gallos Cæsar vicit.
3. Cæsar vicit Gallos.
4. Gallos vicit Cæsar.
5. Vicit Cæsar Gallos.
6. Vicit Gallos Cæsar.

It is difficult to express these diversities in English, without turning the active voice into the passive, in some cases; but the following version will convey an idea of the change of emphasis.

1. Cæsar conquered the Gauls.
2. The Gauls were conquered by Cæsar.
3. It was Cæsar who conquered the Gauls.
4. It was the Gauls who were conquered by Cæsar.
5. Cæsar *did* conquer the Gauls.
6. The Gauls *were* conquered by Cæsar.

129. But just in proportion as there are fewer inflections in English, so the position becomes important to determine the sense.

Because, where there are no changes in the form of the word itself, to denote various relations, these relations must

E

be marked either by particles, as for example by prepositions, or by the position of the words themselves. In the sentences, 'John beats Peter,' and 'Peter beats John,' there is nothing but the position to show which gives the blow, and which receives it. Whereas in Latin the *form* of the words would show the distinction :—

Johann*es* Petr*um* verberat.
Petr*us* Johann*em* verberat.

130. Hence* it is that, in English, the order of words becomes most important; for in very many instances *bad order* is not merely an inelegance, but it is positively *bad grammar*.

As a general rule the English language follows the logical order of subject and predicate. The subject-nominative comes first; then we have the predicate-verb, or the predicate-verb followed by a predicate-nominative, as the case may be. If the verb is transitive, the object generally follows the verb.

A change in the order of words often takes place to mark emphasis. The very change itself awakens attention; and, generally, importance is assigned to those words which occupy the first place. Hence, we often find the predicate, or portions of the predicate preceding the subject; as,—

Great is Diana of the Ephesians.—*Acts* xix. 34.

In another passage our translators have not been so successful. We read, *Rev.* xviii. 4, ' Babylon the great is fallen, is fallen,' where the repetition at the close weakens the emphasis. But on the other hand, ' Fallen, fallen is Babylon the great ' would call attention to the most emphatic word in the sentence; and this, indeed, is the order of the original :—
Ἔπεσεν, ἔπεσε Βαβυλὼν ἡ μεγάλη.

131. In indicative sentences the predicate-verb precedes the subject-nominative, when the sentence or clause opens with ' neither,' or ' nor,' (used in the sense of ' and not') : as,—

Thou know'st that all my fortunes are at sea;
Neither *have I* money, nor commodity
To raise a present sum.
Merchant of Venice, i. 1.

My ventures are not in one bottom trusted,
Nor to one place; nor *is* my whole *estate*
Upon the fortune of this present year.—*Ibid.*

So too after the particle ' there,' used not as an adverb of place, but by way of introducing a sentence :

There *was* a *king* in Thule.

There *came* a *philosopher* from India.

When a conditional clause is employed without the conjunction ' if,' an auxiliary verb may stand first : as,

Were he present, he would say so.

Had I been there I should have seen him.

When other parts of the predicate, as, for example, the object, are placed first for the sake of emphasis, the predicate-verb will often precede the subject-nominative, in order to keep the various parts of the predicate as near together as possible :

Other refuge *have I* none.

　　　　　　　　　　　　Charles Wesley.

So when an adverb, or an adverbial clause, stands first, the verb may precede the subject-nominative : as,

Here *followed* a long *train* of officials.

In this unhappy battle of Newbury, *was* slain the Lord Viscount *Falkland*.

Cautions.

132.—1. Take care that there be a subject-nominative in the sentence.

The following sentence occurs in a well-known passage, where the historian Robertson is describing the character of Mary Queen of Scots :—

Polite, affable, insinuating, sprightly, and capable of speaking and of writing with equal ease and dignity.

The context shows that we must supply the words ' she was.' The whole passage reads thus :

To all the charms of beauty, and the utmost elegance of external form, she added those accomplishments which render their impression irresistible. Polite, affable, insinuating, sprightly, and capable of speaking and of writing with equal ease and dignity. Sudden, however, and violent in all her attachments; because her heart was warm and unsuspicious. Impatient of contradiction; because she had been accustomed from her infancy to be treated as a queen. No stranger, on

E 2

some occasions, to dissimulation; which, in that per-
fidious court where she received her education, was
reckoned among the necessary arts of government. Not
insensible of flattery, or unconscious of that pleasure
with which almost every woman beholds the influence
of her own beauty. Formed with the qualities which
we love, not with the talents that we admire, she was
an agreeable woman rather than an illustrious queen.
—Robertson, *History of Scotland*, book vii.

Grammatically considered, the whole passage from ' Polite,
affable,' to ' illustrious queen,' forms one long sentence, of
which ' she' is the subject-nominative, and ' was' is the predicate-verb.

This form of composition is highly rhetorical, and is admired
by some critics; but youthful composers should be cautious
in imitating this style.

133.—2. Take care that there be a predicate in the sentence.

In other words, having a subject to speak about, take care
to say something about it. This rule is more frequently
violated than the former. It is often observable in answers
to questions in examination. Pupils should be habituated to
give full answers; that is to say, each answer should form a
complete sentence.

Take this instance:

> The poems of Homer, which have exercised an im-
> portant influence upon the literature of the world.

But what of the poems of Homer, which have exercised an
important influence upon the literature of the world? There
is, indeed, a verb, 'have exercised;' but it occurs in the adjective-clause qualifying the subject-nominative ' poems.' But
nothing is *predicated*. Nothing is *stated*, nothing is affirmed
or denied respecting the poems of Homer.

The verses containing the remonstrance addressed to
Richard II. by Old John of Gaunt, 'time-honoured Lancas-
ter,' are sometimes quoted thus:—

> This royal throne of kings, this scepter'd isle,
> This earth of majesty, this seat of Mars,
> This other Eden, demi-paradise;
> This fortress built by Nature for herself
> Against infection and the hand of war;
> This happy breed of men, this little world;

This precious stone set in the silver sea,
Which serves it in the office of a wall,
Or as a moat defensive to a house,
Against the envy of less happier lands;
This blessed plot, this earth, this realm, this England.

But what about 'this England?' If we refer to the original, we find that the remonstrance does not end there; but
goes on as follows:—

This blessed plot, this earth, this realm, this England,
This nurse, this teeming womb of royal kings,
Feared by their breed, and famous by their birth,
Renownéd for their deeds as far from home
(For Christian service and true chivalry)
As is the sepulchre in stubborn Jewry
Of the world's ransom, Blessed Mary's Son;
This land of such dear souls, this dear, dear land,
Is now leased out (I die pronouncing it)
Like to a tenement, or pelting farm;
England, bound in with the triumphant sea,
Whose rocky shore beats back the envious siege
Of watery Neptune, *is now bound in* with shame,
With inky blots, and rotten parchment bonds:
That England, that was wont to conquer others,
Hath made a shameful conquest of itself.
Ah, would the scandal vanish with my life,
How happy then were my ensuing death!
Richard II., ii. 1.

This passage contains three distinct propositions, followed
by an exclamation:

1. This royal throne of kings . . . is now leased out.
2. England . . . is now bound in with shame.
3. England . . . hath made a shameful conquest of itself.

Then follows the exclamation 'would the scandal vanish . . .
how happy were my . . . death!'

134. 3. The careless use of the Case Absolute gives occasion to a class of errors, into which Latin scholars are pecu-
liarly liable to fall. As the Latin language has no perfect
participle active, the perfect participle passive is used in its
stead; but both the participle and the substantive, with which
it agrees, are put in the ablative case. Now, in Latin, this
ablative case is a safeguard; because the noun or pronoun,
so used absolutely, can never be mistaken for a nominative.

But when this construction is imitated in English, the safe-guard is lost. Some grammarians tell us that nouns so employed are in the *Nominative Absolute* in English. If, then, a so-called nominative absolute be employed in the beginning of a sentence, the reader may mistake it for a subject-nomina-tive; and afterwards, when the true subject-nominative is introduced, perplexity may arise. (See § 27.) The confusion is made worse when a participle is used, unconnected with any substantive at all. Here is part of an advertisement, pub-lished by the proprietor of an educational establishment:

> ' Having to pass an examination for admission, a few
> months' preparation at —— is strongly recommended.'

In this sentence the participle is used without any substan-tive at all. Of course, the meaning is, ' As pupils have to pass an examination for admission, a few months' preparation, &c.:' and the form which the writer had in his mind was ' Pupils having to pass an examination —— ' By further license, the writer omits the word ' pupils,' and the phrase stands ' Having to pass,' without stating *who* is to pass.

135. So here:

> Having found that there were great difficulties on both
> sides, it was resolved to proceed no further in the
> business.

From this collection of words we infer that a resolution was formed to proceed no further in a certain business. But we are not told *who* found difficulties, or *who* resolved to proceed no further; although the participle ' having found ' leads us to expect a subject-nominative indicating *persons*. The pas-sage is quoted from the Report of a Committee, who were ashamed to confess that they had abandoned the business in question. If they had said, ' *we* resolved to proceed no further,' they would not only have written correctly, but they would have told the whole truth. This confession, however, did not suit the purpose of the Committee; and, as one fault leads to another, their dissimulation led them into bad grammar.

136. In the early part of a sentence, before the introduction of the subject-nominative, it is dangerous to use the Case Absolute; and it is equally dangerous to employ introductory participles, referring to any noun, other than the subject-nominative: for example,

> ' Having gone through this amount of villany, King George
> thought he was qualified to represent him at the court

of Lisbon, and thither Lord Tyrawley proceeded accordingly.'—Doran, *Annals of the Stage*, ii. 275.

The context shows that it was not King George, but Lord Tyrawley, who had gone through an amount of villany ; and that therefore the King thought Tyrawley a suitable representative. But the phrase 'having gone through this amount of villany,' stands in treasonable proximity to King George; and there is nothing in the *form* of the sentence to guard us against making a wrong application of the phrase.

POSSESSIVE CASE.

137. The Possessive in English corresponds to the Genitive in Latin and other languages; and is the only case in English nouns where we find a change of termination. The form in *'s* is the only case-ending in our nouns. These exhibit no difference in form between the nominative and objective cases. The possessive alone exhibits a variation.

In Anglo-Saxon there are several declensions. Some nouns form their genitive singular in -*es*, as *smith*, *smithes*; others in *an*, others in *e*. But in the transition from Anglo-Saxon to English, the form in *es* seems to have been preferred in all instances; it was written -*es*, -*is*, -*ys*, and finally *'s*.

According to Ben Jonson, (*English Grammar*, c. xiii.) the change from *es* to *is* was the cause of a singular grammatical error, and 'brought in first the monstrous syntax of the pronoun *his* joyning with a noune betokening a possessor, as the *Prince his* house, for the *Prince's* house.'

Dr. Lowth thinks that '*Christ his* sake' in our Liturgy is a mistake of the printers, or of the compilers. He compares, 'Nevertheless, Asa *his* heart was perfect with the Lord,' 1 *Kings* xv. 14; and 'To see whether Mordecai *his* matters would stand,' *Esther* iii. 4; where, however, our more recent copies read 'Asa's heart,' and 'Mordecai's matters.'

Donne says :

> Where is this mankind now ? Who lives to age
> Fit to be made Methusalem *his* page ?

Pope, in his translation of the Odyssey, has,

> By young Telemachus *his* blooming years.

Addison writes :

> My paper is the *Ulysses his* bow, in which every man of wit or learning may try his strength.—*Guardian*, 98.

And it is evident that Addison thus wrote advisedly; for elsewhere he tells us that 'the same single letter *s* on many occasions does the office of the whole word, and represents the *his* and *her* of our forefathers.' (*Spectator*, 135.)

'The latter instance,' says Dr. Lowth, 'might have shown him how groundless this notion is; for it is not easy to conceive how the letter *s* added to a feminine noun should represent the word *her*, any more than, if added to a plural noun, as 'the children's bread,' it can stand for *their*. But the direct derivation of this case from the Saxon genitive is sufficient of itself to decide the matter.' (See Lowth, *English Grammar*, p. 32.)

138. But along with the form in *'s*, we have another method of expressing the genitive case, namely by means of the preposition *of*; we say 'the master's house,' and 'the house *of* the master.'

The origin of this second form is an interesting question. Dr. Adams says (*Elements*, § 144), 'The use of the preposition *of* to express the genitive was unknown in Anglo-Saxon. It was introduced from the Old Norse by the Danes.' Other grammarians think that it was introduced by the Normans, and that it is a translation of the French *de*.

There is a fashion in grammar, as in other things. Some grammarians have a tendency to trace everything to a Saxon or Danish origin; and some of them maintain that the Norman-French has had no influence upon our grammar. They cannot deny that our vocabulary is made up to a great extent of Anglo-Saxon and Norman-French; but they tell us that the same combination finds no place in our grammatical forms.

Professor Max Müller holds that there is no such thing as a mixed language. Of course he does not dispute the mixture of words in a vocabulary; he admits that we can detect Celtic, Norman, Greek, and Latin ingredients in the English dictionary; but he denies the mixture of grammatical forms in a language. For he calls grammar the 'blood of the language;' and he asserts that, in this sense, the English language is Teutonic. He maintains (*Science of Language*, 1st Series, p. 70), that 'not a single drop of foreign blood has entered into the organic system of the English language. The grammar, the blood and soul of the language, is as pure and unmixed in English, as spoken in the British Isles, as it was when spoken on the shores of the German Ocean by the Angles, Saxons, and Juts of the Continent.' Again he says expressly (p. 74), 'Languages, though mixed in their dictionary, can never be mixed in their grammar. For,' he adds, ' we may form whole sentences in English consisting entirely of Latin or Romance words, yet whatever there is left of grammar in English bears unmistakeable traces of Teutonic workmanship.'

139. We shall test this principle as we go along; but we premise that the argument from analogy leads us to regard the doctrine with suspicion. The English language, like the constitution, the law, the custom of the country, partakes of the nature of a compromise. We have commons and barons, common law and feudal tenure, democracy and aristocracy; so, too, in our vocabulary we have English words and French derivatives. It would, therefore, be strange if there were no traces of French idiom in our grammar. There are some forms which can be explained on no other principle ; and I am inclined to think that, wherever we have *double forms* in English grammar, one of them has arisen from the Norman-French.

140. So much for the argument from analogy. Then, if we may quote one authority against another, Mr. Marsh is decidedly of opinion that the English grammar is mixed ; that although the traces of foreign idiom may not be numerous, they are still to be found.

He admits that grammatical structure is a much more essential and permanent characteristic of languages than the vocabulary; and that, therefore, it is alone to be considered in tracing their history and determining their ethnological affinities. But this theory, he thinks, is carried too far when it is insisted that *no* amalgamation of the grammatical characteristics of different speeches is possible. The English language has been affected, in both vocabulary and structure, by the influence of all the Gothic and Romance tongues with which it has been brought into long and close contact. Doubtless, this influence is most readily perceived in the stock of words ; but the same influence, though smaller in extent, is not less unequivocal in its effects upon the syntax.

He then gives instances ; as, the double forms in the comparison of adjectives : (1) By the terminations *-er* and *-est* ; (2) by prefixing the adverbs *more* and *most*. So also the double forms in the genitive of nouns. He says, ' the possessive relation between nouns was expressed in Anglo-Saxon by a regular possessive or genitive case, and not by a preposition ; in Norman-French, in general, by a preposition only.

In English both modes are used.' (Marsh, *Origin and History of the English Language*, pp. 45–48.)

141. The Germans can place their genitive before or after the noun on which it depends. They can say, *Gottes Gnade*, ' God's grace,' and *die Liebe Gottes*, literally ' the love God's,' for ' God's love,' or ' the love of God.' But in English we have not the power of placing the possessive immediately after the governing noun: we may say, 'this work is Cicero's;' but not ' this is a work Cicero's.'

And yet we can say, ' this is a play *of* Shakespeare's.' I have sometimes suspected that this phrase has resulted from an amalgamation of the two idioms; and that our grammarians, finding the anomaly in existence, have turned it to use, and put a new meaning upon it. For they explain the phrase as signifying ' a play of Shakespeare's plays;' that is, ' one of the plays written by Shakespeare.' As they correctly remark, we may say, ' a son of your's,' but not ' a father of your's;' for a man may have several sons, but he can have only one father. And thus they distinguish ' a bust of Cicero,' that is, ' a bust representing Cicero,' from ' a bust of Cicero's,' meaning ' one of the busts in the possession of Cicero.'

I believe that this distinction, however ingenious, is an after thought; and that the form has arisen from a mixture of two constructions.

142. In older English we find a genitive of *juxta-position*: so Chaucer says, of the Knight,

> He never yit no vilonye ne sayde
> In al his lyf unto no *maner wight*.
> *Canterbury Tales, Prologue*, 70.

that is, ' to any manner *of* person.' And so again, ' a manere serjeant,' that is, ' a kind *of* servant.'

This is the usual idiom in Welsh, in which language there is no case-ending to mark the genitive.

In the phrases ' for conscience' sake,' ' for righteousness' sake,' it is usual to employ a mark of apostrophe. Those who are curious in minute points may inquire whether the mark is necessary. It might be argued that the word ' conscience' acquires, by position, the force of a genitive case; just as in composition we say the ' house-top ' for the ' house's-top.' In composition sometimes the form in -*s* is used, and sometimes not; as

wolf's-bane	=	wolf's poison.
hen-bane	=	hen's poison.

143. In some instances, we find the preposition *of* used, where we might expect a noun in apposition; as 'The city *of* Rome' for 'The city Rome,' *Urbs Roma.*

We may term this the *apposition genitive.* We find it used,

1. In geographical descriptions: as,

> The city *of* London.
> The town *of* Liverpool.
> The borough *of* Wigan.

But we are not consistent; for we say, 'The river Thames,' not 'The river *of* Thames;' and 'The Hill *of* Howth,' but 'Mount Lebanon.'

2. In descriptions of persons or things: as,

> A rogue *of* an attorney.
> A monster *of* a man.
> A brute *of* a dog.
> A rag *of* an umbrella.

We employ this second construction chiefly in a humorous or satirical sense; but in Welsh the construction is idiomatic, and employed generally. Thus Rowland tells us, (*Welsh Grammar,* § 411) 'two nouns are set in apposition by means of the preposition *o*, (' of'), when the one describes the *character, occupation,* &c. of the other; and when one of them may be converted into an adjective, or, in fact, frequently omitted; thus *gwr o brophwyd,* 'a man *of* a prophet,' is equivalent to *gwr prophwydol,* 'a man prophetic,' or simply *prophwyd,* 'a prophet.'

I do not venture to say that this idiom has come in from the Welsh; but I certainly think that the British element in our history and our language demands more careful attention than it has yet received.

144. We have, then, five constructions of the genitive case in English:

1. The form in '*s* : Milton's poem.
2. With the preposition *of*: The life of Dryden.
3. A combination of the two: A work of Cicero's.
4. By juxta-position: A many people, (for 'many' is an old noun, signifying a 'multitude').
5. By apposition: The city of Paris.

Compare the French, *La ville de Paris.*

145. With regard to meaning we observe that the genitive has a double force.

1. The *subjective* genitive, as it is termed, indicates some quality of the noun on which it is dependent; and as, among other qualities, it denotes possession, this kind of genitive has given rise to the term *possessive* case, and is generally expressed in English by the form *'s*; as 'the master's house.'

2. The *objective* genitive expresses the object of some feeling or action. It is commonly rendered in English by the preposition 'of;' as 'the love *of* fame;' 'the pursuit *of* wealth.' In fact, if the governing noun were turned into a verb, the objective genitive would be turned into the objective (or accusative) case. For example, 'he has a love of fame' is equivalent to 'he loves fame.' Sometimes the same relation is expressed by other prepositions: as 'longing *for* rest,' 'remedy *for* pain,' 'love *to* virtue.'

146. As the form in *'s*, called the possessive case, chiefly denotes possession, its use is generally limited to words which denote *persons* or *living beings*: as,

> The master's house.
> The lion's mouth.

But in older English, and in poetry, the form is often applied to words denoting *things* or *abstract notions*: as,

> The house's beauty.
> Sin's poison.

With pronouns, the form in *'s* is often used objectively: for instance, *his* stands for 'of him:' thus,

> His virtues
> Will plead like angels, trumpet-tongued, against
> The deep damnation of *his* taking off.
>> *Macbeth,* i. 6.

147. When a compound name is used, the final word alone takes the termination *'s*: as, 'the Bard of Lomond's Lay.'

If two nouns used in apposition are thrown into the genitive case, and if the principal noun comes last, that noun alone takes the termination *'s*: as,

> For thy servant David's sake.
>> *Psalm* cxxxii. 10.

But when the principal noun comes first, and the apposition noun follows, we find diversity of usage. Some would employ the form *'s* with the last word: as,

>   1. I bought it at Tonson the bookseller's.
> would prefer:
>   2. I bought it at Tonson's the bookseller.

While others would repeat the form with each word: as,

     3. I bought it at Tonson's the bookseller's.

The first and third examples are the most defensible in theory; for in the first case, we may regard ' Tonson the bookseller' as one compound term; and the 's follows regularly at the end. In the third case, we have an ordinary instance of apposition.

But the second case, though the least defensible in theory, is the most convenient in instances where two or more words in apposition follow the principal possessive: as,

    I bought it at Tonson's, the bookseller and stationer.

148. When two possessives are used, coupled by the conjunction *and*, we have to consider whether the governing noun applies to them jointly or severally.

    1. If the governing noun applies to the possessives jointly, it is sufficient to affix the form 's to the final possessive: as,

        William and Mary's house.
        The King and Queen's marriage.

    2. But when the governing noun applies to the possessives severally, the form 's should be attached to each:

        The Parliament's and the King's forces approached each other.
        The work was neither Cicero's nor Seneca's.

So, too, when any words intervene, throwing a pause upon the first possessive, the form 's should be used in both instances: as,

    These are William's, as well as Mary's books.

149. The construction involving the form which we call the ' infinitive, or gerund in *-ing* ' demands careful consideration. Take, for example:

    What is the meaning of this *lady's holding up* her fan?
    These are the rules of Grammar, by *the observing of which* you may avoid mistakes.

Some grammarians call this form in *-ing* a Gerund; others a Participle; and others, a Verbal, or a Verbal Substantive.

Dr. Lowth says (*English Grammar*, p. 125):—' The participle with an article before it, and the preposition *of* after it, becomes a substantive, expressing the action itself which the verb signifies; as, "These are the rules of Grammar by *the observing of* which you may avoid mistakes." Or it may be expressed by the participle or gerund; "by *observing* which;" not, "by *observing of* which;" nor, "by *the observing* which;" for either of those two phrases would be a confounding of two distinct forms.'

He then states the principle on which this rule is founded: 'a word which has the article before it, and the possessive preposition *of* after it, must be a noun; and if a noun, it ought to follow the construction of a noun, and not have the regimen of a verb.'

But Dr. Lowth seems to confound a 'noun' with a 'substantive;' the infinitive mood of a verb may be used substantively, yet without losing its powers as a verb. Beside, the prefixing of the article does not turn any part of a verb into a substantive; but, on the contrary, because it is used substantively, it is capable of taking the article.

Hence all the four forms may be defended:

1. by *observing* which.
2. by *the observing of* which.
3. by *observing of* which.
4. by *the observing* which.

1. We have the simple infinitive, or gerund, governing the objective 'which.'
2. The infinitive, with the article, is used substantively, and followed by the genitive, 'of which.'
3. The infinitive, without the article, is used substantively, and followed by the genitive, 'of which.'
4. The infinitive is used substantively, with the article, but still retains its powers as a verb, and governs the objective, 'which.'

POSITION.

150. The form in -*s* precedes the governing word: as 'the father's house,' 'the master's dog.' In German the corresponding form may follow the governing noun: as 'ein Werk Schiller's,' literally 'a Work Schiller's,' where we say, 'a work of Schiller,' or 'a work of Schiller's.' And it is curious that both these English phrases are questioned; some grammarians doubt the one, and some the other. One says that 'a work of Schiller' is absolute nonsense, and not English. Another maintains that 'a work of Schiller's' is a blunder, and not to be allowed. I have already stated my opinion, that 'a work of Schiller's' has arisen from a confusion of the two forms; and it certainly is warranted by the authority of good writers. On the other hand, I see no reason to condemn 'a work of Schiller,' meaning 'a work written by Schiller.'

151. But as we have two forms in English, we should be careful to avail ourselves of this advantage, in order to guard against ambiguity of expression.

For example, where Hume says, 'They attacked Northumberland's house, *whom* they put to death,' we observe a little awkwardness in that form of expression. It seems better to say, 'They attacked the house of Northumberland, whom they put to death.' For although the gender of the pronoun shows that Northumberland is referred to, yet we are so accustomed in English to find the antecedent coming immediately before the relative, that the position of 'house' between the two makes us fancy that there is something wrong. It is a good rule that, if we can make any alteration which will prevent the attention of the reader from being called to the mere form of words, we ought to avail ourselves of the privilege, and to fix his attention, not upon the sign, but upon the thing signified.

OBJECTIVE.

152. We saw, § 13—20, that there may be various kinds of Objectives in a sentence; and we distinguished three; the Primary and Secondary Objectives, and the Complement-Objective.

As an example of the care required to distinguish Objectives, we may take the following passage :—

> *Lafeu.* They say miracles are past; and we have our
> philosophical persons to make modern and familiar
> things supernatural and causeless. Hence it is that
> we make trifles of terrors; ensconcing ourselves into
> seeming knowledge, when we should submit ourselves
> to an unknown fear.—*All's Well*, ii. 3.

In some editions the words are pointed thus :—' to make modern and familiar things, supernatural and causeless.' But the meaning is just the contrary : 'to make modern and familiar, things supernatural and causeless.'

The word 'modern' is used in the literal sense of 'daily,' 'trivial,' 'common-place,' and the meaning is 'to modernise

and familiarise things, which are really above nature, and
beyond the laws of cause and effect, as commonly understood
by us.'

So also the phrase 'we make trifles of terrors' means, 'we
turn terrors into sport.' The adjectives 'supernatural' and
'causeless' are used to qualify the objective 'things;' while
the adjectives 'modern' and 'familiar' are complement-
objectives, to be taken in connection with the verb 'make.'

153. In our version of the Scriptures, we read:

> Who maketh his angels spirits; his ministers a flaming
> fire.—*Psalm* civ. 4.

It has sometimes been suggested that this passage might be
taken just the other way:

> Who maketh the winds his messengers; the flames of
> fire his ministers.

But I have some doubts as to the latter clause. Compare,
too, *Hebrews* i. 7, 8.

154. As there is, in English nouns, no distinction of form
between nominative and objective, the order of words is a matter of great importance. In the following passage from Gibbon,
objectives are immediately followed by nominatives; and the
reader is obliged to peruse the sentence more than once, in
order to discover where the objectives end, and the nominatives begin. Speaking of Theodoric, he says:

> The ambassadors who resorted to Ravenna from the most
> distant countries of Europe admired his wisdom, mag-
> nificence and courtesy; and if he sometimes accepted
> either slaves or arms, white horses or strange animals,
> the gift of a sun-dial, a waterclock, or a musician,
> admonished even the princes of Gaul of the superior
> art and industry of his Italian subjects.
> *Decline and Fall of the Roman Empire*, c. 39.

After a little reflection, it is easy to see that the objectives
end at *animals*, and the nominatives begin with *the gift of a
sun-dial*. But a writer should not cause his readers to
hesitate, even for a moment, upon mere points of grammar.

155. As a general rule, transitive verbs govern an objective, and intransitives do not. But we must be very careful to watch the change of construction in verbs. For an
intransitive verb, when compounded with a preposition, may
acquire a transitive force; and as, in English, the preposition

is generally not attached to the verb, but *put after* it, the construction is sometimes misunderstood.

For instance, *run* is an intransitive verb; but *run through* is transitive, in the sense of (1) *pierce*, (2) *waste* : as,

> They *ran* him *through*, with a sword.
> He *ran through* his property.

Here *him* is the objective, governed by the compound verb *ran through*; and *property* is the objective, governed, not by the preposition *through*, but by the compound verb *ran through*.

For we might turn the sentences thus :

> They *pierced* him with a sword.
> He *squandered* his property.

See §§ 490, 491.

156. These constructions should be distinguished from others, where the intransitive, used with a preposition, still remains intransitive : as ' depart from,' ' despair of.' But one remark is common to both ; that this *appending* of a preposition gives rise to the idiom of throwing a preposition to the end of the sentence : as,

> *This* I was afraid *of*.
> *That result* I despaired *of*.

Those grammarians who derive their notions from the idiom of the Latin language, condemn this usage of the preposition as inelegant ; but more recent investigations, in the Germanic dialects, have proved that this is an old English idiom.—See §§ 483–485.

157. A noun denoting *time, space,* or *measure* is often used absolutely ; and from the analogy of similar constructions in Latin, we say that such nouns are in the objective case : as,

> They rode *all day*.
> That tower was *twenty feet* high.
> In 1661, the justices fixed the labourer's wages at seven shillings *a week*, wheat seventy shillings *the quarter*, and the labourer worked *twelve hours a day*.—*Macaulay*.

It has been surmised, that *a*, in these constructions, is not the indefinite article, but a remnant of the Anglo-Saxon preposition *an*, ' in,' ' on.' But see § 304.

158. Dr. Angus remarks, (*Handbook,* § 413) that the preposition *of* is sometimes erroneously used with an adjective, in such constructions as the following :

> Let a gallows be made *of* fifty cubits *high*.—*Esther* v. 14.
> To an infant *of* two or three years old.—Wayland.

But in the present state of our knowledge, we must guard against hasty judgments. We must not rashly condemn an idiomatic usage, if it be really idiomatic; but we must examine the custom of old writers, before we arrive at a final conclusion.

159. A noun in the objective case is often found with an intransitive verb, when the noun and the verb are akin in meaning. This is called in Latin grammar the Cognate Accusative: as, 'to dream a dream,' 'to run a race.' So,

> Let me *die* the *death* of the righteous, and let my last end be like his.—*Numbers* xxiii. 10.

160. The infinitive mood, used substantively, can stand as an objective: 'John loves *to study*;' and the infinitive so employed does not lose its power as a verb, but may have another objective dependent upon itself: as,

> Ladies, you deserve
> *To have* a temple built you.
> > *Coriolanus*, v. 3.

Occasionally, we find a forerunning *it* employed to show that an infinitive phrase is coming: as,

> Thou dost; and think'st *it* much *to tread the ooze*
> Of the salt deep. *Tempest*, i. 2.

161. We saw, §§ 37, 38, that when a sentence takes the place of an objective, there are three forms in which the subordinate clause may appear:

1. I know [he is eloquent].
2. I know [that he is eloquent]
3. I know [*him* to be eloquent].

We have termed the objective *him*, in the third example, a 'subject-accusative,' because it forms the subject of the subordinate clause, and yet it stands in the accusative or objective case before the infinitive *to be*. This mode of explanation is borrowed from the Latin grammarians, and is the most satisfactory that can be offered.

POSITION.

162. As a general rule, the objective follows the governing verb; but sometimes for the sake of emphasis, the order is reversed, and the objective stands first: as,

> *Honey* from out the gnarled hive I'll bring.
> > **Keats**, *Endymion*, 4.

Such sober *certainty* of waking bliss
I never heard till now.

Milton, *Comus*, 263.

As pronouns often exhibit variations to mark difference of case, there is, with them, less danger of confusion ; and a pronoun in the objective is freely placed before the verb : as,

Him the Almighty Power
Hurled headlong flaming from the ethereal sky.

Milton, *Paradise Lost*, i. 44–5.

So, too, when the subject-nominative denotes a person, and the objective a thing or quality : as,

Equal *toil* the good commander endures with the common soldier.

Interrogative and relative pronouns, when used in the objective, occupy the first place in the sentence or clause; as, '*whom* did he mean ?' 'this is the man *whom* I mentioned.'

THE SECONDARY OBJECTIVE.

163. In Latin, some verbs govern two accusatives; others an accusative and a dative; others an accusative and a genitive. What we have termed the 'secondary objective' corresponds to the second accusative, to the dative, or to the genitive in the Latin construction.

The employment of the secondary objective, in place of a dative, is particularly observable in the usage of personal pronouns; for, *me* and *thee* are old datives, as well as accusatives; and *him* is a true dative, though we commonly employ it as an accusative.

164. The secondary objective is formed after verbs of 'giving,' 'telling,' 'showing :' as,

Give *me* that book.
I will tell *thee* a tale.
They showed *him* all.

Give *sorrow* words : the grief that does not speak,
Whispers the o'erfraught heart, and bids it break.

Macbeth, iv. 3.

165. The secondary objective, in the case of personal pronouns, is often used to represent the person for whom, for whose benefit, or at whose request anything is done. This corresponds to what is called the *dativus commodi* : so,

Prince Henry. I am good friends with my father, and
may do anything.

Falstaff. Rob *me* the exchequer the first thing thou doest.

1st Hen. IV. iii. 3.

Talbot. Convey *me* Salisbury into his tent.

1st Hen. VI. i. 4.

Petruchio. Villain, I say, knock *me* here soundly.

Grumio. Knock you here, sir ! why, sir, what am I, sir,
that I should knock you here, sir?

Petruchio. Villain, I say, knock *me* at this gate,
And rap *me* well.

Taming of the Shrew, i. 2.

166. The secondary objective is found after the verbs *list*
and *like*, both in the sense of '*please*;' after *seem* and *think* in
the sense of 'appear:' as,

> And al that likith *me*, I dare wel sayn
> It likith *the.*

Chaucer.

i.e., 'all that pleaseth me, pleaseth thee.'

> When in Salamanca's cave
> *Him* listed his magic wand to wave,
> The bells would ring in Notre Dame.

Scott, Lay of the Last Minstrel, ii. 13.

> Yet there, *meseems,* I hear her singing loud.

Sidney.

Hotspur. By heaven, *methinks,* it were an easy leap
To pluck bright honour from the pale-faced
moon.

1st Henry IV. i. 3.

Hamlet. Madam, how like you this play ?

Queen. The lady protests too much, *methinks.*

Hamlet, iii. 2.

In such phrases as 'methinks,' 'meseems,' 'meseemeth,' the
pronoun *me* is a dative, and the sense is 'it appears to me,'
'it seems to me.' Some grammarians have found a difficulty
in the form 'methinks,' from not being aware that in Anglo-
Saxon there are two verbs, *thencan,* German *denken,* 'to
think,' and *thincan,* German, *dünken,* 'to seem.' It is from
the latter verb that we have our phrase *me-thinks,* corresponding to the German *mir dünkt,* or *mich dünkt,* 'it seems to me.'
We may remark that the Germans can use, in this construction, either the dative *mir* or the accusative *mich.*

167. In such phrases as 'woe is *me*,' 'woe worth *the day*,' we have similar instances; for they signify 'woe is *to me*,' 'woe be *to the day*.' Here *worth* is a form derived from the Anglo-Saxon weorðan, 'to become.'

> Much wo *worth* the man,
> That misruleth his inwitte;
> And well *worth* Piers Plowman,
> That pursueth God in his going.

That is to say,

> Much woe betide the man,
> That misruleth his conscience;
> And fair befall Piers Plowman,
> That followeth God in his conduct.

Sir Walter Scott, imitating the language of the old ballads, nas the following passage :—

> I little thought, when first thy rein
> I slacked upon the banks of Seine,
> That Highland eagle e'er should feed
> On thy fleet limbs, my gallant steed !
> Woe *worth* the chase, woe *worth* the day,
> That costs thy life, my gallant grey !
>
> *Lady of the Lake*, i. 9.

Some adjectives govern an objective case; as *like, nigh, near, worth* : 'It is *like him*;' 'This is *near me*;' 'That is *worth* twenty pounds.' Analogy would lead us to the conclusion that these objectives represent dative cases; and the argument is corroborated by the fact that the preposition *to* is sometimes added, *like to, near to*.

CHAPTER VI.

ADJECTIVES.

168. 'AN Adjective is a word *added to* a substantive to express its quality.' (Lowth, *Grammar*, p. 44.)

This definition is founded upon the literal meaning of the word *adjective*, which is derived from the Latin *ad-jectus*, 'put on,' 'added to.'

But we must bear in mind the distinction between the

Attributive and the *Predicative* use of the Adjective. When we speak of ' the *good* boy,' ' the *red* apple,' we qualify the words ' boy ' and ' apple.' This is called the *attributive* use of the adjective; and it was treated under the head of Qualifications, §§ 4, 7, 14. But when we assert that ' the boy is *good*,' and ' the apple is *red*,' we employ the adjective as a predicate, and this is termed the *predicative* use of the adjective. See Predicate-nominative, §§ 5, 6.

In short, the so-called copula *is*, and an adjective, are together equivalent to a verb; as may be seen by comparing English with Latin forms :—

is wise = sapit.
is white = albet.
is green = viret.

169. But we have now to consider the *substantive* use of the Adjective. Becker says :

' Adjectives are termed Substantive adjectives when *substantively* used, that is to say, when expressing a person or thing; e. g. *der Gute*, " the good man," *die Kranken*, " the sick persons," *das Schöne*, " the beautiful," or " the beautiful thing." '—*German Grammar*, Fraedersdorf's Transl. § 127.

Dr. Lowth remarks (*English Grammar*, p. 44, *note*), that ' Adjectives are very improperly called *Nouns*, for they are not the *Names* of things. The adjectives *good* and *white* are applied to the nouns *man*, *snow*, to express the qualities belonging to those subjects; but the names of those qualities in the abstract, that is, considered in themselves, without being attributed to any subject, are *goodness*, *whiteness*, and these are Nouns or Substantives.'

Dr. Lowth does not accurately distinguish between Nouns and Substantives. But, to pass over that point, his argument depends upon the principle that *nouns* are *names of things*; and that words which are *not* names of things are *not* nouns.

But this again depends upon the meaning of the word *thing*. If the word be restricted to material or physical things, then Dr. Lowth's rule is not correct: for *virtue*, *wisdom*, *pride*, are not names of material things, and yet they are nouns. If, on the other hand, we extend the term *thing*, to make it include ' thoughts,' ' feelings,' and ' qualities,' why may not an adjective be the ' name of a thing?'

There seems to be no reason why an adjective should not represent a quality in the abstract. In Greek and Latin the neuter of the adjective is constantly so used. And though in Greek the adjective used substantively is always accompanied by the article, that is no warrant for supposing that the article and the adjective are together equal to a substantive; or that the substantive force is due to the presence of the article. The case may be just the other way; because the adjective is used substantively, it is capable of receiving the article.

Besides, the neuter adjective is constantly used as a substantive in Latin, where no article whatever is found. *Utile* and *honestum* are used by Cicero for 'expediency' and 'honour;' and so Horace—

Omne tulit punctum qui miscuit *utile dulci.*

De Arte Poetica, 343.

'Profit with pleasure.'

. . . *molle* atque *facetum*
Virgilio annuerunt gaudentes rure Camœnæ.

Sat. I. x. 44.

'Tenderness and grace.'

They used to tell us at school, that with an adjective so employed, a substantive must be 'understood;' and as *res* is unfortunately feminine, we were bidden to supply *negotium,* which does not suit the meaning. But why must a substantive be understood? Only because the grammarians are determined not to admit the claim of the adjective. If we may 'understand' and 'supply' words at pleasure, it is easy to prove anything. Even when an adjective stands as the predicate of a proposition, as 'Snow is *white,*' this is sometimes explained by grammatical ellipsis: as, 'Snow is a white (thing),' or 'a white (substance),' or 'a white (object).'

The poets, however, have no scruple. Milton, in particular, is very fond of this construction:

Who shall tempt with wandering feet,
The dark unbottomed infinite abyss,
And through the palpable *obscure* find out
His uncouth way?

Paradise Lost, ii. 404–407.

Dark with excessive *bright* thy skirts appear.

Ibid. iii. 380.

So much of death her thoughts
Had entertained, as dyed her cheeks with *pale.*

Ibid. x. 1009.

So Shakespeare:

Call you me fair? That 'fair' again unsay:
Demetrius loves your *fair.* O happy fair!
Your eyes are lodestars, and your tongue's sweet air
More tuneable than lark to shepherd's ear,
When wheat is green, when hawthorn buds appear.

Midsummer Night's Dream, i. 1.

And so Spenser, where the adjective used substantively may be taken in the concrete:

'The lyon, lord of everie beast in field,'
Quoth she, 'his princely puissance doth abate,
And mightie *proud* to humble *weake* does yield.'

Faerie Queene, I. iii.

If it be urged that this is merely poetic license, we may quote the '*deep*' used for the 'sea,' the *waste* for the 'desert,' with the philosophic terms, 'the good,' 'the true,' 'the beautiful.'

POSITION.

170. Adjectives generally stand before the nouns which they qualify; as, ' the *bright* sky,' 'the *distant* shore.' But, in poetry, the order is often changed, to vary the diction, and to raise it above ordinary prose; as, ' O lady *fair*,' ' my father *dear*.'

It is a common practice with Milton to place an adjective both before and after a noun; as,

> At length a *universal* hubbub *wild*
> Of stunning sounds and voices all confused,
> Borne through the hollow dark, assaults his ear
> With loudest vehemence.
> > *Paradise Lost*, ii. 951–4.

> Thus with the year
> Seasons return, but not to me returns
> Day, or the sweet approach of ev'n or morn,
> Or sight of vernal bloom, or summer's rose,
> Or flocks, or herds, or *human* face *divine*.
> > *Ibid.* iii. 40–4.

So, too, he alludes to Isocrates as 'that *old* man *eloquent*,' where, however, ' old man' may be considered almost one word, equivalent to the Latin *senex* :

> . . . as that dishonest victory
> At Chæronea, fatal to liberty,
> Killed with report that *old* man *eloquent*.
> > *Sonnet* ix.

Even in prose, participles are often found after a noun: as, the persons *named*,' ' the reasons *mentioned*.'

171. Chaucer uses an adjective with the indefinite article after a noun: as,

> A monk there was *a fayre*.
> > *Canterbury Tales, Prologue*, 165.

> A frere there was *a wanton and a mery*.—*Ibid*. 208.

And, in more modern English, it is not unusual for one adjective to precede the noun, while others follow connected by *and*: as,

> A dark prince, and infinitely *suspicious*.—*Bacon*.

When the adjective or participle is itself qualified it follows the noun : as,

Out flew
Millions of flaming swords *drawn* from the thighs
Of mighty cherubim.

Milton, *Paradise Lost*, i. 664.

172. When two numerals qualify one noun, the ordinal adjective generally stands first, and the cardinal second : as, ' the last three chapters of John,' ' the first two of Matthew.' Strictly, there cannot be ' three *last* chapters,' or ' two *first* chapters.' And yet the terms ' three last' and ' two first,' might occur in another construction, and with a different meaning. For instance, if there were three classes in a school, the boys at the bottom of each might be termed the ' three last.' Or if there were two classes, the boys at the head of each might be styled the ' two first.'

DEGREES OF COMPARISON.

173. English adjectives have no changes to express gender, number, or case; but they undergo changes, to denote Degrees of Comparison.

There are three Degrees of Comparison, in English :

1. The *Positive*, which gives the word in its simplest form ; as *bright*.
2. The *Comparative*, which ascribes a quality in a higher degree ; as *brighter*.
3. The *Superlative*, which ascribes a quality in the highest degree ; as *brightest*.

We have two methods of denoting comparison in adjectives; one, derived from the Anglo-Saxon, by adding terminations to the positive ; the other, borrowed from the Norman-French, by prefixing to the positive the adverbs *more* and *most*.

Formation of Comparison by adding *Terminations*.

First Rule. In Adjectives, which end in a consonant, the comparative is formed by adding -*er*, and the superlative by adding -*est* to the positive ; as *bright, bright-er, bright-est*.

Obs.—When an adjective ends in -*e*, the vowel *e* of the termination -*er*, -*est*, is dropped, or, practically, -*r* and -*st* are added to the positive : as *wise, wise-r, wise-st*.

F

Second Rule.—When the positive ends in *d*, *g*, or *t*, preceded by a single vowel, the final consonant is doubled in form-ing the comparative and superlative: as,

red	redder	reddest.
big	bigger	biggest.
hot	hotter	hottest.

But if the *d*, *g*, or *t* be preceded by another consonant, or by more than one vowel, the final consonant is not doubled: as,

kind	kinder	kindest.
neat	neater	neatest.

Third Rule.—When the positive ends in *y*, preceded by a consonant, the *y* is changed to *i* before -*er* and -*est*: as,

lovely	loveli-er	loveli-est.

These rules are applicable to adjectives of one or two syllables, which very commonly are of Anglo-Saxon deriva-tion. With adjectives containing more than two syllables, it is usual to prefix *more* and *most*. The Germans, indeed, append the terminations -*er* and -*est* to all adjectives, no matter how many syllables they may contain. But in Eng-lish, custom has ruled that the terminations -*er* and -*est* shall be restricted to adjectives of one and two syllables.

174. In the Indo-European family of languages, a few ad-jectives exhibit peculiarities of comparison : and it is curious to remark that these adjectives, in the several languages, cor-respond in meaning. For our purpose, it will be sufficient to compare the English with the Latin.

good	better	best.
bonus	*melior*	*optimus.*
bad	worse	worst.
malus	*pejor*	*pessimus.*
much		
or	more	most.
many		
multus	(*plus*)	*plurimus.*
little	less	least.
parvus	*minor*	*minimus.*

Some grammarians maintain that these forms as, for example, *good* and *better*, are derived from distinct roots. Dr. Latham says that *good* has no comparative or superlative : and that *better* has no positive.—Latham, *English Grammar*, § 110.

Professor Key, in an able treatise appended to his *Alphabet*, endeavours to prove that ' good, better, best,' ' bonus, melior, optimus,' owe their variety of form to two principles: (1) the difference of pronunciation, called ' dialect;' (2) those euphonic changes which grow out of the approximation of particular sounds. Professor Key's arguments are highly ingenious; I wish I could add that they are equally convincing.

175. The following peculiarities of comparison deserve notice, especially in reference to the use of the termination -*most*:

aft	after	aftermost.
far	farther	farthest, farthermost.
fore	former	first, foremost.
forth	further	furthest, furthermost.
hind	hinder	hindmost, hindermost.
in	inner	inmost, innermost.
late	later, latter	latest, last.
out	outer, utter	utmost, outermost.
up	upper	upmost, uppermost.

Grimm doubts whether such words as ' after-most,' ' inmost ' are formed immediately by the addition of -*most*. He finds in Gothic and in Anglo-Saxon superlative forms *aftuma*, *innema*, and, what he considers double superlatives, *æftemest*, *innemest*. According to this view, both the letter *m*, and the termination -*est*, are marks of the superlative degree. Then he thinks that the English forms ' aftermost,' ' inmost,' &c., have arisen by corruption, or by false analogy. To use his own expression, the English termination -*most* in these words is ' an unorganic -*most*.' See Grimm, *Deutsche Grammatik*, vol. iii. pp. 628–631 : and compare Latham, *English Language*, § 481, *English Grammar*, § 117.

176. We must beware of supposing that comparison necessarily involves the notion of greater or less; for in the sentence, ' He is *as* tall *as* I am,' we have as truly a comparison as in the sentence, ' He is *taller than* I am.' In other words, there may be a comparison of equality; and in the Welsh language there is a fourth degree of comparison, with a distinct form, to express the relation which we denote by prefixing *as* or *so* to the positive. See Rowland, *Welsh Grammar*, § 149.

Hence, before we make use of a comparison, involving the notion of greater or less, we should consider whether the quality expressed by the adjective admits of degrees. Strictly speaking, *perfect* is an absolute term : that which is not ' perfect' is 'imperfect,' and although a thing may be brought nearer to perfection than it was before, it cannot properly be called 'more perfect.' Yet Addison writes :

> Our sight is the *most perfect* and most delightful of all our senses.—*Spectator, No.* 411.

Similarly *extreme* is ' uttermost,' and yet many persons write *most extreme*, that is literally 'most uttermost.' In the following passages we find *extremest* :

> While the *extremest* parts of the earth were meditating a submission.—Atterbury, *Sermons*, i. 4.
>
> That on the sea's *extremest* border stood.
>
> Addison, *Travels.*

177. Cobbett well remarks, (*English Grammar*, § 220):— ' But our ears are accustomed to the adverbs of exaggeration. Some writers deal in these to a degree that tires the ear and offends the understanding. With them every thing is *excessively* or *immensely* or *extremely* or *vastly* or *surprisingly* or *wonderfully* or *abundantly*, or the like. The notion of such writers is, that these words give *strength* to what they are saying. This is a great error. Strength must be found in the *thought*, or it will never be found in the *words.* Bigsounding words, without thoughts corresponding, are effort without effect.'

178. The word *chief*, derived from the French *chef*, ' head,' denotes primacy ; and as there can be no more than one ' first' in the same series, it is not strictly correct to say *chiefest.* Yet we read :

> Whosoever of you will be the *chiefest*, shall be servant of all.—*Mark* x. 44.

One of the first and *chiefest* instances of prudence.

> Atterbury, *Sermons*, iv. 10.

> But first and *chiefest* with thee bring
> Him that yon soars on golden wing,
> Guiding the fiery-wheeled throne,
> The Cherub Contemplation.
>
> Milton, *Il Penseroso.*

179. When we are comparing things, or classes of things, it is necessary to consider whether our comparison involves the number *two*, or *more than two.*

If we compare two things, or two classes of things; or, if

one individual is contrasted with the rest of a class, we use the comparative degree : as,

> An acre in Middlesex is *better* than a principality in Utopia.

> He is *wiser* than all the rest put together.

But if we mean to express that one of a class, *more than two*, possesses a quality in the highest degree, we employ the superlative : as,

> This was the *noblest* Roman of them all.
> > *Julius Cæsar*, v. 4.

180. As we have seen, there are two methods, in English, of denoting the comparative and the superlative degree; and this is one proof, among others, that English is a mixed language, in its grammar, as well as in its vocabulary. For the Anglo-Saxon, in comparisons, varied the adjective by change of termination only, and not by adverbs corresponding to *more* and *most*, while the Norman-French made use of adverbs. The English employs both methods; the latter uniformly with long words. (Compare §§ 138—140.)

Now some of our older writers, when they wish to be emphatic, employ double comparatives or superlatives; so Shakespeare:

> Timon will to the woods ; where he shall find
> The unkindest beast *more kinder* than mankind.
> > *Timon of Athens*, iv. 1.

> This was the *most unkindest* cut of all.
> > *Julius Cæsar*, iii. 2.

181. When both forms are used in the same phrase, it is better to put the adjective ending in *-er* or *-est* first, and then the adjective combined with *more* or most; as,

> He was the wisest and most learned of them all.

Otherwise it is desirable to repeat the article :—

> He was the most learned, and the wisest of them all.

182. In using comparatives and superlatives, we ought to take care that the construction be consistent with itself.

When a superlative is used, the class which furnishes the objects of comparison, and which is introduced by *of*, should always include the thing compared. Yet Milton, imitating a Greek idiom, writes:

> Adam the goodliest man, of men since born
> His sons; the fairest of her daughters, Eve.
> > *Paradise Lost*, iv. 323.

If these lines be construed literally, Adam is one of his own sons, and Eve is one of her own daughters.

Some writers use the superlative, when only two objects are implied : as,

> The question is not whether a good Indian or bad Englishman be *most* happy, but which state is *most* desirable, supposing virtue and reason to be the same in both.—Johnson.

Here, others would say 'be the *more* happy,' 'is the *more* desirable.' And, no doubt, the comparative degree is preferable, because *two* individuals and *two* states are compared.

183. The following is an example of wrong construction in the comparative :

> This noble nation hath *of all others* admitted *fewer* corruptions.—Swift.

The construction is not consistent with itself; for the phrase ' of all others' would lead us to expect a superlative degree ; but even that would not mend the sentence, because ' this nation ' is here confounded with ' all others.'

The writer meant to say :

> This noble nation hath admitted *fewer* corruptions *than any other.*

So here :

> The vice of covetousness is what enters deepest into the soul *of any other.*—*Guardian*, No. 19.

First of all, the phrase ' of any other' is most unfortunately placed ; for it might mean ' the soul of any other person.' But the chief fault is, that covetousness is classed among *all other* vices ; and is then said to enter the deepest of those vices.

The writer might have said :

> The vice of covetousness enters *deeper* into the soul, *than any other.*

or,

> *Of all vices*, covetousness enters *deepest* into the soul.

184. In comparisons of equality, the second clause is introduced by *as* ; in comparisons of greater or less, the second clause is introduced by *than*. Sometimes awkwardness results from coupling these two kinds of phrase in one construction : as,

Will it be urged, that the four gospels are *as old* or even *older than* tradition ?—Bolingbroke, *Essays*, iv. 19.

The words ' as old' and 'older' cannot have a common construction : the one should be followed by *as*, the other by *than*. If Bolingbroke had said ' *as old as* tradition and even *older*,' there would have been no error.—See Campbell, *Philosophy of Rhetoric*, pp. 182—187.

185. We have seen, § 64, that the word *than*, commonly called a conjunction, is a later form of the adverb *then*. Hence, ' this is better *than* that' means, ' first this is better ; *then* that [is good].'

The same word *than* is used after *other, rather, else, otherwise*, and all forms of speech implying comparison :

> Ye watch, like God, the rolling hours,
> With larger *other* eyes *than* ours,
> To make allowance for us all.
>> Tennyson, *In Memoriam*, 50.

> Style is nothing *else than* that sort of expression which our thoughts most readily assume.—Blair, *Lecture* 10.

When a comparative is used with *than*, the thing compared must always be excluded from the class of things with which it is compared. Take this sentence :

Jacob loved Joseph more than all his children.

But Joseph was one of those very children. Therefore, if he loved Joseph more than all, he loved Joseph more than his other children, and Joseph to boot. If we read ' than his other children ' or ' than all his other children,' there could be no room for objection.

The noun or pronoun that follows *than*, will be in the nominative or objective according to the construction of the subordinate clause. Thus,

> I esteem you more than *they*,

means,

> I esteem you more than they [esteem you].

But,

> I esteem you more than *them*,

means,

> I esteem you more than [I esteem] them.

186. Dr. Priestley seems to have had a notion that *than*, in some cases, is a preposition ; and this view is very properly rejected by Dr. Campbell, *Philosophy of Rhetoric*, pp. 182, 183.

Yet there is one construction in which the objective has been so commonly used after *than*, that we can hardly refuse to accept the anomaly, though it cannot be justified by rule. In the best authors we find such phrases as these:

The Duke of Argyle, *than whom* no man was more hearty in the cause.—Hume.

Cromwell, *than whom* no man was better skilled in artifice.—Hume.

Pope, *than whom* few men had more vanity.—Johnson.

Dr. Lowth says, (*Grammar*, p. 154):

'The relative *who*, having reference to no verb or preposition understood, but only to its antecedent, when it follows *than* is always in the objective case; even though the pronoun, if substituted in its place, would be in the nominative; as,

Beelzebub, *than whom*,
Satan except, none higher sat.
Milton, *Paradise Lost*, ii. 299.

which, if we substitute the pronoun, would be,
'none higher sat than *he*.'

It is evident that there is no reason for using the objective in this construction. I suspect that this peculiarity has resulted from confounding the English idiom with the Latin, where the comparative is followed by the ablative *quo*. In Latin *quo* means 'than who,' and *than* is expressed by the ablative. Our classical scholars, writing in English, have supplied *than*, and yet, with the Latin syntax in their minds, have retained the oblique case. The influence of Latin idioms upon English style would form an interesting subject of inquiry; and I think that when boys are translating upon paper, they should not be allowed to follow the original so closely as to violate the English idiom. 'Which when Cæsar saw,' and similar phrases, are not English. They may pass in oral construing, but not in written translation.

CHAPTER VII.

PRONOUNS.

187. A PRO-NOUN is defined as a word used instead of a noun.

Buttmann, however, says, ' Pronouns cannot be so precisely defined as not to admit many words which may also be considered as adjectives.'—Angus, *Handbook of the English Tongue,* p. 179.

Grammarians are not all agreed upon the meaning of the word *noun.* According to some it comprises both substantives and adjectives; and those who take this view distinguish ' nouns substantive' and ' nouns adjective.'

To avoid controversy, we have uniformly used the word *noun* in the sense of a ' noun substantive; ' but we shall extend the term ' pronoun' to comprise ' pronouns substantive,' and ' pronouns adjective.'

Pronouns are divided into the following classes :—

1. Personal.
2. Possessive.
3. Demonstrative.
4. Interrogative.
5. Relative.
6. Reflective.
7. Reciprocal.

We shall consider, in a separate chapter, words which have been variously termed Adjective Pronouns or Pronominal Adjectives.

PERSONAL PRONOUNS.

188. There are three persons which may form the subject of any discourse :

1. The person who speaks, may speak of himself.
2. He may speak of the person to whom he addresses himself.
3. He may speak of some other person, or of some thing.

These are called, respectively, the first, second, and third persons.

The persons speaking and spoken to, being at the same time the subjects of the discourse, are supposed to be present; hence their sex is commonly known, and needs not to be marked by a distinction of gender in the pronouns; but the third person or thing spoken of, being absent and in many respects unknown, needs to be marked by a distinction of gender. Accordingly the pronoun of the third person has, in the singular, three genders; but in the plural, we have only one set of forms for all the genders.

189. In pronouns, we have some remains of the variations used in Anglo-Saxon. Thus in the First Personal Pronoun, we have,

	Singular.	*Plural.*
Nom.,	I	we
Gen.,	mine	our
Dat.,	me	us
Acc.,	me	us

We shall remark upon the genitives *mine* and *our* under the head of Possessive Pronouns.

The old dative *me* appears in such forms as *me-seems*, *me-thinks*, meaning 'it seems to me,' 'it appears to me.' For here 'thinks' is derived not from *thencan*, 'to think,' but from *thincan*, 'to seem.'

The same dative is frequently used as a secondary objective: 'Give *me* the book,' 'Tell *me* the story.' In like manner the old dative *us* is employed as a secondary objective: as, 'He gave *us* good words.'

190. In the Second Personal Pronoun we have the following forms:—

	Singular.	*Plural.*
Nom.,	thou	ye (you)
Gen.,	thine	your
Dat.,	thee	you
Acc.,	thee	you

In former times in England, *thou* was used as a mark of endearment among relatives; and the corresponding pronoun is still so used in France, Germany, and other countries. Perhaps one reason why it has gone out of common use with us, is that being adopted by the Society of Friends, and used by them on all occasions, it became a token of sectarian distinction.

But, beside expressing affection, it was used, in old times; to denote familiarity; and the transition from familiarity to contempt is soon made:

> If thou *thouest* him some thrice, it shall not be amiss.—*Twelfth Night*, iii. 2.

We shall discuss *thine* and *your* under the head of Possessive Pronouns.

Thee and *you*, old forms of the dative, are commonly used as secondary objectives.

Thou and *ye* are very commonly used in solemn language, and in poetry:

> *Thou* sun, said I, fair light!
> And *thou* enlightened earth, so fresh and gay!
> *Ye* hills and dales! *Ye* rivers, woods, and plains!
> And *ye* that live and move, fair creatures, tell,
> Tell if *ye* saw, how came I thus, how here?
> > Milton, *Paradise Lost*, viii. 273–7.

It is a common error with young writers to begin by using *thou* in the early part of a sentence; and then, forgetting the commencement, to slide into *you*; and sometimes even to mix up 'thou' with 'your,' or 'you' with 'thy' in the same clause.

In poetry this licence is sometimes taken: as,

> I pr'ythee give me back my heart,
> Since I can not have *thine*;
> For if from *yours you* will not part,
> Why then should'st *thou* have mine?
> > Sir John Suckling.

In older English *ye* was the nominative of the plural, and *you* the objective: as, 'I know *you* not, whence *ye* are.' But the forms were confounded, and in Shakespeare we find *ye* employed as an objective: so,

> The more shame for *ye*; holy men I thought *ye*.
> > *Henry VIII.*, iii. 1.

On the stage it is very common for actors to utter *ye* in the objective, where the copies have *you*. They seem to think it more rhetorical.

191. The forms of the Third Personal Pronoun are made up from the Anglo-Saxon personal *he, heó, hit,* and the demonstrative *se, seó, thæt.* We have,

| | *Singular.* | | | | *Plural.* |
	Masc.	*Fem.*	*Neut.*		*M. F. N.*
Nom.	he	she	it	. . . .	they
Gen.	his	her	its	. . . .	their
Dat.	him	her	it	. . . .	them
Acc.	him	her	it	. . . .	them.

In Old English the neuter nominative was *hit,* and the neuter genitive *his*. This neuter form of the genitive constantly occurs in our English Bible: as,

> The fruit-tree yielding fruit after *his* kind, whose seed is in *itself*.—*Gen.* i. 11.

> *It* shall bruise thy head, and thou shalt bruise *his* heel.—*Gen.* iii. 15.

> If the salt have lost *his* savour.—*Matt.* v. 13.

The word *its* does not occur in the original edition of the English Bible. In one passage, where our modern copies have *its*,

> That which groweth of *its* own accord—*Leviticus* xxv. 5.

the original copy reads,

> That which groweth of *it* own accord.

(See Alford, *The Queen's English*, p. 7, *note.*)

Shakespeare often uses *his* in the neuter: as,

> And that same eye, whose bend doth awe the world,
> Did lose *his* lustre.
> *Julius Cæsar*, i. 2.

> In such a time as this it is not meet
> That every nice offence should bear *his* comment.
> *Ibid.* iv. 3.

But he also has *its*: as,

> Heaven grant us *its* peace, but not the King of Hungary's.
> *Measure for Measure*, i. 2.

Before the form *its* came into full use, there seems to have been a period of transition, when *it* was used as a 'genitive by juxta-position:' thus,

> *It* knighthood and *it* friends.
> Ben Jonson, *Silent Woman*, ii. 3.

> Go to *it* grandam, child . . . and *it* grandam will give it a plum.—Shakespeare, *King John*, ii. 1.

It will be observed that the forms of the plural *they, their, them*, wherein *th* is found, are derived from the Anglo-Saxon demonstrative.

192. In nouns, there is no difference in form between the nominative and objective cases; but as in pronouns such a distinction exists, we must be careful to observe it, especially in compound sentences. 'She is as tall as *me*,' should be, 'as tall as *I*,' meaning 'as I am.' And so where the poet Thomson says,

The nations not so blest as *thee*,
  Must in their turn to tyrants fall ;
Whilst thou shalt flourish great and free,
  The dread and envy of them all :

he makes ' thee ' rhyme with ' free ; ' but his grammar is wrong ;
he should have said ' as *thou*,' because he means ' as thou art.'

So again, no one would think of saying ' let *I* go,' instead
of saying ' let *me* go ; ' and yet many persons think it right to
say, ' let you and I go.' Charles Dickens systematically adopts
this construction, and he may think that it is correct. And so
Southey :

. Let you and *I* endeavour to improve the inclosure of the
  Carr.—*The Doctor.*

But a little reflection must convince us, that if it is correct to
say ' let *me* go,' the addition of ' you ' can have no power to
turn an objective into a nominative construction. Besides,
in this case, *let* is properly a verb in the imperative mood, *go*
is an infinitive dependent upon that imperative ; and the construction is, ' grant me to go,' or ' allow me to go.' Similarly,
' let you and me go ' means ' grant you and me to go.' If, indeed, we could suppose *that* introduced, the case would be
quite altered : ' grant that you and I go ; ' but such a phrase
as ' let that ' is unwarranted, and is barely intelligible.

193. The construction after *but* is more doubtful. The word
was originally a preposition *be-utan*, ' by-out,' akin in signification to *with-utan*, ' with-out : '

For warld's wrak *but* welfare nought avails.
                                                    Dunbar.

that is, ' without well-being.'
So Gawin Douglas,

Admonist us *but* mare delay to ga.   *Book 4.*

' without more delay.'
Now if we admit that ' but ' still retains its force as a preposition, we may say, ' there was no one present but *me*,' that
is, ' beside me.' If on the other hand we do not allow the
prepositional force of ' but,' we must consider ' but ' as nothing
else than a conjunction, and say, ' there was no one present
but I,' that is, ' but I was present.'
So Shakespeare :

Which none but heaven, and you, and *I* shall hear.
                                                    King John, i. 1.

And so Coleridge :

Which none may hear but *she* and *thou*.—See § 478.

194. The rules that regulate the use of a verb, in the singular or in the plural, after two or more nouns, or after a collective noun, apply also to the use of pronouns in the singular, or in the plural; as,

Every one must judge of *his* own feelings.

But as ‘every one’ must include women as well as men, and as the singular preserves the distinction of gender, there is a tendency to avoid the difficulty by using the plural:

If an ox gore a man or woman, so that *they* die.
Exodus xxi. 28.

Not on outward charms alone should man or woman build *their* pretensions to please.—Opie.

In such instances, Cobbett would repeat the pronoun, in different genders, in the singular: ‘so that he or she die,’ ‘build his or her pretensions;’ for he argues that, however disagreeable repetition may be, it is better than obscurity or inaccuracy.

This point is not omitted in the parody upon Cobbett's style in the *Rejected Addresses*:

‘I take it for granted that every intelligent man, woman, and child, to whom I address myself, has stood severally and respectively in Little Russell Street, and cast their, his, her, and its eyes on the outside of this building before they paid their money to view the inside.’
Hampshire Farmer's Address.

CAUTIONS.

195. In using pronouns we should constantly remember to what words they refer; and examine whether the reference be consistent with other parts of the sentence, as well as with the clause in which the pronoun itself is found. For want of proper attention errors frequently occur in the use of pronouns. Take, for example, the following sentence from Addison:

‘There are, indeed, but very few who know how to be idle and innocent, or have a relish of any pleasures that are not criminal; every diversion *they* take is at the expense of some one virtue or other, and *their* very first step out of business is into vice or folly.’—*Spectator*, No. 411.

Of this passage Dr. Blair says (*Rhetoric*, Lecture 20):—
‘Nothing can be more elegant, or more finely turned than this sentence. It is neat, clear, and musical. We could hardly

alter one word, or displace one member, without spoiling it. Few sentences are to be found more finished or more happy.'

But to what persons does the pronoun *they* relate in that sentence? Surely not to the good 'few' who know how to be innocent, but to the wicked 'many' who plunge into vice. As Cobbett justly remarks (*Grammar*, § 176) the meaning of the sentence is this: ' that but few persons know how to be idle and innocent; that *few persons* have a relish of any pleasures that are not criminal; that every diversion *these few persons* take is at the expense of some one virtue or other, and that the very first step of *these few persons* out of business is into vice or folly.' Hence he adds, ' the sentence says precisely the contrary of what the author meant; or rather, the whole is perfect nonsense. All this arises from the misuse of the pronoun *they*. If, instead of this word, the author had put *people in general*, or *most people*, or *most men*, or any word, or words, of the same meaning, all would have been right.'

Yet I have often asked persons to examine this sentence; and at the first reading scarcely any one has been able to detect an error. We are so accustomed to use *they* in a general sense, that the grammatical reference to the ' few ' does not readily occur to the mind. A critic, with whom I conversed on one occasion, undertook to defend Addison against Cobbett, on the ground that the pronoun *they* is here used indefinitely, like *on* in French, and *man* in German. The defence is more ingenious than sound. It is better candidly to admit that Addison tripped; and that Dr. Blair, being occupied with the harmony of the sentence, did not observe the error. In his remarks upon this passage, Cobbett is very droll; but he is too severe upon Dr. Blair.

196. Where several persons are spoken of in the same sentence, the reference to each is sometimes doubtful, especially if the reader is not well acquainted with the matter in question. Take this passage from Sir W. Blackstone :

> For, the custom of the manor has, in both cases, so far superseded the will of the lord, that, provided the services be performed, or stipulated for by fealty, *he* cannot, in the first instance, refuse to admit the heir of *his* tenant, upon *his* death; nor, in the second, can *he* remove *his* present tenant so long as *he* lives.
>
> Kerr's Blackstone, ii. 94.

This means that ' the lord cannot, in the first instance, refuse to admit the heir of his tenant, in case of that tenant's death;

nor, in the second, can he remove his present tenant, during the lifetime of that tenant.'

197. When a personal pronoun refers to a collective noun, we must be consistent in our usage.   We may generally take our choice, whether we mean to consider the collective noun as singular or plural ; but having once made our election, we ought to persevere in the same : we must not mix up together ' they ' and ' its,' or ' it ' and ' their.'

198. When two nouns in the singular are coupled by the conjunction *and*, the pronoun referring to them both ought, strictly, to be in the plural.   But ' double-barrelled ' substantives, as Sydney Smith terms them, are often taken as making one idea ; for example, Dr. Blair says of Lord Shaftesbury :

> He was fonder of nothing than of *wit* and *raillery* ;
> but he is far from being happy in *it.—Rhetoric,*
> Lecture 19.

It may be argued, that if *wit* and *raillery* are different things, the pronoun should have been *them* : ' he is far from being happy in *them.*'   If, on the other hand, *wit* and *raillery* are the same, one of the terms is unnecessary.   See Cobbett, *Grammar,* § 179.

This, no doubt, is the strict law ; and in composition we ought to be severe critics of our own work.   But in the writings of the last century we may find scores of passages parallel to that of Dr. Blair.

When, however, nouns in the singular take the alternative conjunction *or,* the pronoun must be in the singular : as, ' when he shoots a partridge, a pheasant, or a woodcock, he gives *it* away.'

IT.

199. This convenient little word is constantly misused by careless writers.   We ought never to use *it,* without being quite sure that we know what we are doing, and that our construction is accurate.

We shall examine the causes of error, and try to discover some useful cautions.

1. The pronoun *it* is often used to represent a person or persons unknown, where the gender and the number are alike uncertain.   Thus when we ask, ' Who is it ? ' the answer may be, ' it is I,' ' it is he,' ' it is she,' or ' it is they.'   In these *sentences,* as the verb stands between two nominatives, it *might, strictly,* agree with either of them.   In Anglo-Saxon

we find *ic sylf hit eom*, 'I self it am' ('it is myself'), *Luke*
xxiv. 39. Chaucer says 'it *am* I,' and the Germans say 'es
sind Männer,' 'it *are* men,' where we say '*there* are men.'
In all such cases we make the verb agree with *it*, no matter
what person or number may follow.

Some critics have entertained doubts about the propriety of
this usage. Dr. Johnson says, 'This mode of speech, though
used by good authors, and supported by the *il y a* of the
French, has yet an appearance of barbarism.'

Dr. Lowth thinks that the phrases which occur in the following examples, though pretty common and authorised by
custom, are yet somewhat defective.

> '*Tis they*, that give the great Atrides' spoils;
> '*Tis they*, that still renew Ulysses' toils.
>
> Prior.
>
> '*Tis two* or *three*, my lord, that bring you word
> Macduff is fled to England.
>
> *Macbeth*, iv. 1.

200. Dr. Campbell, in reviewing the question, observes,
that the indefinite use of the pronoun *it* may have a reference,

1. To persons as well as to things.
2. To the first person and the second, as well as to the
   third.
3. To a plural as well as to a singular.

Against the first application to persons as well as to things,
neither Dr. Johnson nor Dr. Lowth seems to have any objection; and both these critics speak with some hesitation about
the other two. Yet, in the opinion of Dr. Campbell, if one be
censurable, they are all censurable; and if one be proper,
they are all proper. For the distinction of genders is as
essential as the distinction of persons, or that of numbers.

Besides, where a personal pronoun must be used indefinitely,
as when we ask a question about a person or persons unknown, we are obliged to use one person for all the persons,
one gender for all the genders, and one number for both numbers. Now, in English, custom has chosen, for this indefinite
use, the third person, the neuter gender, and the singular
number—namely, the pronoun *it*.

201. Accordingly, in asking a question, no one censures
this use of the pronoun; as, for example, in the interrogation
'Who is *it*?' Yet the answer may show that *it* represents *I*,
he, or *she*, *one* or *many*. But whatever be the answer, we are

justified in beginning that answer by the same indefinite
form, which appeared in the question. The words *it is* are
consequently warrantable here, whatever be the words which
ought to follow, whether *I* or *he, we* or *they.*

And if there be nothing faulty in the expression, when it is
an answer to a question actually proposed, there can be no
fault in it when used absolutely. Nor is there any reason
why one number may not as well serve indefinitely for both
numbers, as one person for all the persons, and one gender
for all the genders.

202. Writers have been more scrupulous about the difference of number, in this construction, than about the variations
of person or gender; probably because they disliked to use a
verb in the singular followed by a plural nominative. In
order to avoid this supposed incongruity, the translators of
the Bible have employed the unusual phrase ' they are they '
for ' it is they: '

> Search the scriptures, for in them ye think ye have
> eternal life; and *they are they* which testify of me.—
> *John* v. 39.

In the other applications they have not hesitated to use the
indefinite form *it,* as in this expression, ' *It* is *I,* be not afraid.'
(*Matt.* xiv. 27.) Yet the phrase ' they are they ' in the first
quotation is no better English than ' I am I ' would have been
in the second.

A convenient mode of speech, which custom has established,
and for which there is frequent occasion, ought not to be
hastily given up, especially when the language does not furnish us with another equally simple to supply its place.—See
Campbell, *Philosophy of Rhetoric,* pp. 208–211.

203.—2. Frequently, the pronoun *it* refers, not to a single
noun, but to a phrase, or to a sentence: as, ' Walking before
breakfast is healthy, and he is very fond of *it,*' *i. e.* ' walking
before breakfast: ' ' I told them so before, and they know *it,*'
i. e. ' that I told them so before.'

We should take care that the reference be clear; and there
is risk of error, if, in the same sentence, we have one *it* referring to a single noun, and another *it* referring to a phrase.

204.—3. The pronoun *it* is frequently employed as a *fore-
runner,* to represent a coming phrase or sentence: as,

> *It* is pleasant *to ride on horseback.*
> *It* is true *that the war is over.*

Here the meaning is 'to ride on horseback is pleasant,' 'that the war is over is true.' In this construction subordinate clauses are commonly introduced by *that*, but other particles, as *if*, *whether*, may be used in the same way:

> *It* is uncertain *if he will come.*
> *It* is doubtful *whether he will go.*

205. We may easily see that the various references of this pronoun are a frequent cause of ambiguity; for we are often unable to tell which of the several possible references a writer has in view, when he uses the word. For instance:

> There are so many advantages of speaking one's own language well, and being a master of *it*, that let a man's calling be what *it* will, *it* cannot but be worth while taking some pains in *it*.

The first *it* refers to ' language; ' the second to ' calling; ' the third is a forerunner and stands for ' taking some pains; ' the fourth goes back to ' language.'

206. We should avoid using *it* in relation to different nouns in the same sentence; and when we are obliged to employ *it* in reference to a preceding noun, we should not introduce a forerunning *it* in addition.

So in this passage:

> The best way in the world for a man to seem to be anything is really to be what he would seem to be. Besides that *it* is many times as troublesome to make good the pretence of a good quality as to have *it*; and if a man have *it* not, *it* is ten to one but he is discovered to want *it*, and then all his pains and labours to seem to have *it* are lost.

POSSESSIVE PRONOUNS.

207. Possessive pronouns have arisen from the genitive cases of the personal, or of other pronouns, used as adjectives. Thus, for example, in Anglo-Saxon, *min*, the genitive case of the first personal pronoun *ic*, is used as an adjective and regularly declined: masc. *min*, fem. *mine*, neut. *min*. Similarly, in Latin, *cujus*, the genitive of the relative pronoun, is declined like an adjective, *cujus*, *cuja*, *cujum*; as in Virgil,

> *Cujum* pecus? an Meliboei?
> *Eclogue*, iii. 1.

We shall not consider the pronoun *whose* in this place; but we shall confine our attention to those possessive pronouns which have arisen from personals or demonstratives. And first we remark that many of the possessive pronouns in English have two forms; as *my, mine; thy, thine; her, hers; our, ours; your, yours; their, theirs.*

As a general rule, the shorter form is used before a noun; and the longer form when no noun follows.

Of *his* and *its* there are no second forms: we may say 'that is *his* book,' and 'that book is *his*.' But instead of 'that is *my* book,' we cannot say 'that book is *my*;' but, 'that book is *mine*.'

208. It will be necessary to consider these forms more particularly.

Mine is from the Anglo-Saxon *min*; it is sometimes used as an adjective, and sometimes it retains the force of a genitive. In the sentence 'that book is *mine*,' it is an open question, whether 'mine' is the genitive of the personal, or an adjective. In early English, the true genitive force is exhibited, in such phrases as 'maugre *myne*,' *i. e.* 'in spite *of me*,' used by Robert de Brunne.

As we trace the history of the language, we find the form *mine*, used adjectively, still remaining before nouns beginning with a vowel, or with the letter *h*: as 'myn helthe' for 'my health:' and so,

> Shall I not take *mine* ease in *mine* inn, but I shall have my pocket picked?—*1st Hen. IV.* iii. 3.

But it became customary, before nouns beginning with a consonant, to use the shortened form *my*. In the following passage both forms are used, one before a consonant, the other before a vowel:

> *Mine* eye also shall see *my* desire upon *mine* enemies, and *mine* ears shall hear *my* desire of the wicked that rise up against me.—*Psalm* xcii. 11.

In modern English, *mine* is the form employed as a predicate, when used absolutely, that is without a following noun: as, 'that book is *mine*.'

It also occurs in such idiomatic phrases as 'that is a book *of mine*,' which I explain in the same way as the sentence 'that is a play of Shakespeare's,' namely, that we have a double form of the genitive. (See § 141.) Grammarians expound the idiom thus: 'that is a book of my books;' but I believe that this is an afterthought; and that the old genitive *mine* was used with the preposition *of*, by a confusion of the two kinds of genitive.

209. *Thine.* Similar remarks apply to this word. It is derived from the Anglo-Saxon *thin*, the genitive of the second personal pronoun *thu*, 'thou.' Its true character as a genitive is seen in the old English phrase ' maugre *thin*,' *i. e.*, ' in spite *of thee.*' (*Havelok the Dane.*) In modern English, it stands alone as a predicate : ' that book is thine ; ' and in the phrase ' that is a book *of thine.*' Before nouns, where it has the force of an adjective, it is shortened to *thy*; as ' that is *thy* book.'

210. *Our* is from the Anglo-Saxon *ure*, genitive plural of *ic*, which was also used as an adjective.

In Old English we find *oure* : as,

> Gif he passeth with honour
> *Oure* is the deshonour.
>
> > *Kyng Alisaunder.*

That is,

> If he passes with honour
> *Our* is the dishonour.

And so,

> *Oure* is the maistry of the felde.
>
> > *Ibid.*

That is,

> *Our* is the mastery of the field.

In modern English *our* is used before a noun; but when the word is used absolutely, it takes the form *ours*, where the *s* is said to represent the possessive case. If so, we have here a sort of double genitive; for *our* itself is derived from a genitive plural, and if *s* is the mark of possession, that is equivalent to a genitive.

In some counties of England the form *ourn* may be heard ; this is probably formed by the adjective termination *en*, *ouren* contracted to *ourn*. Etymologically, *ourn* is just as good a word as *ours* ; perhaps even better; and if it were only customary, we should think it quite correct.

211. *Your* is from the Anglo-Saxon' *eower*, the genitive plural of the second personal pronoun. I cannot find any adjective form of this word in Anglo-Saxon. In Old English it is used absolutely, as a predicate : so Chaucer,

> Fro that blisfull hour
> That I you swore to be all freely *your*.

And again,

> I am and will be *your* in will and herte.

In modern English, when the word is used absolutely, that is without a following noun, the form of the double genitive *yours* is employed: as ' I am yours; ' and there seems to be no necessity for using the apostrophe in these cases, *your's*; at all events, the best writers do not introduce it.

The adjective form *yourn* occurs in some provincial dialects: as ' that's none o' yourn.'

212. *His* is from the Anglo-Saxon *hys*, or *his*, the genitive of the masculine *he* and of the neuter *hit*. In Anglo-Saxon it does not appear to have been declined like an adjective; but Dr. Adams thinks that in Old English it received inflectional endings like an adjective: as,

> And *hise* disciples camen and took *his* body.—Wycliffe.

The adjective form *hisn* occurs in provincial dialects.

Her is from the Anglo-Saxon *hyre* or *hire*, the genitive of the feminine *heo*, a word still preserved in Lancashire, and pronounced *hoo*. When this pronoun is used absolutely, it takes the form of the double genitive *hers*: ' that is hers.'

Its. This form is comparatively modern, not much more than three hundred years old. It is employed both before nouns and absolutely; and strictly it is rather the genitive of a personal, than a possessive pronoun.

Their : this is formed from *thara*, the genitive of the Anglo-Saxon demonstrative, and not from the genitive of the personal *hira* or *heora*.

When the word is used absolutely, it takes the form *theirs* : ' the estate was theirs.'

We have then the following forms :—

Before a Noun.					Used absolutely.
my	.	.	.	.	. mine
thy	.	.	.	.	. thine
our	.	.	.	.	. ours
your	.	.	.	.	. yours
his	.	.	.	.	. his
her	.	.	.	.	. hers
their	.	.	.	.	. theirs

DEMONSTRATIVE PRONOUNS.

213. Demonstrative Pronouns are used to 'point out' (*demonstrate*) the objects to which they refer; more especially to show the locality of objects. They vary their forms to denote number, but not to denote gender or case:

Singular.	*Plural.*
1. This	These.
2. That	Those.

This and *these* are used to point out objects near the speaker; *that* and *those* to point out objects at some distance from the speaker.

214. Some grammarians deny that *this* and *that* are pronouns. Professor Bain classes them under Adjectives, and terms them Pronominal Demonstratives. His reason for placing them under adjectives, and not under pronouns, is that they 'require a noun after them which the proper pronouns do not.' —*English Grammar,* p. 28.

But as he cannot deny that these words often appear to stand alone, he says, (p. 29) 'The frequent ellipsis of the noun with the demonstrative adjectives is what gives them the character of demonstrative pronouns: "after *that,* I shall say no more;" "*this* being granted."'

Here, as usual with grammarians, he has recourse to the artifice of 'understanding' a noun.

215. Crombie, quoted by Kerchever Arnold, (*English Grammar,* § 71) says: 'it is abundantly evident that *this* and *that* are not pronouns, for they never represent a noun.'

'But surely,' replies Mr. Arnold, 'to go no further, "that" does stand for a noun in the example quoted by himself:

the only good on earth
Was pleasure; not to follow *that* was sin.

Here *that* stands simply for *pleasure*; there is no ellipse, for we cannot put in the word *pleasure* without striking out *that*. *That* stands for *pleasure*, and not for *that pleasure*. So in such sentences as, "the first opportunity was *that* of the Prince of Denmark's death," *that* stands for *the opportunity*.'

216. Dr. Lowth is of opinion that these words are Adjectives, and not Pronouns; he says (*English Grammar,* p. 40), 'Beside the foregoing, there are several other Pronominal Adjectives; which, though they may sometimes *seem* to stand by themselves, yet have always some Substantive belonging to them, either referred to or ' understood;' as, *This, that, other, any, some, one, none.*

217. Sir John Stoddart rejoins (*Universal Grammar*, p. 44), 'Almost all pronouns, except the first and second personals, are clearly adjectives in origin; but we cannot admit that they continue to be such when they stand by themselves, or as Lowth rather singularly expresses it, " seem to stand by themselves." It is true that, in such cases, they often have " some substantive . belonging to them, either referred to or understood ; " but this only proves that they are pronouns. Whether we say " *this* is good," " *it* is good," or " *he* is good," there is always some noun referred to or understood; and the words *it* and *he* " seem to stand by themselves," just as much as the word *this* does.'

218. The whole difficulty arises from the unwillingness of grammarians to admit that the term *noun* may comprise adjectives as well as substantives. They further maintain that an adjective can never stand alone, but must always have a substantive, either expressed or understood.

As before stated, we do not scruple to extend the term pronoun; hence, we call *this* and *that* pronouns; and we say that they are used sometimes as substantives, sometimes as adjectives; in other words, sometimes absolutely, and standing by themselves; sometimes with a following noun.

219. In the plural number, the substantive use is very common, and is admitted by some grammarians who question the same usage in the singular : so,

> Some place the bliss in action, some in ease;
> *Those* call it pleasure, and contentment *these*.
>
> <div align="right">Pope, <i>Essay on Man</i>, iv. 21, 22.</div>

In the singular the substantive use is more common in reference to things, or to thoughts : as,

> *Self-love*, the spring of motion acts the soul;
> *Reason's* comparing *balance* rules the whole;
> Man, but for *that*, no action could attend ;
> And, but for *this*, were active to no end.
>
> <div align="right"><i>Ib.</i> ii. 59—62.</div>

Often, too, *that* is used referring to a phrase, or to an entire sentence : as,

> To be or not to be, *that* is the question.
>
> <div align="right"><i>Hamlet</i>, iii. 1.</div>

In reference to *persons*, when *this* and *that* are used substantively, it will be found, as a general rule, that a noun is used as a predicate-nominative in the sentences: as, ' *this* is my brother,' ' *that* is my friend.' We cannot say, ' *this* did the deed,' meaning ' this man ; ' or ' *that* shall be punished,' meaning that person.'—See Mason, *English Grammar*, § 157.

220. A very common use of *that* is before a genitive case, in order to avoid the repetition of a noun : as,

He mistook his own room for *that* of the stranger.

We might express this more briefly by saying 'for the stranger's.' Professor Bain suggests (*English Grammar*, p. 20), that the form 'that of the stranger' is derived from the French.

So in the plural :

The rules of style, like *those* of law, arise from precedents often repeated.

221. *This* and *that* are also used as ' logical' pronouns; that is, they refer to some word or words, which have occurred in discourse : as,

The general was in command of a large force. *This* force consisted of infantry and cavalry.

Cromwell, I charge thee, fling away ambition :
By *that* sin fell the angels.　　　*Henry VIII.* iii. 2.

222. When two objects are named, *this* represents the latter; *that* the former; like *hic* and *ille* in Latin : as,

This can unlock the gates of Joy ;
Of Horror *that*, and thrilling Fears.
　　　　　Gray, *Progress of Poetry*.

223. The singular *this* is sometimes used with a plural noun and an adjective, when they mark a period of time :

This *seven years* did not Talbot see his son.
　　　　　1st *Henry VI.* iv. 3.

224. The adjective use of *this* and *that* is so common as hardly to need exemplification :

Beneath *those* rugged elms, *that* yew-tree's shade,
　Where heaves the turf in many a mouldering heap,
Each in his narrow cell for ever laid,
　The rude forefathers of the hamlet sleep.
　　　　　Gray, *Elegy.*

G

CAUTIONS.

225. Younger pupils must learn to distinguish between the demonstrative *that*, the relative *that*, and the conjunction or connective particle *that*.   Probably these forms have all arisen from the Anglo-Saxon demonstrative *thæt*; but diversity of usage has given them a different character.   At present, it will be enough to furnish an example of each:

Demonstrative .	*That* man told me so.
Relative . . .	He is the man *that* told me so.
Conjunction . .	He said *that* he would come.

226. Some difference of opinion prevails respecting the use of the demonstrative followed by a relative : as, *those who, those that ;* and in particular, whether it be correct to say *they who, they that,* using *they* in the sense of *any persons,* or *persons in general.*

Cobbett draws a distinction : in the sentence ' We ought always to have a great regard for *them* who are wise and good,' he maintains that we ought to say 'for *those* who are wise and good ' if we mean 'those ' persons in general 'who are wise and good.'   But in reference to particular persons, who are stated to be wise and good, and who are also beloved, we may say 'I love *them* who are wise and good,' where the pronoun ' who ' has a co-ordinating force.

Hence he condemns this passage in Dr. Blair's *Rhetoric* (Lecture 21) : ' The two paragraphs are extremely worthy of Mr. Addison, and exhibit a style which *they* who can successfully imitate may esteem themselves happy.'   He thinks that *they* ought to be *those ;* and in commenting upon another passage he remarks, ' It is truly curious, that Lindley Murray should, even in the *motto* in the title-page of his *English Grammar,* have selected a sentence containing a grammatical error ; still more curious, that he should have found this sentence in Dr. Blair's *Lectures on Language ;* and most curious of all, that this sentence should be intended to inculcate the *great utility of correctness* in the composing of sentences ! *" They* who are learning to compose and arrange their sentences with accuracy and order, are learning, at the same time, to think with accuracy and order." '—Cobbett, *Grammar,* § 210.

227. But we must not be too hasty in condemning Lindley

Murray and Dr. Blair; we may do well to inquire whether
there be a grammatical error in this sentence; whether, in
fact, this use of *they* may not be warrantable.

228. Etymologically, *they* is a demonstrative pronoun: it
is inaccurate to consider *they* the plural of *he.* The words belong to different systems; and *they* is formed fiom the Anglo-
Saxon demonstrative *se, seó, thœt.*—See Latham, *English
Grammar,* § 81.

229. The question resolves itself into one of usage; and
there can be no doubt as to the phrase *they that* in the older
stages of the language. Professor Bain advocates the use of
that instead of *who,* in what he calls the restrictive use of the
relative in adjective clauses. In accordance with that view,
he argues (*English Grammar*), p. 192: 'The form "those
who," applied in a restrictive sense, is the modern substitute
for the ancient idiom "they that," an idiom in accordance
with the true meaning of "that:" "*they that* told me the
story said;" "blessed are *they that* mourn;" "and Simon
and *they that* were with him;" "I love *them that* love me,
and *they that* seek me early shall find me." '—See § 92.

We have, then, authority for *they that*; and the modern
those who is unquestioned. *They who* is frequently employed
by Dr. Johnson, in those general propositions which he is fond
of enunciating; and, as we have seen, it has the authority of
Dr. Blair.

The phrase is not so manifestly wrong as Mr. Cobbett sur-
mises; but, in practice, it is safer to write *those who,* or *those
that,* in general statements.

230. *That* is used after relative pronouns and relative adverbs, in a manner which seems to us superfluous; but this
usage was very common in older English : as,

> In olde dayes of the Kyng Arthour,
> Of *which that* Britouns speken gret honour,
> Al was this lond fulfilled of fayrie.
> Chaucer, The Wyf of Bathes Tale.

> Wot ye not wher ther stent a litel toun,
> *Which that* icleped is Bob-up-and-doun.
> Chaucer, Prologue of the Maunciples Tale.

> *When that* the poor have cried, Cæsar hath wept.
> Julius Cæsar, iii. 2.

In modern English we have still the phrases *now that, so that.*
—See Adams, *Elements,* § 531.

231. *Yon, yond*, and *yonder* are forms derived from the Anglo-Saxon adverb *geond*, which appears in our word *be-yond*. In practice, however, these forms are sometimes used with the force of demonstrative pronouns :

Yond Cassius hath a lean and hungry look.
Julius Cæsar, i. 2.

Near *yonder* copse, where once a garden smiled,
And still where many a garden flower grows wild.
Goldsmith, *Deserted Village*.

INTERROGATIVE PRONOUNS.

232. Interrogative pronouns, used in asking questions, are *who* and *what*. We have also to consider *which* and *whether*; and we shall find that, etymologically, *which* is not the neuter of *who*, but a compound word. *Whether* is a derivative.

233. Of the pronoun *who, what*, the following forms remain, common to the singular and plural :

Masc. and Fem.					*Neut.*
Nom.	who .	.	.	.	. what
Gen.	whose	.	.	.	. (whose)
Dat.	whom	.	.	.	. —
Acc.	whom	.	.	.	. what

There are doubts whether *whose* may be used in the neuter gender; but, etymologically, there is no reason against it. And, practically, the usage in the neuter is very convenient; for otherwise we are obliged to say ' of which;' as for example, instead of ' the trees whose leaves are withered,' we must turn the phrase, ' the trees the leaves of which are withered.'

These forms are used in the singular and in the plural. *What* may be employed adjectively; the rest are used as substantives.

When *what* is used as a substantive, it is singular and neuter; when used as an adjective, it may be joined to a noun of any gender, and of either number.

234. *Which* is properly a compound word, from the Anglo-Saxon *hwilc*, contracted from *hwa-lic* 'what-like,' corresponding to the Latin *qua-lis*. As an interrogative it may be used

substantively or adjectively, for any gender, and for either
number: as,

> *Which* was it?
> *Which* of you will go?
> *Which* will you have?
> *Which* place did he choose?
> *Which* numbers did she select?

In asking questions we distinguish between *who* and *which*.
For example, 'who spoke?' asks the question generally; 'which
spoke?' inquires for a particular individual of a number or
class.

235. *Whether*, Anglo-Saxon *hwæther*, is the interrogative pronoun *hwa*, 'who,' with the old termination *-ther*, which denotes
'one of two,' as we see it in 'o-*ther*,' 'ei-*ther*.' In modern
English its force as a pronoun has been lost, and it is employed
adverbially; but in older English it is seen as a true pronoun:

> *Whether* of them twain did the will of his father? i.e.
> '*which* of the two?'

Caution.

236. When an interrogative pronoun introduces a dependent
clause, there is danger of mistaking it for a relative.

To determine whether 'who,' 'which,' or 'what' is an interrogative, turn the sentence into a question. If the dependent
clause gives the answer to such a question, the pronoun is an
interrogative: as,

> I asked *who* was there.
> *Question.*—What did you ask?
> *Answer.*—Who was there.
>
> They inquired *what* he was going to do.
> *Question.*—What did they inquire?
> *Answer.* What he was going to do.

In these sentences *who* and *what* are interrogative pronouns.
—See Arnold, *English Grammar*, § 78.

237. When the interrogatives *who* and *whom* are placed
near the words with which they are joined in construction,
there is not much risk of error: as '*Who* was there?' '*Whom*
did you see?' '*To whom* did he give it?' But when the
interrogatives stand at some distance from the related words,
the ear gives no assistance, and mistakes may arise as, who

did he give it *to* ' for ' *whom* did he give it *to.*' In spite of
Lindley Murray, it is idiomatic, in English, to throw a preposition to the end of a clause or sentence; but then we must
carefully remember the government : ' *whom* did he give it
to ? ' exhibits precisely the same government as ' *To whom* did
he give it ? '

Take these instances : ' *Whom* do men say that *I am* ?
But *whom* say ye that *I am* ? '—*Matt.* xvi. 13–15. ' *Whom*
think ye that *I am* ? '—*Acts* xiii. 25. In these places *whom*
ought to be *who*, for the pronoun is not governed by the
verb *say* or *think*, but enters into the construction of the subordinate sentence. For, in an indicative sentence, we might
have ' Ye say that I am *he* :' then, in the way of interrogation,
the nominative *he* being thrown to the beginning of the question
becomes *who*, not *whom* :—

> ' *Who*, say ye, that I am ? '—See Lowth, *English Gram-
> mar*, p. 110.

RELATIVE PRONOUNS.

238. Etymologically, we have no true relative pronoun in
English ; but we borrow other pronouns, and use them as
relatives. In our earliest writings, *that* is so employed ; in
course of time, the interrogatives *who* and *what*, with the compound pronoun *which*, were also used ; and although, in
practice, *which* serves as a neuter, this was not the original
force of the word.

But, what is the meaning of the word *relative*, in the term
'relative pronoun ? ' Other pronouns may involve a *reference*
to some word which has gone before in a sentence, and which
might be termed the *antecedent*, that is, the ' fore-goer,' or the
' fore-runner.'

239. The distinctive character of ' relative pronouns,' properly so called, is that they cannot be used to form the subject
of an independent sentence ; but that they are employed to
introduce a subordinate sentence, otherwise termed a dependent clause. And as they must, of necessity, look for
some subject to which they *relate*, they are called *relative*.

For example, the *interrogative* ' who' may be used alone in
an interrogative sentence ; as, ' *Who* did it ?' But the *relative*
' *who* ' *cannot* be used alone in an indicative sentence : to say.

'Who did it' would have no meaning; but the sentence, 'I know the man *who did it*,' is intelligible.

The noun or pronoun, to which the relative points, is usually called the *antecedent*, because it commonly 'goes before' the relative. But sometimes the noun or pronoun 'comes after' the relative, in which case the term *ante*-cedent is not literally correct.

Sometimes a relative pronoun refers to a phrase, or to a whole sentence, which then takes the place of an antecedent.

240. We shall consider the origin and the uses of the forms *that, who, what,* and *which*. *That* is from the Anglo-Saxon *thæt*, the neuter of the demonstrative *se, seó, thæt*.

In Anglo-Saxon, the relative is expressed sometimes by the demonstrative, and at other times by the indeclinable particle *the*: as,

> Se *the* of heofone cóm, se ys ofer ealle.
> He *that* from heaven came, he is over all.
> > *John* iii. 31.

> Thæt *the* acenned is of flæsc, thæt is flæsc.
> That *which* born is of flesh, that is flesh.
> > *Id.* iii. 6.

Sometimes we find *thæt* doubled:

> Ic sende eow to rypanne, *thæt thæt* ge ne beswuncon.
> I sent you to reap *that that* ye ne belaboured.
> > *Id.* iv. 38.

i.e. 'that for which he have not laboured.'

This will explain the use of *that* in older English, where the one word is made to do double duty:

> To consider advisedly of *that* is moved.—Bacon, *Essay* xxii.

> We speak *that* we do know, and testify *that* we have seen.
> —*John* iii. 11.

where Wycliffe reads, 'that that we witen.'

A nice question might be raised, one more curious than useful, whether the first or second *thæt* was omitted: the antecedent *thæt* or the relative *thæt*.

In like manner, the neuter pronoun *it* is used where we should employ *that which*, or *what*:

> By this also a man may understand, when it is that men may be said to be conquered; and in what the nature of a conquest and the right of a conqueror consisteth; for this is *it* implieth them all.—Hobbes, *Leviathan*.

And this is *it* men mean by distributive justice, and is
properly tempered equity.—Hobbes, *Elements of Law*,
part i. chap. iv. 2.

The English relative *that* is used for all genders, and for
either number; hence it is conveniently used for *who* or *which*,
when we do not wish to discriminate gender; and in instances
where the antecedents refer to things, as well as persons : thus,

Ulysses spoke of the men and the cities *that* he had seen.

241. *Who* is derived from the interrogative *hwa*, ' who ? '
In the authorised version of the Bible, the relative *who* is occasionally employed, but the more usual relative is *that*. *Who*
is never used as an adjective.

The genitive *whose* is used as the possessive case of the
relative pronoun ; and in prose, custom has been in favour of
restricting it to the masculine and feminine genders. Etymologically, it might be used of all genders, for, in Anglo-Saxon,
the genitive *hwœs* was employed for the neuter as well as for
the masculine or the feminine. In the poets, we constantly
find *whose* referring to neuter nouns : as,

But that I am forbid
To tell the secrets of my prison-house,
I could a tale unfold, *whose* lightest word
Would harrow up thy soul.—*Hamlet*, i. 5.

But that the dread of something after death,
The undiscovered country, from *whose* bourn
No traveller returns, puzzles the will ;
And makes us rather bear those ills we have,
Than fly to others that we know not of.—*Id*. iii. 2.

Of man's first disobedience, and the fruit
Of that forbidden tree, *whose* mortal taste
Brought death into the world and all our woe,
With loss of Eden, till one greater man
Restore us, and regain the blissful seat,
Sing, heavenly Muse.

Milton, *Paradise Lost*, i. 1-6.

242. *What* is derived from *hwœt*, the neuter of the interrogative : it is nominative or objective, singular and neuter.

When used as a relative, *what* may be used substantively
or adjectively. But it has a peculiar force ; it appears to be
equivalent to an antecedent and a relative combined : ' *What*
I said was this,' i.e. ' *that which* I said was this ;' ' *what* time
I am afraid, I will trust in thee,' i.e. ' *at that* time *at·which* I

am afraid, I will trust in thee.' But it is a mistake, says Mr. Mason (*English Grammar*, § 161), to parse the word *what*, as though it were made up of *that which*. In such a sentence as 'I know *what* is correct,' it is wrong to say that *what* is in any sense governed by the verb *know*. *What* is the subject of the verb *is*, and is in the nominative case.

We may suppose that this use of *what* originated from the employment of *that* in two co-ordinate sentences : as,

> *That* he bids, *that* thou shalt do.
> *What* he bids, *that* thou shalt do.
> *What* he bids, thou shalt do;

and by conversion,

> Thou shalt do *what* he bids.

But let us consider this passage :

> *What* he bids be done is finished with his bidding.—
> *Coriolanus*, ⅴ. 4.

Here we want a nominative to the verb *is* ; and we also want an objective dependent upon the verb *bids*, or to stand as a subject-accusative to the infinitive *be done* : hence there is a strong temptation to resolve *what* into *that which* :

> That, which he bids be done, is finished with the bidding.

If we say, that *what* is here the objective, then the nominative of the sentence (*that*) is omitted, and we have a sentence without an apparent nominative.

243. *Which*, as we have seen (§ 234), is a compound word, and is used both as an adjective and a substantive. Although, in practice, its use is limited to inanimate and irrational beings, yet it is not properly the neuter of *who*.

Hence 'Our Father *which* art in heaven' is grammatically accurate ; although it appears that the Americans have thought right to alter *which* into *who*. Cobbett says (*English Grammar*, § 65), 'This application of the relative *which* solely to irrational creatures is, however, of modern date; for, in the Lord's Prayer, in the English Church Service, we say, "Our Father *which* art in heaven." In the American Liturgy this error has been corrected; and they say, "Our Father *who* art in heaven."' But there was no error, and consequently no necessity for change. Still the usage of the language has varied, and by present custom *who*, *whose*, *whom* are now limited, in prose, to rational beings; *which* to irrational beings, inanimate objects, and collective nouns, when the idea of personality is not prominent; while *that* may represent nouns of any kind.—See Angus, *Handbook*, § 435.

244. When inanimate objects are personified, *who*, *whose*, and *whom* may be employed; but we should avoid a confusion of genders: as,

> 'Twas Love's mistake, *who* fancied what *it* feared.
> > *Crabbe.*

Connection of the Antecedent and the Relative.

245. The Antecedent may be a noun, a pronoun, an infinitive used substantively, a phrase, or a sentence.

> Some men are too ignorant *to be humble*, without *which* there can be no docility and no progress.—*Berkeley.*
>
> Homer is remarkably concise, *which* renders him lively and agreeable.—*Blair.*

Here the antecedents are the 'being humble' and the fact of 'being concise.'

246. Every relative must have an antecedent to which it refers, either expressed or understood: as,

> *Who* steals my purse, steals trash.
> > *Othello*, iii. 3.

that is, *the man who*, or *he who*.

247. The relative is of the same person with the antecedent; and the verb agrees with it accordingly: as,

> Who is *this that cometh* from Edom; *this that is* glorious in his apparel? *I that speak* in righteousness.
> > *Isaiah* lxiii. 1.
>
> O shepherd of Israel; *Thou that leadest* Joseph like a flock; *Thou that dwellest* between the Cherubims, shine forth.—*Psalm* lxxx. 1.

Now take this passage:

> I am *the Lord that maketh* all things; *that stretcheth* forth the heavens alone; *that spreadeth* abroad the earth by myself.—*Isaiah* xliv. 21.

In the first part of the sentence 'I am the Lord *that maketh* . . . *that stretcheth*,' all is right: *the Lord* in the third person is the antecedent, and the verb agrees with the relative in the third person: 'I am the Lord, *which Lord*, or *he, that maketh* all things.' It would have been equally right, if *I* had been made the antecedent, and the relative and the verb had agreed with it in the first person: '*I* am the Lord, *that make* all things.' But when it follows, '*that spreadeth* abroad the earth *by myself*,' there arises an apparent confusion of the third and first persons.—See Lowth, *English Grammar*, p. 145.

But in Hebrew poetry we often find an alternation of persons, not in accordance with formal grammar, but quite intelligible, and conducive to poetical ornament: as,

> O that my people had hearkened unto me, and Israel had walked in my ways! *I* should soon have subdued their enemies, and turned *my* hand against their adversaries. The haters of the Lord should have submitted themselves unto *him*; but their time should have endured for ever. *He* should have fed *them* also with the finest of the wheat; and with honey out of the rock should *I* have satisfied *thee*.
>
> *Psalm* lxxxi. 13–16.

248. Our own poets sometimes take a license which is not so warrantable, because it exhibits rather confusion than alternation : as,

> *Thou* great first cause, least understood,
> *Who* all my sense *confin'd*,
> To know but this, that *Thou* art good,
> And that myself am blind :
> Yet *gave* me in this dark estate, &c.
>
> Pope, *Universal Prayer*.

In strict grammar, the poet should have written *confinedst* or *didst confine, gavest* or *didst give*.

And so here :

> *O thou* supreme! high throned all height above!
> O great Pelasgic, Dodonean Jove!
> *Who* midst surrounding frost, and vapours chill,
> *Preside* on bleak Dodona's vocal hill.
>
> Pope, *Iliad*, xvi. 284.

where the grammar requires *presidest*.

249. A collective noun, representing a class or group of individuals, is referred to by *which*, and the verb follows in the singular; but when the idea of plurality is intended, the notion of personality also comes in; and then the reference is by means of the pronoun '*who*,' and the verb follows in the plural :

> The committee, *which was* appointed last session, *reports* in favour of the bill.

The ministry, *who were* divided among themselves, *were* obliged to resign.

Care must be taken not to combine the two constructions: as,

> That ingenious nation, *who have done* so much for modern literature, *possesses* in an eminent degree the talent of narration.—*Blair.*

250. In older English, *which* and *that* are frequently found after *such* : as,

> Avoid *such* games, *which* require much time or long attendance.—*Jeremy Taylor.*

> But with *such* words *that* are but rooted in your tongue.

251. Instead of a relative pronoun, we more commonly use the relative adverb *as*, after the antecedents *such*, *same* : as,

> Tears, *such as* angels weep, burst forth.
> > Milton, *Paradise Lost*, i. 620.

i. e. ' tears like those which angels weep.'

> > Art thou afeard
> To be the *same* in thine own act and valour,
> *As* thou art in desire? *Macbeth*, i. 7.

In like manner *but* is frequently equivalent to a relative and a negative :

> There is no vice so simple, *but* assumes
> Some mark of virtue on his outward parts.
> > *Merchant of Venice*, iii. 2.

252. But although *as*, after *such* and *same*, has the force of a relative, we cannot admit that it is a relative *pronoun*. Dr. Adams (*English Grammar*, § 253) and Professor Bain (*English Grammar*, p. 24) are careful to use the term ' relative,' and not ' relative pronoun.' So too Dr. Angus (*Handbook*, § 227). But the latter adds, ' The use of *as* and *so* with a pronominal force, is justified by analogous forms in the Gothic languages.'

No doubt there is a tendency in the Germanic languages to employ an adverb where other languages would use a pronoun. We say ' wherein,' ' whereby,' for ' in which,' ' by which; ' and the Germans are fond of using such forms as ' dazu,' ' dabei,' ' dadurch,' equivalent to ' thereto,' ' thereby,' ' therethrough.'

Compare also the following passages:

> I have heard
> *Where* many of the best respect in Rome,
> (Except immortal Cæsar), speaking of Brutus,
> And groaning underneath this age's yoke,
> Have wished that noble Brutus had his eyes.
>
> *Julius Cæsar*, i. 2.

> The abuse of greatness is, *when* it disjoins
> Remorse from power; and, to speak truth of Cæsar,
> I have not known *when* his affections swayed
> More than his reason.
>
> *Ibid.* ii. 1.

But it is one thing to say that an adverb is used where we might expect a pronoun, or where other languages would employ a pronoun; and it is another thing to maintain that an adverb is a pronoun. I have sometimes suspected that, in an older stage of the language, the phrases ' as *that*,' ' but *that* ' may have occurred in such constructions; but I have not yet been able to find instances.

Omission of the Antecedent.

253. When the antecedent is *he, they,* or *those,* it is often omitted: as,

> *Who* steals my purse, steals trash.
>
> *Othello*, iii. 3.

When the neuter antecedent *that* is omitted, the relative form is *what* and not *which*: as, ' He knows *what* he wants.' In older English, *that* sometimes stands alone in such constructions: as, ' we speak *that* we do know;' and grammarians generally regard *that* in such instances as an antecedent, with omission of the relative. Hence, Dr. Angus lays down the following rule: ' These sentences are best read by pausing *after* " that," and *before* " what," thus treating them as antecedent and relative respectively: as,

> We speak—what we know.
> We testify that—we have seen.'
>
> Angus, *Handbook*, § 227.

This is a good practical rule; but the theory might be matter of controversy.

The antecedent is very seldom omitted when governed b preposition ; but Milton writes,

> How wearisome
> Eternity so spent in worship paid
> *To whom* we hate.
>
> *Paradise Lost*, ii. 247.

i. e. ' *to him whom.*'

Dr. Adams remarks (*English Grammar*, § 546), that ' antecedent is sometimes implied in a possessive pronoun : '

> And do you now strew flowers in *his* way,
> *That* comes in triumph over Pompey's blood ?
>
> *Julius Cæsar*, i. 1.

But this passage is capable of another interpretation : may be taken as the genitive of the personal pronoun ═ *him* : and then the construction would be ' in the way *of h* that comes, &c.'

Omission of the Relative.

254. The relative is frequently omitted, when, if express it would stand in the objective case : as ' The man I saw,' ' the man *whom* I saw : ' so ' the horse I bought,' ' the bc I gave.'

But where the omitted relative would, if expressed, be pendent upon a preposition, there is an awkwardness in om ting the preposition as well as the relative : so,

> Had I but served my God with half the zeal
> I served my king, he would not in mine age
> Have left me naked to mine enemies.
>
> *Henry VIII.* iii. 2.

Here the meaning is ' with half the zeal *that* I served my ki *with*,' or ' *with which* I served my king.'

> In the temper of mind he was.
>
> *Spectator*, 54.

for ' *that* he was *in*,' or ' *in which* he was.'

The omission of the relative, when, if expressed, it wou stand in the nominative case, is much less frequent : as,

> In this 'tis *God directs*, in that 'tis man ;

i. e. ' 'tis God *who* directs.'

In some few instances, where the relative is omitted, antecedent is attracted into the case of the relative ; that it is put into the case in which the relative would have stood : as,

Him I accuse

The city ports by this hath entered.

Coriolanus, v. 5.

i. e. 'he, *whom* I accuse . . . hath entered.'

POSITION.

255. The relative pronoun usually stands immediately after the antecedent; but when the sense of the passage clearly indicates the antecedent, qualifying words, or phrases, are sometimes interposed.

But here there is great risk of error. A careless writer often introduces qualifying phrases, and then employs a relative pronoun referring to some word in the former part of the sentence, but without considering whether the reader may not apply the pronoun to some word in the qualifying phrase. Classical scholars are liable to errors of this kind. For they have been accustomed to the construction of the Greek and Latin languages, in which the varieties of termination, the concords of gender and number, are a guide to the sense; hence, when composing in English, they are apt to forget that the position of words is the great safeguard.

Therefore, as a general rule, it is well to place qualifying phrases in some other part of the sentence, and not between the relative and its antecedent; unless those qualifying phrases have exclusive reference to the antecedent, and do not involve a new subject.

256. The order of words, in the government of a relative pronoun by a preposition, demands attention, as showing a remarkable difference between *that* and *who*.

We can use a preposition before 'whom' and 'which,' but not before 'that.' We cannot say, 'the man *of that* I told you;' but the preposition must be thrown to the end of the clause, 'the man *that* I told you *of*.' The same construction may be found with 'whom·:' as,

Horace is an author *whom* I am much delighted *with*.

The world is too well bred to shock authors with a truth, *which* generally their booksellers are the first that inform them *of*.—Pope, *Preface to Poems*.

But there is this distinction : the preposition may stand before 'whom,' 'which,' or it may be thrown to the end of the clause: with 'that' there is no choice ; the preposition must be thrown to the end.

This is an idiom which prevails in common conversation, and accords with similar constructions in German ; but, about two hundred years ago, an opinion began to prevail that this usage was inelegant, if not incorrect. Dryden published two editions of his ' Essay on Dramatic Poesy,' the first in 1668, and the second sixteen years afterwards, in 1684. The alterations made by Dryden in the second edition are carefully noted by Malone, and are very suggestive. Among other changes, the idiom of ending a sentence with a preposition is rejected. Thus, ' I cannot think so contemptibly of the age I live in,' is altered to ' the age in which I live.'—See §§ 483–485.

257. When the antecedent is governed by a preposition, it often happens that the preposition is not repeated after *that*, although such repetition would be necessary before *whom* or *which* : as,

> In the day *that* thou eatest thereof, thou shalt surely die.
> —*Genesis*, ii. 17.

i. e. ' in the day *in which.*'

REFLECTIVE PRONOUNS.

258. A Reflective pronoun refers to the subject of the preposition in which it stands.—Matthiæ, *Greek Grammar*, § 117.

Reflective pronouns refer to the person or thing expressed in the nominative case. In English the word *self* is used for this purpose.—Key, *Latin Grammar*, § 278.

Professor Key argues (§ 279) that Reflective pronouns, from their very nature, can have no nominative or vocative. But for the sake of emphasis, the Greek αὐτός and the English *self* are constantly found in opposition with the subject-nominative.

259. There is no distinct reflective pronoun in Anglo-Saxon, or in modern English :

> thæt folk hit reste ;
> the folk *it* rested ;

i. e. ' rested itself.'

> tha theowas wyrmdon hig ;
> the servants warmed   *them* ;

i.e. ' warmed themselves.'

So in older English, and in poetry, the personals are employed where the agent is acting upon himself, or makes reference to himself: as,

I thought *me* richer than the Persian king.—*Ben Jonson.*

He sat *him* down at a pillar's base.—*Byron.*

But commonly the word *self* is added in such instances; and confusion has arisen from not clearly determining the force of this word. '*My-self*' would lead us to think *self* a substantive; but 'himself' looks as if self were an adjective; indeed, in some provincial dialects, we find '*his*-self' uniformly used for '*him*-self.' Nor should we despise these dialectic varieties; they sometimes throw light upon grammatical theories.

260. Let us examine the history of *self.* In Anglo-Saxon *sylf* appears to be an adjective, and it agrees with the pronoun to which it is joined. Rask says (*Anglo-Saxon Grammar,* § 141) *sylf* is usually added to the personal pronoun in the same case and gender; as

ic sylf hit eom;
I   self it am.—*Luke* xxiv. 39.

i. e. ' it is I myself.'

ic swerige thurh me sylfne;
I   swear   through me self.

Gen. xxii. 16.

i. e. ' by myself.'

Sometimes however, adds Rask, the dative of the personal pronoun is prefixed to the nominative of *sylf*: as,

ic com me-*sylf* to eow
I come *myself* to you.

Ælf. N. T. p. 35.

1. e. ' of my own accord.'

ær thu *the-self* hit me   gerehtest
ere thou *thyself* it to-me didst-explain.

Boethius, v. 1.

261. In Layamon's *Brut* the word sometimes has the meaning of ' alone;' thus when Cordelia is sent away to be married to the French king Aganippus, King Leir sends her,

mid *seolven* hire clathen;
with *selves* her clothes;

that is, with the clothes she wore, but without any outfit, or anything in the way of dowry.

262. Besides the emphatic forms used to strengthen the nominative *ic me-sylf* and *thu the-sylf*, we also find *ic sylf*, ' I self' and *thu sylf*, ' thou self.'

In early English, *me-sylf* and *the-sylf* passed into *mi-sylf*, *my-sylf*, *thi-sylf*, *thy-sylf*; whence it was thought that *self* had a substantive force, and that *my*, *thy* were possessive pronouns. Hence too, by analogy, such forms as *our-selves* and *your-selves* arose.

In older English we find *his-self* and *their-selves*, which are formed on the analogy of *my-self* and *yourself*, and are theoretically defensible, though not allowed in modern English :—

> Every of us, each for *hisself*, laboured how to recover him.

> That they would willingly, and of *theirselves,* endeavour to keep a perpetual chastity.

263. It is worth remarking that, in modern English, the first and second persons exhibit the substantive force of *self*: as *my-self*, *thy-self*, *our-selves*, *your-selves*; where Dr. Latham remarks (*English Grammar*, § 331) that the word *self* (or *selves*) governs the words *my*, *thy*, *our*, *your*, just as in the expression *John's hat*, the word *hat* governs the word *John's*; so that *my*, *thy*, are possessive cases.

On the other hand, in the third person, we find the word used apparently as an adjective, but added to the *objective* case of the pronoun, in the forms *him-self*, *them-selves*. This presents no difficulty when the pronouns are used as the object of a verb : ' He crowned *himself*;' 'They praised *themselves*.' But it is very difficult to justify the use of *himself* as a nominative in the sentences, ' He *himself* said so,' ' *Himself* bare our sins.' We can only say that it is the custom of the language, one of the many anomalies that have crept in.

264. The word *her-self* is ambiguous; since it is doubtful whether *her* be a possessive or an objective case.

In like manner it is doubtful whether *it-self* was originally *it-self*, or *its-self*.

One-self and *one's self* are both used; though *one-self* is the more common.

In the poets we find *self* sometimes as a substantive, and sometimes as an adjective : as,

> Swear by thy gracious *self*.

Being over full of *self* affairs
My mind did lose it.
Midsummer Night's Dream, i. 1.

265. Whenever any words are interposed between the pronominal part and *self*, the substantive force of *self* predominates. We say *him-self*, but ' *his* own *self*,' ' *his* own dear *self*.' So *them-selves*, but ' *their* own precious *selves*.'

266. To express the adjectival Reflective (Lat. *suus*) we use the word *own* (Anglo-Saxon *agen*) with the possessive pronoun, or the genitive of the personal : as, ' That is *my own* book ; ' ' Virtue is *its own* reward.'

RECIPROCAL PRONOUNS.

267. A Reciprocal pronoun is said to be one that implies the mutual action of different agents ; but we have no forms, in English, to which this term can strictly be applied. With us, reciprocity of feeling or action is expressed by the combination *each other*, *one another*.

In the constructions, ' They love *each other*,' ' They love *one another*,' we consider *each* and *one* as nominatives, in opposition with the subject-nominative *they*; and *other*, *another*, objectives governed by the verb *love*.

In such expressions as ' after each other,' ' to one another,' the place of the preposition has been disturbed. The real construction is ' each after other,' ' one to another,' as we actually find in older English:

A thousand sighes, hotter than the glede,
Out of his breast *each after other* went.
Chaucer.

Some grammarians assert that *each other* strictly refers to two, and *one another* to any number more than two ; but this distinction is not always observed.

CHAPTER VIII.

WORDS VARIOUSLY TERMED ADJECTIVE PRONOUNS, OR PRONOMINAL ADJECTIVES.

268. When England and Scotland were distinct kingdoms, and often at war with one another, there was a belt of land on the Border, absolutely held by neither nation, and termed the 'Debateable Land.'

So there are words which lie on the border line, between two Parts of Speech; sometimes found on one side of the line, and sometimes upon the other; but obstinately refusing allegiance to either.

Grammarians have led us astray, by wishing to make it appear that the Parts of Speech are something more than an artificial division of their own; and as though there were some corresponding natural division. Hence they have gravely discussed the question, whether the Parts of Speech are *eight* or *nine* in number. But, all along, they take for granted that the parts of speech can be clearly defined; that all words can be brought under one heading or another; and in order to make out their case, they have recourse to forced explanations.

269. For example, in many languages, adjectives are used substantively; but the grammarians labour hard to show that, in such instances, a *noun* is always *understood.* They argue thus: that in speaking we do not always express all that we have in our thoughts; but, very often, our words indicate what is meant, though not expressed. Hence adjectives are very often used, when the nouns to which they relate are not expressed. In such cases, the adjective is said to be used substantively; that is, *as though it were* itself a substantive; the real explanation being that the substantive, to which the adjective belongs, is *not expressed.*—See Mason, *English Grammar,* §§ 97–99.

But grammarians are obliged to admit, that some adjectives are used so completely as substantives as to have the ordinary inflections of nouns; when in fact the adjective becomes, to all intents and purposes, a noun substantive. Thus the words *subject* and *individual* are proper adjectives; but they are also nouns in such phrases as, ' A *subject's* duties,' 'The *subjects* of the Queen,' ' Some *individuals.*'

Where are we to draw the line? It may be urged, that *proper* adjectives cannot have the inflections of a noun; that where such inflections are used, the word ceases to be an adjective, and becomes a substantive.

270. But, on the other hand, we must be careful not to confound *meaning* with *form*. No doubt, when we speak of 'the good,' we mean 'good *men*' or 'good *persons*;' but there seems to be no reason, why we should insist upon supplying a word, a grammatical form, merely because we are unwilling to admit that the adjective may stand in the place of a substantive.

In the same way, because *each, other,* &c., are constantly used as Substantives, some grammarians do not like to call them *adjectives*, but contend that they must be *pronouns* at all events; and some, by way of compromise, have termed them Adjective Pronouns.

Others again, thinking that most of these words are originally adjectives, have stated the compromise in the other way, and called them Pronominal Adjectives. In truth, grammarians have hardly known what to call them. But this very difficulty should have led grammarians to reflect, and to inquire whether the distinction between Parts of Speech is, or is not, absolute.—See §§ 403, 404.

271. We shall divide these words, accordingly, as they denote quality or quantity.

I. Words denoting quality: *such, same, only.*

SUCH means literally 'so-like,' and is derived from the Anglo-Saxon *swa-lic, swilc.*

It is commonly used as an adjective: as,

> *Such* harmony is in immortal souls.
>
> *Merchant of Venice,* v. 1.

It is also used as a substantive: as,

> Mere strength of understanding would have made him *such* in any age.—*De Quincey.*

i. e. 'such a person.'

The adverb *so* is frequently found where we might expect *such*: as,

> We think our fathers fools, so wise we grow;
> Our wiser sons, no doubt, will think us *so.*
>
> Pope, *Essay on Criticism,* 438, 439.

> In these [free states] no man should take up arms, but with a view to defend his country and its laws: he puts not off the citizen, when he enters the camp; but it is because he is a citizen, and would wish to

continue *so*, that he makes himself for a while a soldier.
—Kerr's *Blackstone*, i. 414.

Cobbett ventures to correct Sir William Blackstone, saying that *so* ought to be *such*; but the custom of the language warrants this use of *so*.

Lindley Murray unfortunately took it into his head to order *such* to be turned into *so*, whenever it was found in company with another attributive. The notion has no foundation in truth or reason; and the construction is constantly found in our best writers: '*such* worthy attempts,' *Milton*; '*such* great and strange passages,' *South*.—See Kerchever Arnold's *English Grammar*, § 72.

272. SAME is called by some grammarians a demonstrative pronoun. It is used both as an adjective and as a substantive; and is usually preceded by *the*, *this*, or *that*.

The two men were of *the same* nature.

He that abideth in me, and I in him, *the same* bringeth forth much fruit.—*John* xv. 5.

> *Obs.*—The Anglo-Saxon *same* is an adverb. The corresponding adjectives are *sylf*, 'self,' and *ylc*, the Scottish *ilk*, as 'Glengarry of that ilk,' i.e. 'of the same' or 'Glengarry of Glengarry.'

273. ONLY (Anglo-Saxon *an-lic*, 'one-like') is a derivative of *one*. The original pronunciation of the word (ōne) is preserved in this derivative, and in ALONE, 'all-ōne.' It is not used substantively, but as an adjective; 'the *only* son,' 'an *only* child.' It is also used as an adverb.—See §§ 434–438.

II. Words denoting quantity, or number.

274. *Indefinites.* These might be called Indefinite Numerals, as they have reference to number or quantity, without however 'defining,' that is, 'marking out' or 'determining' the precise number.

ONE. The numeral *one* is often used substantively, meaning a single individual of some kind already mentioned. When thus used, it may even take the plural form: 'Give me another pen; 'this is a bad *one*,' or 'these are bad *ones*.'

ONE = French *on*. We must not confound this word (which is said to be derived ultimately from the French *homme*, 'man') with the numeral just mentioned. It is never found in the plural, but admits the possessive case singular: as,

One does not like to lose *one's* property.

Some writers consider this use of the possessive inelegant;

but it is still more awkward to introduce the genitive of a personal pronoun in its stead: as, ' *One* does not like to lose *his* property.' In such instances, perhaps the best way is to give the whole sentence a turn: as, ' Loss of property is not agreeable to any one.'

This word is always used substantively.

275. NONE is compounded of *ne-one*; that is, *not-one*. And although, if *one* be singular, we might expect *not one* to be also singular; yet when this word is used substantively, it is sometimes followed by a plural verb. Indeed, this is almost invariably the case when a genitive plural intervenes: as, ' None of the castles *were* taken.' This is literally ' *not-one* .... *were*; ' but an idea is suggested to the mind, ' that *all* the castles *were safe* ; ' ' that *all* were *un*-taken ; ' and so the verb runs into the plural.

This usage is so common, with good writers, that I suppose we must allow it.

When this word is used adjectively, it is interchanged with *no*; that is, *none* differs from *no*, as *mine* differs from *my*. *No* is used when the noun which it qualifies is expressed; and *none* when the noun is not expressed: as, ' I have *no* book, and my friend has *none*.'

276. ANY is from the Anglo-Saxon *æn-ig*, which is derived from *an* or *æn*, ' one,' with the adjective termination -*ig*; so that the word *any* is originally an adjective. With nouns in the singular it often implies quantity; but, with nouns in the plural, it always refers to number. Its general signification is *any whatever*: as,

> Mere strength of understanding would perhaps have made him such in *any* age.—*De Quincey*.

With words of negation it excludes all: as, ' He has *not* received *any* letters.'

The substantive use of the word is very common: as,

> *Brutus.* Who is here so base, that would be a bondman ? If *any*, speak; for *him* have I offended. Who is here so rude, that would not be a Roman? If *any*, speak; for *him* have I offended. Who is here so vile, that will not love his country? If *any*, speak; for *him* have I offended. I pause for a reply.
> *Citizens.* None, Brutus, none.
> *Brutus.* Then *none* have I offended.
> *Julius Cæsar*, iii. 2.

277. AUGHT is in Anglo-Saxon *a-wiht*, *aht*.

The Anglo-Saxon *wiht* is the English *whit* and *wight*,
'thing' and 'person.' Hence *aught* means 'anything.'

The derivation is in favour of writing *aught*, rather than
ought; and convenience dictates the same spelling; for *ought*
is employed as part of the verb 'owe,' and there is an advantage in keeping distinct forms for distinct meanings.

NAUGHT is compounded of the negative *ne* and *aught*, meaning 'not anything.'

These words *aught* and *naught* are originally substantives,
and not adjectives. The true adjective formed from 'naught'
is *naughty*, literally meaning 'of no value,' 'worthless.' Where
we read 'It is *naught*, it is *naught*, saith the buyer,' we may
explain the construction thus: that a substantive in the predicate has often the force of an adjective.

278. SOME, Anglo-Saxon *sum*, is used as an adjective and
as a substantive: '*Some* men were there;' '*some* said so, and
some said not.

In the singular, when employed as a substantive, it usually
implies quantity: as,

> *Some* of his skill he taught to me.
>
> > *Scott.*

In the plural it implies number: as, '*Some* wish to be rich.'

There is a distinction between *some* and *any*:

> *Some* means 'not none,' 'one or more.'
> *Any* means 'some, no matter which.'

Professor Bain says (*English Grammar*, p. 81), '"Some"
denotes an uncertain portion of an entire collection.

'In strict logic it signifies "not none," that is, *some at least*.
There is a more popular meaning, which implies less than the
whole, *some only*, or *some at most*. "Some men are wise"
insinuates that there are other men not wise. Hence the
alternative signification: "some believed, and some (others)
believed not."'

279. OTHER. The derivation of this word seems doubtful;
but it is probably derived from the root of the word *one*, with
the termination *ther*, which denotes 'one of two,' as in 'ei-ther,'
corresponding to the *ter* in the Latin *u-ter*, *neu-ter*.

But, in practice, the word *other* is not restricted to instances
where two alone are in question; it may apply to any number, and means 'some one, but not this;' 'any, but not this.'

The ordinary use of the word as an adjective before a substantive is well known; 'the *other* day,' 'the *other* way.' But

.when it stands alone, referring to a preceding substantive, as 'He had no taste for poetry dramatic or *other*,' some writers appear to think this construction bald, and would even write, 'dramatic or *otherwise*.' But, strictly speaking, 'otherwise' is an adverb, meaning 'in another way;' whereas, in this construction, we want an adjective. The only way of defending 'otherwise' in this connection, would be to contend that here it means 'of another kind.' Such an interpretation, however, is doubtful; and it is better to say 'dramatic or other.'

So also, in phrases involving a comparison, we should distinguish *other than* from *otherwise than*: as,

(*Adjective*) . . He had no books *other than* classical.

(*Adverb*) . . . He never spoke *otherwise than* persuasively.

280. When *an* precedes *other*, the two are often written as one word, *another*; and observe, that *the other* means 'the second of *two*;' *another* means 'one of *any* number *above two*:' as,

Two women shall be grinding at the mill; the one shall be taken, and *the other* left.—*Matt.* xxiv. 41.

One generation passeth away, and *another* generation cometh.—*Ecclesiastes* i. 4.

Care must be taken not to confound the ideas of 'two' and 'more than two,' and so to misapply the words 'the other' and 'another.' For example, in this passage,

And the house of Baal was full from one end to *another*. —2 *Kings* x. 21.

we are ready to ask, what other? It should be 'from one end to *the other*.'

In short, 'another' is Indefinite; 'the other' is Alternative.

281. *Many*. In Anglo-Saxon there are two words: (1) an adjective, *manig*, or *mænig*, 'many,' 'much;' (2) a substantive, *mænigeo*, 'a multitude,' 'crowd.'

Both these words appear to have given rise to our word *many*, which is used sometimes as a substantive, and at other times as an adjective: as,

(*Adjective*) . . . *Many* men, *many* minds.—*Proverb*.

(*Substantive*) . . The *many* rend the skies with loud applause.—Dryden, *Alexander's Feast*.

The use of *many* in construction with the indefinite article

H

will be considered in the next chapter; at present, we compare the following phrases :—

    (1) Many men.
    (2) Many a man.
    (3) A many men.

(1). In the first example, *many* is an adjective agreeing with men.

(2). In the second, *many* is also an adjective; and by an idiom, to be discussed in the next chapter, the indefinite article comes between the adjective and the substantive : so,

> Full *many* a gem of purest ray serene
> The dark unfathomed caves of ocean bear :
> Full *many* a flower is born to blush unseen,
> And waste its sweetness on the desert air.
> > Gray, *Elegy.*

(3). In the third example, *many* is a substantive derived from *mænigeo*, denoting multitude ; and *men* is a genitive by juxtaposition, dependent upon 'many.' Hence, 'a many men' means 'a multitude of men.'

282. *Few*, derived from the Anglo-Saxon adjective *feawa*, still appears as an adjective in 'few persons,' 'few things.' It is employed in connection with the indefinite article in such phrases as ' *a few* years,' ' *a few* apples,' where the construction presents some difficulty. For there is no authority for calling *few* a substantive ; and, on the other hand, if *few* be an adjective, it must be in the plural to agree with 'pears' or 'apples;' whereas the indefinite article *a* requires that *few* should be in the singular.

283. *Distributives*; ' each,' ' every.' These words have reference to the members of a class, or to the parts of a whole, and are thus distinguished :

> *Each* means ' every ' individual of a certain class, viewed *separately.*
> *Every* means ' each ' taken *collectively.*

EACH is derived from the Anglo-Saxon *ælc.*
It is used adjectively and substantively ; as,

> > *Each* man had his weapon.
> > *Each* had his appointed place.

It is properly singular ; and the correlative is ' other,' as in the phrase ' bear *each other's* burdens.'

But though *each* is properly singular, the best writers are liable to err in the use of pronouns referring to this word. Addison writes,

> *Each* of the sexes should keep within *its* particular bounds, and content *themselves* to exult within *their* respective districts.—*Freeholder*, No. 38.

It is very doubtful whether, under any circumstances, *themselves* and *their* could grammatically refer to each ; but there can be no doubt at all, that it is a glaring error to use *its* in one part of the sentence, and *themselves* in another, both referring to the same word, *each.* For even if, in the first instance, we might take our choice of singular or plural, we ought to be consistent.

And so Crabbe :

> Now either spoke, as *hope* or *fear* impressed
> ' Each ' *their* alternate triumph in the breast.

The same caution applies to the use of ' every ' :

> And they were judged *every* man according to *their* works.—*Revelation*, xx. 13.

284. EVERY is derived from the Anglo-Saxon *æfre,* ' ever,' *ælc*, ' each,' *i. e.* ' ever each.'

In Early English, it appears in the forms ' ever-ilk,' ' ever-ich.'

In modern English, the word is used as an adjective only, and on that ground has been excluded by some writers from the class of pronouns. But in Early English it is frequently employed as a noun : so Chaucer,

> And *everich* had a chaplet on her head.

When ' each ' denoted ' one of two,' as seems to have been the case at one period in the history of the language, there was a difference in meaning between ' each ' and ' every,' which does not appear to exist any longer. At present, the difference is chiefly one of usage : ' each ' may be used sub-stantively and adjectively ; ' every ' only as an adjective.

' Every ' is an emphatic word for ' all,' and makes a direct appeal to individuals ; as,

> England expects *every* man to do his duty.

285. *Alternatives* ; ' either,' ' neither.'

EITHER. The element *æg* in composition signifies ' ever,' ' all ' ; as *æghwa*, ' ever who,' that is ' every one ' ; *æghwær*, ' every where.' In like manner from *hwæther*, ' which of two,'

we have *æghwæther*, *ægther*, ' every one of two,' 'each,' ' either.'
See Bosworth, *Anglo-Saxon Dictionary*; and Hensleigh Wedgwood, *Dictionary of English Etymology*.

But Dr. Bosworth gives another form—*athor, auther, awthær*,
' either,' ' other,' ' both.' And we may observe that the pronunciation of the word *either* is various: some say *ĕther*,
others *ĭther*, and in some counties the people say *ŏther*.

It is used both as an adjective and as a substantive :

Adjective . . *Either* way is good.
Substantive . But never *either* found another
To free the hollow heart from paining.
Coleridge.

Very commonly we find the alternative *either*, where we
might expect the distributive *each* : as,

On *either* side
Is level fen, a prospect wild and wide,
With dike on *either* hand.   *Crabbe.*

Elated with this easy conquest, and presuming on the
distresses or the degeneracy of the Romans, Sapor
obliged the strong garrisons of Carrhæ and Nisibis to
surrender, and spread devastation and terror on *either*
side of the Euphrates.—Gibbon, *Decline and Fall*, c. 10.

According to modern usage,

either means ' one *or* other.'
each means ' one *and* other.'

Now Gibbon does not intend to tell us, that Sapor carried
devastation on ' one *or* other ' bank of the Euphrates, but
upon both banks of the river; and therefore we might have
expected *each* instead of *either*.

Still, as the older forms of the language exhibit *either* in the
sense of ' each,' I do not venture to say that Gibbon is wrong.

286. NEITHER is compounded of *ne* ' not,' and *either*; and
we remark, that while *either* means ' one *or* other,' *neither* means
' not one *and* not the other '; for the negative excludes each.

Either and *neither* refer strictly to one of two objects :
hence the following sentence is inaccurate :

Injustice springs only from *three* causes. . . . *Neither* of
these causes for injustice can be found in a Being
wise, powerful, benevolent.

We cannot say ' Neither of three ': we should read, ' No
one of these causes.'

CHAPTER IX.

ARTICLES.

287. Professor Max Müller remarks, that though the general outline of grammar existed at an early period in the schools of the Greek philosophers, yet the critical study of Greek took its origin at Alexandria, and was chiefly based on the text of Homer.

Plato recognised the 'noun' and the 'verb' as the two component parts of speech; Aristotle added 'conjunctions' and 'articles.' But with Aristotle, the word *rhema* (ῥῆμα), commonly translated by the term *verb*, is little more than a 'predicate.' For, in such a sentence as 'snow is white,' he would have called 'white' a *rhema* (ῥῆμα); and under the head of 'articles' he would have comprised many words, which modern grammarians classify among other parts of speech.

When the scholars of Alexandria were engaged in publishing critical editions of the Greek classics, they were obliged to discuss the various forms of Greek grammar. They raise such points as these: Did Homer use the *article*? Did Homer use the *article* before proper names? Here the term 'article' had obtained a more precise meaning, as distinguished, for example, from the demonstrative pronoun.

Article is a literal interpretation of the Greek word *arthron* (ἄρθρον), which literally signifies the 'socket of a joint.' The word was first used by Aristotle, and was fancifully applied to words which formed the 'sockets' in which the members of a sentence were supposed to move. Before the time of Zenodotus, the first librarian of Alexandria, 250 B.C., all pronouns were simply classed as 'sockets,' *arthra*, or 'articles' of speech. Zenodotus was the first to introduce a distinction between personal pronouns and the mere articles or articulations of speech, which henceforth retained the name of *arthra*. (See Max Müller, *Science of Language*, First Series, pp. 87—89.)

288. In English we have two articles, *an* (sometimes contracted to *a*) and *the*.

An, called the Indefinite Article, is used in speaking of any individual of a class. The old notion was, that the Indefinite Article was *a*, but that *n* was added (*an*) before a word beginning with a vowel or silent *h*. The fact is just the contrary; the article is *an*, and *n* is dropped before a word beginning with a consonant, or with vocal *h*.

The, called the Definite Article, is employed in speaking of a particular object, or class of objects. It is regarded as 'defining,' that is 'marking out,' the object in question.

INDEFINITE ARTICLE.

289. AN is a modification of the numeral *one*; Anglo-Saxon, *an* or *œn*; Old English, *ane, an, a*.

When it comes before a word beginning with a consonant, or with *h* vocal, *w* or *y*, the letter *n* is dropped: as 'a man,' 'a horse,' 'a wall,' 'a year.'

In older English it is frequently written before *h* vocal, as 'an house'; and even yet, some writers think proper to say, 'an historical account.'

It was also common to write *an* before a word beginning with the letter *u*: as, 'an University.' But where the initial *u* has the force of *yu*, it is now customary to omit *n*: as, 'a Union,' 'a University.'

When several objects are separately specified, the indefinite article is usually placed before each :—

> Leave not *a* foot of verse, *a* foot of stone,
> *A* page, *a* grave, that they can call their own.—*Pope*.

Hence, when the indefinite article is expressed before the first only of two or more nouns, the reader will infer that the nouns are to be taken together, as referring to the same person or thing. Thus, 'a priest and king' will be interpreted to indicate the same individual holding the offices of priest and king combined. Similarly, 'a coachhouse and stable' implies that the two form one building, or one tenement, or that they are in close connection. Consequently, if we wish to mark separation, we must repeat the article: ' *a* priest and *a* king'; ' *a* coachhouse and *a* stable.' By this rule, 'a black and a white horse' means *two* horses; 'a black and white horse' means *one* horse.

The same rule applies to the use of the Definite Article: ' *the* secretary and treasurer' would lead us to suppose that one person occupied a twofold position; but ' *the* secretary and *the* treasurer' would point to two distinct persons.

290. If two nouns are applied to the same person, by way of comparison, the article is used only once: as,

> *Southey* is *a* better prose writer than poet.

Not that it would be wrong to say, 'a better prose writer than a poet'; for we might turn the sentence thus:—

Southey is more successful *as a* prose writer than *as a* poet.

291. The force of *a*, prefixed to a noun, is to represent that noun as belonging to a class; for instance, 'Gold is *a* metal,' means, 'Gold is *one* of the class of metals.' It is therefore very frequently found with *common* nouns, that is nouns which are employed in a *general* sense, as representing a class.

Sometimes in poetry, or in oratory, a proper name is used with the indefinite article, and thus receives something of the force of a common noun, indicating a character like that of the person named :—

> 'Frenchmen, I'll be *a Salisbury* to you;' that is, as terrible as the Earl of Salisbury.

> He may be *a Newton* or *a Herschel* in affairs of astronomy, but of the knowledge of affairs of the world he is quite ignorant.—*Burke.*

That is, 'as profound as Newton or Herschel.'

This use of the Indefinite Article may sometimes be employed with good effect; but it has been so hackneyed by rhetoricians and declaimers, that a man of taste will be very careful in imitating this construction.

292. As the Indefinite Article indicates *one* thing of a kind, it must not be joined with a word denoting a whole kind or class. We say ' the unicorn is a kind of rhinoceros,' but not ' the unicorn is a kind of *a* rhinoceros.'

293. When two or more objects are distinctly specified, and attention is drawn to each, the Indefinite Article should be repeated : as,

> Burleigh had *a* cool temper, *a* sound judgment, and *a* constant eye to the main chance.—*Macaulay.*

294. When an indefinite article is used with a noun, and the noun is qualified by several adjectives, the construction will depend upon the force of those adjectives :—

> 1. If the adjectives are all to the same purpose, so that one merely amplifies the other, it is sufficient to prefix the article to the first alone : as,
>> There is about the whole book *a* vehement, contentious, replying manner.—*Macaulay.*

> 2. But where there is a marked emphasis, or contrast, the article is usually repeated : as,

He went like one that hath been stunned,
    And is of sense forlorn;
A sadder and a wiser man
    He rose the morrow morn.
                    Coleridge, *Ancient Mariner.*

There is a difference between *a* liberal and *a* prodigal
hand.—*Ben Jonson.*

295. In Early English, when a noun is qualified by the
article *a*, and an adjective follows the noun, it is customary to
repeat the article; as,

A monk there was, *a* fayre.
        Chaucer, *Canterbury Tales, Prologue.*

Therefore he was *a* prickasoure *a* right.—*Ibid.*
that is, 'a good hard rider;' where, however, the more recent editions have ' aright.'

When several adjectives follow the noun, the article is repeated with each : as,

A Frere there was, *a* wanton, and *a* mery.—*Ibid.*

In later English, it is not uncommon to find the usual
order—article, adjective, noun, and then another adjective
with the article repeated : as,

> *Falstaff*: And yet there is a virtuous man, whom I
> have often noted in thy company, but I know not his
> name.
> *Prince Henry*: What manner of man, an it like your
> majesty ?
> *Falstaff*: *A good portly* man, i' faith, and *a corpulent.*
>   *1st Hen. IV.,* ii. 4.

A very *good* piece of work, I assure you, and *a merry.*
            Midsummer Night's Dream, i. 2.

POSITION

296. When the indefinite article is used in connection with
an adjective and a noun, where the adjective qualifies the
noun, varieties of position are observable.

In Early English, we sometimes find the same order as in
our modern language—article, adjective, noun : for example,

to hare feire burge,
to *a fair* burgh.
        Layamon, *Brut,* 3553, vol. i. p. 151.

to hare ægene burh,
to *a high* burgh.
Layamon, *Brut*, 3610, vol. i. p. 153.

At other times, we have the article placed between the adjective and the noun: as,

he heo wolde habben.
hæge to are queene.
he her would have.
high to *a* queen.
Ibid. 3132, vol. i. p. 133.

that is, 'for a noble queen.'

And we may remark that similar variations occur in the position of pronouns :—

his drichliche lond.
his lordly land.
æthele his meiden.
noble his maiden.

that is, ' his noble maiden.'

297. Now, although the former construction has become the general rule in modern composition, we still have vestiges of the latter; for with the words *many*, *such*, and *what* joined with nouns, and accompanied by the article, we find the article in the middle place : as,

When the merry bells ring round,
And the jocund rebecks sound,
To *many a* youth, and *many a* maid,
Dancing in the chequered shade.
Milton, *L'Allegro.*

I had rather be a dog and bay the moon,
Than *such a* Roman.—*Julius Cæsar*, iv. 2.

What a piece of work is man !—*Hamlet*, ii. 2.

A similar order occurs, when an adjective is qualified by the words *too*, *so*, *how*, *as*.

You hold *too* heinous *a* respect of grief.
King John, iii. 4.

Ye see *how* large *a* letter I have written unto you with mine own hand.—*Galatians*, vi. 11.

298. Curiously enough, in some passages of Early English we find instances of the other construction ; as,

A such will brought this lond to gronde.
Robert of Gloucester.

Mony blessyng
He hadde, for he delivered men of *an so foul* thyng.
Robert of Gloucester.

A so grete beast.—*Chaucer.*

Hence the phrase 'many a youth' is quite in accordance
with the older forms of the language; 'many' is here a true
adjective, while the article stands between the adjective and
the noun.

299. Archbishop Trench (*English Past and Present*, pp.
160–162, ed. 1859) explains 'many a youth' as arising from
confusion of thought, and forgetfulness of original form.

In the phrase 'many a youth,' he observes that the following
points are perplexing to the student :—

1. The *place* of the indefinite article *between* the adjective
   and the substantive.
2. That it is not lawful to change the order, and to bring
   back the article to its ordinary position. We cannot
   say, 'a many youth,' or 'a many maid.'
3. That the junction of 'many,' an adjective of number,
   with 'youth' and 'maid' in the singular, seems inconsistent; for withdraw that 'a,' and it is not lawful to
   say 'many youth,' or 'many maid.'

300. Now the first and second objections are met by comparing the older forms of the language, where we observe a
variation in the order of words : the article takes sometimes
the first place, and sometimes the middle place.

In reply to the third objection, we admit that the form
'many youth' is not customary, but it would be warranted
by the analogy of *plurimus puer*, in Latin. And so Virgil :

Crudelis ubique
Luctus, ubique pavor, et *plurima* mortis *imago*.
Aeneid, ii. 369.

where Heyne paraphrases *plurima mortis imago*, h. e. ubique
cædes facta cernitur; passim cæsorum cadavera projecta.

So Ovid :

Plurima lecta *rosa* est; sunt et sine nomine flores;
Ipsa crocos tenues liliaque alba legit.
Fast. iv. 441.

301. The explanation offered by Archbishop Trench is
this—that 'many' was originally a substantive, the Old
French 'mesgnée,' 'mesnie,' and signified a 'household,' which

meaning it constantly has in Wycliffe, and which it retained down to the time of Spenser :

> Then forth he fared with all his *many* bad.
> *Shepherd's Calendar.*

We still recognise its character as a substantive in the phrases 'a good many,' 'a great many,' and, in Old English or Scottish, even 'a few many.'

There can be no doubt that 'many' is often used as a substantive; though it may be derived from the Anglo-Saxon *mænigeo*, 'a multitude,' rather than from the Norman-French *mesnie*, '*meinie*,' 'a household,' 'a retinue.'

302. Then Archbishop Trench argues, truly enough, that *a* is sometimes a corrupted form of the preposition *on* or *of* : in this instance he considers it to stand for *of*, quoting Wycliffe,

> I encloside man ye of seintis [*multos sanctorum*] in prisoun.
> *Acts,* xxvi. 10.

He concludes, there can be no reasonable doubt that such a phrase as 'many a youth' was once 'many *of* youths,' or 'a many *of* youths.' By much use 'of' was worn away into 'a'; this was then assumed to be the indefinite article, that which was really such being dropped ; and 'youths' was then changed into 'youth' to match : one mistake, as is so often the case, being propped up and made plausible by a second, and thus we arrive at our present strange and perplexing idiom.

This explanation, however ingenious, is wholly unnecessary; because, as we have seen, 'many' can be explained, in this construction, as an adjective.

303. But in the phrases 'a many men,' 'a many ships,' 'a great many years,' we cannot explain 'many' as an adjective; for if so, it qualifies a noun in the plural, and yet it is joined with 'a' (*an* = 'one'), which is singular.

We have seen above, that in Anglo-Saxon *mænigeo* is a noun signifying 'multitude,' 'crowd ;' and even in modern English 'the many' bears this interpretation :

> *The many* rend the skies with loud applause ;
> So love was crowned, but music won the cause.
> Dryden, *Alexander's Feast.*

In these phrases 'a many men,' &c., I consider 'many' a noun, and the words 'men,' 'ships,' &c., as genitives by juxtaposition. According to this view, 'a many men' may be rendered in Latin *multitudo hominum,* whereas 'many a youth' would be *plurimus puer.*

I would apply the same principle to the phrases 'a thousand men,' 'a dozen bottles;' but I must admit that it does not apply to 'a few horses;' for *few* (Anglo-Saxon *feawa*) is properly an adjective; and I can find no authority, beyond this phrase or similar phrases, for the substantive use of that word.

304. We must not lose sight of the fact indicated by Archbishop Trench, that *a* is, in some instances, a contraction of the Anglo-Saxon preposition *an* or *æt.*

For example, we find the particle *a* before nouns which are used distributively; as,

> And passing rich with forty pounds *a* year.
> > Goldsmith, *Deserted Village.*

where 'a year' means 'for each year,' or 'in each year.' So, too, in common conversation we say 'sixpence *a* pound,' 'four shillings *a* bushel.'

It is a nice question whether, in these phrases, *a* is an indefinite article or a preposition. It may possibly be the relic of an old preposition; and the tendency in modern times to introduce the Latin *per,* 'sixpence *per* pound,' appears to show the want of a preposition.

But, on reference to the Anglo-Saxon, we find that, in phrases of this kind, the noun was used in the dative or some other case, without a preposition, and that the word *ælc,* 'ilk,' 'each' was frequently introduced; as *ælce gear,* 'ilk year,' 'each year;' *ælce dæy,* 'ilk day,' 'each day.'

On the whole, I am inclined to think that, in these phrases, *a* is the indefinite article, meaning *one*; and that 'forty pounds a year' means 'forty pounds for one year,' *i. e.* 'for each and every year.'

305. There is more difficulty with those phrases where the particle *a* is joined with numerals; as,

> And it came to pass about *an eight days* after these sayings.—*Luke,* ix. 28.

> There is a vale between the mountains that dureth nere *a four mile.*

> > For him was lever han at his beedes hed
> > *A twenty bokes* clothed in black or red,

Of Aristotle and his philosophie,
Than robes riche, or fidel, or sautrie.
> Chaucer, *Canterbury Tales, Prologue*, 295.

Here Mr. Morris reads, ' Twenty bookes.'

This construction deserves further inquiry. At present we leave it to the judgment of others.

DEFINITE ARTICLE.

306. Etymologically, *the* is derived from a form of the demonstrative pronoun. In modern English it has no distinction of gender, number, or case; but in Early English the following inflections occur :—

Singular.

	Masc.	Fem.	Neut.
Nom.	the	theo (tho)	thet (that).
Gen.	this	thare (there)	this
Dat.	thon (than, then)	thare (there)	thon (than, then).
Acc.	then (thane)	thun	thet (that).

> See Adams, *Elements*, § 237.

307. The pronunciation of *the* is very important, especially in singing. It is *thĕ* before a word beginning with a consonant, and *thē* before a word beginning with a vowel; as,

'thĕ time,' 'thĕ race,' 'thĕ course.'
'thē inn,' 'thē apple,' 'thē orange.'

308. The original use of the definite article is to ' demonstrate,' or ' point out,' a particular object, or class of objects; as,

The man that hath no music in himself,
Nor is not moved with concord of sweet sounds,
Is fit for treasons, stratagems, and spoils.
> *Merchant of Venice*, v. 1.

Hence it is very commonly used in reference to some object previously known or mentioned; as, ' *The* exhibition which you saw yesterday.'

309. In some languages, the definite article is used with proper names of persons, who are distinguished, and well known to all; as ὁ Πλάτων 'the Plato,' which Cicero renders *Ille Plato*. So the Italians speak of *Il Tasso*, and the French of *L'Arioste*.

In English we may employ this construction in the singular, when a qualifying phrase is added; as, 'Handel was *the* Homer of music;' and so,

> Shakespeare was *the* Homer or father of our dramatic poets; Jonson was *the* Virgil, the pattern of elaborate writing; I admire him, but I love Shakespeare.
>
> Dryden, Essay on Dramatic Poesy.

It will be remarked, however, that in such instances, the proper name seems to lose its distinctive individuality, and partakes of the construction of a common noun.

In the plural, this construction is very usual : ' the Smiths,' ' the Jenkinsons,' ' the Macgregors,' ' the Macdonalds.' The chief of a Celtic clan is termed ' The Macarthy,' ' The O'Donoghue,' ' The Douglas,' ' The Mackenzie; ' and the reason is this, that all the members of a clan, however humble they might be, bore the general name of the clan; but the chief was *the* representative clansman.

310. With some geographical terms, as before the names of rivers, mountains, and seas, we find the definite article; as, ' *the* Thames,' ' *the* Rhine,' ' *the* Alps,' ' *the* Baltic.' But observe, that we never employ this construction with names of cities; we never say ' *the* London,' or ' *the* Paris.' Compare the difference of construction in the ' river Thames,' and the ' city *of* London,' § 148.

311. The definite article is used before names which denote a whole class, as, for example, the names of entire nations; often in the plural, as ' *the* French,' ' *the* English; ' and sometimes also in the singular, especially in rhetorical composition, as, ' *the* Briton, and *the* Gael.' The same construction with a singular noun is often found in terms used in the Natural Sciences, denoting a whole class of objects; as, ' *the* lion,' ' *the* eagle,' ' *the* violet,' ' *the* rose.'

Similarly, the article is used with a noun denoting a profession, or the members of a profession viewed collectively; as, ' *the* bar,' ' *the* church,' ' *the* army,' ' *the* navy.'

> *Obs.*—' Man ' and ' woman ' are already class nouns, and do not admit the article, unless we speak of particular individuals; so,

What a piece of work is *man* ! How noble in reason ! how infinite in faculties ! in form, and moving, how express and admirable ! In action, how like an angel !

in apprehension, how like a god! the beauty of the
world! the paragon of animals! And yet, to me, what
is this quintessence of dust? *Man* delights not me, nor
woman neither; though, by your smiling, you seem to
say so.—*Hamlet*, ii. 2.

312. It is not the custom, in English, to employ the definite
article before nouns denoting an abstract notion; we say
'truth,' 'virtue,' 'pride'—not '*the* virtue,' '*the* pride.' This
enables us to make a distinction, which is not observed in
some other languages; for, with us, 'truth' means 'truth
absolutely considered,' 'truth in the abstract;' but '*the* truth'
means 'the truth mentioned before,' or some particular aspect
of truth, 'mathematical, philosophical, or religious truth.'

The French, on the contrary, use the definite article before
abstract nouns; and I suspect that some phrases in older
English, which are condemned as ungrammatical, have come
down to us from the Norman-French. For example,

And I persecuted this way unto *the* death.—*Acts* xxii. 4.

where Dr. Lowth remarks, 'the Apostle does not mean any
particular sort of death, but death in general; the definite
article therefore is improperly used. It ought to be *unto
death*, without any article; agreeably to the original, ἄχρι
θανάτου.' Compare 2 Chron. xxxii. 24, 'In those days
Hezekiah was sick to *the* death;' and Rev. xii. 11, 'And they
loved not their lives unto *the* death.' The French would be
à la mort. See also Prov. xxix. 21, 'He that delicately
bringeth up his servant from a child shall have him become
his son at *the* length.'

313. *The* is often used where we might expect a possessive
pronoun; and this too, among others, may be a construction
derived from the French: as,

Her corpse was the object of unmanly and dastardly ven-
geance: *the* head was severed from the body and set
upon a pole.—*W. Irving.*

I have reserved to myself seven thousand men, who have
not bowed *the* knee to Baal.—*Romans*, xi. 4.

314. When two or more objects are distinctly specified, the
definite article, or some word equally distinctive, should be
used before each: as,

I was with Hercules and Cadmus once,
When in a wood of Crete they bayed the bear

> With hounds of Sparta; never did I hear
> Such gallant chiding; for, beside *the* groves,
> *The* skies, *the* fountains, *every* region near
> Seemed all one mutual cry; I never heard
> So musical a discord, such sweet thunder.
>
> Midsummer Night's Dream, iv. 1.

Hence in the following sentence we observe an ambiguity : ' The Chancellor informed the Queen of it, and she immediately sent for *the* secretary and treasurer.' Here, it is not certain whether the secretary and treasurer be not one and the same person; at all events, it is possible to put that meaning upon the words. If we wish to imply that two distinct persons were summoned, we should repeat the article : ' for *the* secretary and *the* treasurer.'

315. When two or more nouns are used in opposition, qualifying some other. noun, the article is placed before the first alone, of the nouns in opposition :

> He sends a letter to Mr. Larkins, *the* bribe-agent and broker on this occasion.—*Burke.*

Similarly, when several adjectives qualify a noun, the definite article is usually employed before the first alone : as,

> If parts allure thee, think how Bacon shined,
> *The* wisest, brightest, meanest of mankind.
>
> Pope, Essay on Man, iv.

But if we wish to lay emphasis upon the adjectives, we may repeat the article before each : as,

> A name at the sound of which all India turns pale; *the* most wicked, *the* most atrocious, *the* boldest and most dexterous villain that that country ever produced.—*Burke.*

316. When the adjectives cannot be regarded as describing one and the same thing, the article must be repeated if the noun is in the singular, or it must stand before the first adjective only, if the noun is in the plural : as,

> The third and fifth chapters of John.

or,

> The third and the fifth chapter of John.

POSITION.

317. When the definite article and an adjective qualify a noun, the usual order is—article, adjective, noun; sometimes, however, the noun stands first, followed by the article and the adjective; as,

Alonzo *the brave*, and the fair Imogene.

Lewis.

When the words *all* and *both* are used to qualify a noun, the article occupies the middle place ; as,

All the contrivances which we are acquainted with are directed to beneficent purposes.—*Paley.*

He had disobliged *both the* parties whom he wished to reconcile.—*Macaulay.*

Chapter X.

VERBS.

318. Grammarians have not been very successful in their attempts to define the ' verb.'

Plato recognised only two parts of speech, the Name (ὄνομα), and the Saying (ῥῆμα). And in fact, when we say ' Light shines,' *light* is the Name of the thing whereof we speak, while *shines* is our Saying about that thing.

When we are speaking the truth, or what we believe to be true, our Saying is the same as our Thinking. Hence we may conclude, that the Name and the Thought are the two main pillars that support the sentence.

The Name and the Saying are grammatically termed the Noun and the Verb.

But if the term ' Verb' (*verbum*, ' word') is meant as a translation of the term ῥῆμα, it is a questionable translation. We might rather expect *Dictum* (' Saying,' or ' thing said'), than *Verbum* (' word').

There appears to be no truth in the common assertion that the Verb is the chief Word in a sentence. There are two principal words in every sentence, and the Name is as important as the Saying; for if there be no Name, there is nothing to speak about.

Neither is it true that there can be no sentence without a Verb; for in Hebrew and in Latin hundreds of sentences can be produced wherein no verb is found. But then, the grammarians maintain that in such instances a Verb is *understood*; that is, they lay down a definition dogmatically, and then they explain away every passage which does not conform to their definition.

319. Some grammarians have founded their definitions upon the *meaning* of the Verb as a word. As in the old definition,

'A verb is a word which signifies to be, to do, or to suffer;' or as in the theory wherein 'motion' and 'rest' are considered the distinctive characteristics of verbs.

Others have founded their definitions upon the *function* of the verb, that is, upon its power in a sentence; as, 'A verb is a part of speech which makes an assertion.'

320. I. *Definitions founded upon Signification.*

(1). 'A verb is a word which signifies to be, to do, or to suffer.' 'There are three kinds of verbs, Active, Passive, and Neuter verbs.' —Lowth, *English Grammar*, p. 45.

(2). *Theory of Sir Graves C. Haughton.*

'In the infancy of language the Verb merely denoted the modes of action peculiar to the simplest objects of nature—as, *to fly, to run, to strike*, &c.; but in process of time, as language became perfect, the Verb adapted itself to the expression of every want of the human mind, and in this state it is considered as denoting *action, being,* or *suffering.* But it is solely by a metaphorical use that language is fitted for describing abstract ideas; and for this purpose the Verb divests itself of its essential attribute, which is *motion* in a physical sense.

'If a verb denotes any particular kind of motion, depending or conceived to depend on the will of the agent, it is Active, but Intransitive; that is, it implies voluntary motion, which is commonly called Action, as "he runs." And when the motion passes on to an object on which it *reposes*, it is Active and Transitive, as "he strikes the child."

'*Motion* is the essential attribute of the Verb; and those who hold it to be a mere connective, have not perhaps sufficiently considered its origin; and have been led to observe its apparent use, which is often metaphorical, rather than its essential quality, which indicates different kinds of motion.'

'After use had first fixed the forms of the Verb, the rest were easily brought into existence, by that love of analogy which is inseparably connected with the nature of the human mind.'—*Preface to a Dictionary, Bengâli and Sanskrit, by Sir Graves C. Haughton.*

(3) Professor Key gives no general definition of the Verb; but his whole doctrine depends upon the theory of 'motion' and 'rest.' He says, in his *Latin Grammar*, §§ 367–385:

'An *active* verb denotes action or movement: as *caed*, "cut" or "strike;" *curr*, "run."

'The person (or thing) from whom the action proceeds is called the nominative to the verb.

'A *transitive* verb is one which admits an object or accusative after it: as *caedit puerum*, "he strikes the boy."

'An *intransitive* verb is one which does not admit an accusative; as, *currit*, "he runs."

'A *static* verb denotes a state; as *es*, "be"; *dormi*, "sleep"; *vigila*, "be awake"; *jace*, "lie"; *metu*, "fear."'

321. II. *Definitions founded upon the Function of the Verb.*

(1). Sir John Stoddart says :—

'The Verb expresses that faculty of the mind by which we assert that anything exists or does not exist. And as all existence is contemplated by the mind, either simply as existence, or in one of its two distinguishable states, action or passion ; therefore, the common definition of the verb is sufficiently accurate—namely, that "the verb is a word which signifies to do, to suffer, or to be."

'Yet we must observe, that the essence of the verb does not consist in the mere signification or *naming* of existence, or of action, or of passion; because, so far as that goes, the verb is a mere noun. For Mr. Tooke's observation is strictly correct, that "the verb is a noun and something more."

'This "something more," which is the true characteristic of the verb, is the *power of assertion*. It is by this peculiarity alone that the verb is distinguished from the noun.'

Sir John Stoddart then reviews several objections :—

Objection 1. 'We may assert without the express use of verbs. Numerous sentences, with the verb omitted, may be produced from Hebrew, Latin, and English.'

Answer. 'True; but then the verb is *understood*.'

[This is begging the question.]

Objection 2. 'That *connection*, not "assertion," is the distinguishing characteristic of verbs.'

Answer. 'Truly, the verb connects, but it does more ; connection is a secondary characteristic.'

Objection 3. 'That *attribution* is the proper function of a verb.'

Answer. 'But this is an accidental circumstance applying to some verbs, not as to verbs, but in regard to the nouns which they involve.'

Objection 4. 'That to be significant of *time* is the characteristic of the verb.'

Answer. 'No doubt time is a necessary adjunct of assertion, but it is only secondary. Assertion is the appropriate function of the verb.'

Objection 5. 'That the Infinitive mood asserts nothing.' This objection is urged by Dr. Lowth (*English Grammar*, p. 54): 'That the participle is a mere mode of the verb is manifest, if our definition of a verb be admitted. For it signifies being, doing, or suffering, with the designation of time superadded. But if the essence of the verb be made to consist in affirmation, not only the participle will be excluded from its place in the verb, but the Infinitive itself also; which certain ancient grammarians of great authority held to be alone the genuine verb, denying that title to all other modes.'

Answer. 'The Infinitive is not properly a verb, but rather a Verbal Noun ('Ονομα ῥηματικόν).'—Stoddart, *Universal Grammar Encyclopædia Metropolitana*, pp. 45–47.

322. (2). *Theory of Mr. Garnett.*

In the *Proceedings of the Philological Society*, vol. iii., we find several papers by the late Rev. Richard Garnett, on the 'Nature and Analysis of the Verb.' These and other articles have been reprinted by his son, under the title of 'Philological Essays' (Williams and Norgate, 1859).

According to the view taken by Mr. Garnett, 'the true definition of a verb appears to be, that it is a *term of relation* or *predicate* in grammatical combination with a subject, commonly pronominal. In some languages, any word in any given part of speech is capable of being made the basis of a verb, and of being regularly conjugated through moods, tenses, and persons; in others this license is considerably restricted.'

After remarking that there has been much discrepancy of opinion as to what constitutes a verb, and in what essential particular it differs from a noun, he observes, 'that much of the misapprehension and error prevalent on this subject has originated in confounding the *finite verb* with the root from which it is formed. It has been admitted that the essence of this part of speech consists in predication or assertion, a view to which no objection can be made. But this immediately destroys its claim to be considered as a primitive element of speech. There can be no predication in the concrete without a given *subject*; every verb therefore must have its subject—that is, speaking grammatically, it must be in a definite person. The term expressing this person is an element perfectly distinct from the root; and when it is taken away, there is no predication, and consequently no verb. In short, a verb is not a simple but a complex term, and therefore no primary part of speech.'

But while Mr. Garnett considers that the root or predicative part of a simple verb is, or originally was, an abstract noun, he differs from those philologists who analyse the verb as consisting of a noun connected with a subject or nominative by means of a verb substantive understood. He denies that 'Ego (sum) somnium' can be brought to mean 'Ego somnio.' He says: 'Grammarians have not been able to divest themselves of the idea that the subject of the verb must necessarily be a *nominative*; and when it was ascertained that the distinctive terminations of the verb are in fact personal pronouns, they persisted in regarding those pronouns as *nominatives*, abbreviated indeed from the fuller forms, but still performing the same functions.'

Mr. Garnett holds that the personal terminations are pronouns, not however *nominatives* in apposition, but *oblique cases*, or (as he terms it) *in regimine*. He proves his point by an appeal to many languages; but no part of the proof is more satisfactory than his reference to the Welsh. He says: 'The personal terminations in Welsh are pronouns, and they are more clearly so than the corresponding endings in Sanskrit. But it is an important fact, that they are evidently *in statu regiminis*, not in apposition or concord; in other words, they are not nominatives, but oblique cases, precisely such as are affixed to various prepositions. For example, the second person plural does not end with the nominative *chwi*, but with *ech*, *wch*, *och*, *ych*, which last three forms are also found coalescing with various prepositions, *iwch*, "to you," *ynoch*, "in you," *wrthych*, "through you."

'Now the roots of Welsh verbs are confessedly nouns, generally of abstract signification; as, for example, *dysg* is both *doctrina*, and the second person imperative *doce*. *Dysg-och*, or *-wch*, is not, therefore, *docetis* or *docebitis vos*; but *doctrina vestrum*, "teaching *of* or *by* you." This leads to the important conclusion, that a verb is nothing but a *noun* combined with an oblique case of a personal pronoun, virtually including in it a connecting preposition. This is what constitutes the real *copula* between the subject and the attribute. *Doctrina ego* is a logical absurdity; but *doctrina mei*, "teaching of me," necessarily includes in it the proposition *ego doceo*, enunciated in a strictly logical and unequivocal form.'

Mr. Garnett compares the prepositional forms with the verbal forms, thus:

Prepositional forms:

er-ov	'for me.'
er-ot	'for thee.'
er-o	'for him.'
er-om	'for us.'
er-och	'for you.'
er-ynt	'for them.'

Verbal forms:

car-ov	'I will love.'
car-ot	'thou wilt love.'
car-o	'he will love.'
car-om	'we will love.'
car-och	'you will love.'
car-ont or *car-wynt*	'they will love.'

And he concludes: 'No one capable of divesting his mind of preconceived systems, who compares the Welsh prepositional forms with the verbal forms, will deny the absolute formal identity of the respective sets of endings, or refuse to admit that the exhibition of parallel phenomena of languages of all classes, and in all parts of the world, furnishes a strong *primâ facie* ground for the belief of a general principle of analogy running through all.'—Garnett, *Philological Essays*, pp. 289–342.

323. Amid these diversities, we shall proceed rather by way of enumeration than by way of definition. And we say:

  I. With regard to *meaning*;
     A Verb is a word which denotes an action, or a state of being.

  II. With regard to *function*, the Verb has several powers:

     (1). The Indicative mood is used to make an assertion.

(2). The Subjunctive mood is used to make a modified assertion.

(3). The Imperative mood is used to express commands, exhortations, or entreaties.

(4). The Infinitive mood and the Gerunds are Verbal Substantives.

(5). The Participles are Verbal Adjectives.

CLASSIFICATION.

324. We divide verbs into two classes: (1) Transitive; (2) Intransitive.

A Transitive Verb generally requires an object to complete the meaning, and is commonly followed by an Objective—that is, a substantive in the objective case.

An Intransitive Verb frequently furnishes a complete meaning, and does not, as a general rule, admit an objective case.

Transitive Verbs may be used in three relations, which are termed Active, Passive, and Reflective.

In some languages, there are distinct forms, involving changes of termination, to denote the change of relation. These forms are commonly termed Voices; and in Greek grammar, the Reflective form is called the Middle Voice, as though it held a middle place between Active and Passive.

In English we have a distinct form for the Active Voice of verbs Transitive: as,

> William *loves* Mary.
> William *loved* Mary.

The Passive relation is denoted by the verb *be* coupled with the perfect participle, which, in Transitive Verbs, has a *passive* signification; thus,

> Mary *is loved* by William.

The Reflective relation is denoted by the word *self*, used in composition with certain pronouns, and governed by a Transitive Verb, in the Active Voice; as,

> William *loves himself.*
> Mary *loves herself.*

In Early English, the personal pronouns *me*, *him*, *her*, &c., were used with a reflective force, where we employ *myself*, *himself*, &c.; as,

'I was weary forwandred,
And went *me* to reste.'

Piers Plowman, *Vision.*

i.e. ' to rest myself.'

In poetry, the same usage still prevails, as

' I'll lay *me* down, and die.'

Intransitive Verbs are used in one form only, which corresponds, in point of *form*, with the Active voice of verbs Transitive ; as,

The boy runs.
The girls laugh.

Many Transitive verbs in English are used Intransitively ; as,

He *broke* the glass	(*Transitive*).
The glass *broke*	(*Intransitive*).
He *rolled* the stone	(*Transitive*).
The stone *rolled*	(*Intransitive*).

Many Intransitive verbs, compounded with a preposition, become Transitive. And since in English the preposition frequently follows the verb, students are apt to forget that the verb, in such cases, becomes a *Compound Verb* ; so,

He *laughed*	(*Intransitive*).
They *laughed* at him . . .	(*Transitive*).

Intransitive verbs are sometimes followed by a noun in the objective case, when that noun bears a meaning akin to the signification of the verb; as, ' to sleep a sleep,' ' to run a race,' ' to die the death.'

In Latin grammar this objective is called the ' cognate accusative.'

CONJUGATION.

325. To *conjugate* literally means *to yoke together* ; and, as used by grammarians, it means to place under one view the *variations* (or *inflections*) in the form of a verb.

Hence Conjugation is the arrangement of the several inflections of a verb, in its different Voices, Moods, Tenses, Numbers, and Persons.

Until late years, English verbs were commonly divided into two classes, termed *Regular* and *Irregular*. The distinction was thus explained :

Regular Verbs are those in which the past tense and the perfect participle are formed by adding to the verb *-ed*, or *-d* only, when the verb ends in *-e*; as *call, call-ed*; *love, love-d*.

Irregular verbs are those that vary from this rule, in either or both instances.—See Lowth, *English Grammar*, p. 71.

More recent grammarians have contended that verbs of the latter kind are not really irregular, but that they are formed according to rules specially applicable to themselves. And since the verbs termed Regular are formed by addition to the root, while the so-called Irregular verbs are formed, in most instances, by internal change of the root-vowel—as *take, took*; *shake, shook*; the Regulars have been called Weak verbs, and the Irregulars Strong verbs.

But other grammarians consider these terms fanciful and objectionable. They remark, truly enough, that all derivatives, all verbs borrowed from other languages, in short all *new* verbs, are formed in the first method, by adding -*ed* or -*d*. It is also a fact, that many verbs, which once formed their past tense by change of vowel, now take the form in -*ed*, -*d*, or -*t*; as *lep, slep, mew, snew*, now take the form *leapt, slept, mowed, snowed*.

Hence we may infer, ' that there is a tendency for the one form to be displaced by the other ; and the more we compare the older stages of our language with the newer, the more clearly we see that such is actually the case.'—Latham, *English Grammar*, § 136.

For these reasons, some grammarians prefer the terms New and Old Conjugation ; assigning Regular verbs to the New, and Irregular verbs to the Old. But these terms are liable to mislead the student, for many verbs in the New conjugation are historically as old as verbs in the other.

326. We have, then, the following comparison of terms :—

1. Regular . . . Weak . . . New
2. Irregular . . . Strong . . . Old.

Now, we observe that all these terms involve a theory ; and, as a matter of course, the advocates of each fresh proposal condemn their predecessors ; because, unless the former terms were objectionable, there was no necessity for change. But, in the present state of our knowledge, we should beware of giving names which involve any theory whatever, because future investigations may prove that our terms have been unadvisedly imposed.

It appears safer to divide verbs into the First and Second conjugations.

VERBS OF THE FIRST CONJUGATION.

327. Verbs of the First Conjugation form their Past Tense and Perfect Participle by adding *-ed* to the root of the verb, or *-d* alone, if the verb itself ends in *-e* : as,

call	call-ed	call-ed
move	move-d	move-d.

But certain changes take place, according to the *letters* in which the verb itself terminates.

When the verb ends in *-y*, with a consonant immediately preceding, the *y* is turned into *i* in the past tense and the perfect participle : as,

reply	replied	replied.

But if the *-y* be preceded by a vowel, *-ed* is generally added : as,

delay	delayed	delayed
convey	conveyed	conveyed.

Yet not always; for sometimes the *e* is dropped, and the *y* is changed into *i*: as,

lay	laid	laid
pay	paid	paid
say	said	said.

Sometimes, too, authors differ in their way of writing : from the verb *stay*, some will write *stayed*, others *staid*.

328. With reference to verbs ending in a single consonant, the rules are uncertain. We are told that when the verb ends in a single consonant, which has a single vowel immediately before it, the final consonant is doubled in the past tense and the perfect participle : as,

rap	rapped	rapped.

But this rule holds good only for words of one syllable; for with verbs of more than one syllable, the consonant is not doubled, unless the accent be on the last syllable : thus we write,

open	opened	opened,

but

refér	reférred	reférred.

Yet, even here, usage is not consistent. There is a tendency to double the letters *l*, *p*, and *t* : we constantly see *levelled*, *bigotted*, *rivetted*, *worshipped*. Unless my memory deceives

I

me, I have seen *benefitted* in a leading article of the *Times*. The word *unparalleled* is constantly written with one *l* before *-ed*, to avoid an accumulation of consonants. The Americans, following Dr. Webster, generally observe the strict rule, and do not double the consonant, unless the accent falls upon the last syllable of the root.

329. But we have to consider the doctrine of contraction. In all languages, there is a tendency to abbreviation, and we generally pronounce more briefly than we write; we say *lov'd, mov'd* for *lovĕd, movĕd*. Archdeacon Hare proposed that, following the example of Spenser and Milton, we should adopt that form of writing which expresses the sound. For example, Spenser writes *lookt, pluckt, nurst, kist*; and Milton has *hurld, worshipt, confest*. According to this view the rule would be, 'where *e* is omitted in the past tense and perfect participle, the *d* becomes *t* after *l, m, n, p, k, f, gh*, and *s*; as *dealt, dreamt, learnt, crept, crackt, reft, sought, kist.*' At present our usage is not uniform; some write *dropt*, others *dropped*; and many who write *dropt*, would scruple to use *wisht* and *jumpt*, for *wished* and *jumped*. To show the inconsistency of our custom, Archdeacon Hare quotes this stanza from Coleridge's *Genevieve*:

> Her bosom heaved, she *stepped* aside,
> As conscious of my look she *stepped*
> Then suddenly, with timorous eye,
> She fled to me and *wept*.

There is no reason why we should not write *stept*, just as we write *wept*. But the English language is full of these inconsistencies.

If the root of a verb ends in a double consonant, one of the two is always rejected before *-d* or *-t* : as,

dwell	dwelt	dwelt
spill	spilt	spilt.

Hence if the *e* of *dropped* is omitted, the word becomes *dropt*.

330. Many verbs of this conjugation, besides adding *-d* or *-t*, admit changes of the internal vowel. We therefore make the following divisions :

I. Verbs forming their past tense and perfect participle by adding *-d* or *-t*, and by *shortening* the vowel of the root.

(1) Verbs ending in a vowel:

flee	fled	fled
lose	lost	lost.

(2) Verbs ending in -*l*:

| deal | dealt | dealt |
| feel | felt | felt. |

In *dealt* the shortening is not exhibited to the eye; but the word is pronounced *delt*.

(3) Verb ending in -*n*:

| mean | meant | meant. |

(4) Verbs ending in -*p*:

creep	crept	crept
keep	kept	kept
sleep	slept	slept
sweep	swept	swept
weep	wept	wept.

In *bereave* and *leave* there is not only a shortening of the vowel, but a change of consonant, *v'd* becoming *f't*:

| bereave | bereft | bereft |
| leave | left | left. |

331. II. Verbs forming their past tense and perfect participle, by adding -*d* or -*t*, and by *changing* the vowel of the root: as,

| sell | sold | sold |
| tell | told | told. |

With verbs ending in *k*, *g*, *ch*, not only is there a change of vowel, but the final consonant of the root is changed into *gh*.

(1) Verbs ending in -*k*:

seek	sought	sought
think	thought	thought
work	wrought	wrought.

(2) Verb ending in -*g* (or rather in -*ng*):

| bring | brought | brought. |

(3) Verbs ending in -*ch*:

catch	caught	caught
be-seech	be-sought	be-sought
teach	taught	taught.

In Old English, the verb *reach* was conjugated,

| reach | raught | raught. |

So Chaucer says of the Prioresse,

Full semely after her mete she raught.
Canterbury Tales, Prologue.

In the verb *buy* (A. S. *bycg-an*) the consonant *g* does not appear, as a final, in the present tense; but it finds place in the past tense and the perfect participle:

       buy   .   bought   bought.

In the verb *fight*, the letter *t* is an original part of the root; so that, strictly, this verb ought to be classed with verbs ending in *-t*.—See § 333.

The verb *light*, where the *-t* is part of the root, is conjugate

       light   lighted   lighted.

But sometimes the essential character of the *-t* is forgotten, and contraction takes place:

       light   lit   lit.

Verbs ending in *-d* or *-t*.

332. Special attention must be paid to verbs the root of which ends in *-d* or *-t*. If, for example, we take the verbs which are said not to change their form in the past tense and perfect participle, we find that they all end in *-d* or *-t*.

(1) Verbs ending in *-d*:

rid	rid	rid
shed	shed	shed
shred	shred	shred
spread	spread	spread.

(2) Verbs ending in *-t*:

burst	burst	burst
cast	cast	cast
cost	cost	cost
cut	cut	cut
hit	hit	hit
hurt	hurt	hurt
knit	knit	knit
let	let	let
put	put	put
set	set	set
shut	shut	shut
slit	slit	slit
split	split	split
sweat	sweat	sweat
thrust	thrust	thrust.

Dr. Lowth thinks that these forms have resulted from contraction; hence he considers them not as irregular, but as contracted.—See Lowth, *English Grammar*, pp. 73, 74. In fact, not being able to pronounce such an accumulation of consonants as. *burst'd* or *burst't*, we drop the last letter altogether.

333. In the following verbs, the final -*d* of the root is changed into -*t* in the past tense and the perfect participle:

bend	bent	bent
build	built	built
gild	gilt	gilt
gird	girt	girt
lend	lent	lent
rend	rent	rent
send	sent	sent
spend	spent	spent.

In some instances -*d* or -*t* remains throughout, but the internal vowel is shortened:

bleed	bled	bled
breed	bred	bred
feed	fed	fed
lead	led	led
read	read	read (*pronounced* red)
speed	sped	sped
meet	met	met.

In *fight* the internal vowel is changed:

fight	fought	fought.

VERBS OF THE SECOND CONJUGATION.

334. Verbs of the Second Conjugation form the past tense by change of internal vowel, that is, by changing the vowel or diphthong in the root of the verb; as, *break, broke; drink, drank; steal, stole.*

The perfect participle, in verbs of this conjugation, is generally formed by adding -*en* or -*n*, with or without change of internal vowel.

Examples:

break	broke (*or* brake)	broken
choose	chose	chosen
cleave	clove (*or* clave)	cloven
drive	drove (*or* drave)	driven
eat	ate (*or* eat)	eaten

fall	fell	fallén
be-fall	be-fell	be-fallen
freeze	froze	frozen
give	gave	given
for-give	for-gave	for-given
rise	rose	risen
a-rise	a-rose	a-risen
for-sake	for-sook	for-saken
shake	shook	shaken
speak	spoke (*or* spake)	spoken
steal	stole	stolen
strive	strove	striven
strike	struck	stricken (*or* struck)
take	took	taken
thrive	throve	thriven
weave	wove	woven
wake	woke	waken (*or* waked)
a-wake	a-woke	a-waken (*or* awaked).

335. When the verb ends in *w*, *y*, or a vowel, the *e* of the perfect participle is omitted : as,

blow	blew	blown
crow	crew	[crown] (*or* crowed)
fly	flew	flown
grow	grew	grown
know	knew	known
lie	lay	lain (*or* lien)
see	saw	seen
slay	slew	slain
throw	threw	thrown.

The verb *show* had an old form of the past tense *shew*, for which *showed* is now used. The participle *shown* is still preserved.

The same rule affects verbs ending in *-r*: as,

bear (*carry*)	bore (*or* bare)	borne
for-bear	for-bore	for-borne
bear (*bring forth*)	bore (*or* bare)	born
shear	shore (*or* sheared)	shorn
swear	swore	sworn
tear	tore	torn
wear	wore	worn.

336. With the following verbs, ending in *-d* or *-de*, *-t* or

-te, the consonant is doubled before the termination *-en* of the perfect participle.

(1) Verbs ending in *-d*:

bid	bade	bidden
for-bid	for-bade	for-bidden
tread	trod	trodden.

(2) Verbs ending in *-de*:

chide	chid (*or* chode)	chidden
hide	hid	hidden
ride	rode	ridden
slide	slid	slidden.

The verb *abide* is conjugated,

abide	abode	abode.

(3) Verbs ending in *-t*:

get	got (*or* gat)	gotten (*or* got)
sit	sat	sitten (*or* sat)
spit	spat	spitten
shoot	shot	shotten (*or* shot).

The verb *beat* exhibits no change in the past tense:

beat	beat	beaten.

(4) Verbs ending in *-te*:

bite	bit	bitten
smite	smote	smitten
write	wrote	written.

337. With verbs ending in *-n* or *-ne*, *-m* or *-me*, the principle of contraction seems applicable, and the termination *-en* is omitted altogether. If we compare our verb *begin* with the German

beginnen	begann	begonnen,

we may reasonably conjecture that our participle *begun* has been derived by contraction from *begunnen* to *begunn'n*, and finally to *begun*.

(1) Verbs ending in *-n*:

be-gin	be-gan	be-gun
run	ran	run
spin	span	spun
win	won	won.

(2) Verb ending in *-ne*:

shine	shone	shone.

(3) Verb ending in -*m* :

swim	swam	swum.

(4) Verbs ending in -*me* :

come	came	come
be-come	be-came	be-come.

338. The same principle seems to be applicable in cases where the letter *n* immediately precedes a final consonant, as -*nk*, -*ng*.

(1) Verbs ending in -*nk* :

drink	drank	drunken (*or* drunk)
shrink	shrank	shrunken (*or* shrunk)
sink	sank	sunken (*or* sunk)
slink	slank	slunk
stink	stank	stunk.

(2) Verbs ending in -*ng* :

cling	clang	clung
fling	[flang] (*or* flung)	flung
ring	rang	rung
sing	sang (*or* sung)	sung
sling	[slang] (*or* slung)	slung
spring	sprang (*or* sprung)	sprung
sting	stung	stung
string	strung	strung
swing	swung	swung
wring	wrung	wrung.

The verb *hang* is conjugated,

hang	hung	hung ;

and also, according to the first conjugation,

hang	hanged	hanged.

The latter is used in speaking of persons, the former in reference to things.

To these we may add verbs ending in -*nd* :

bind	bound	bound
find	found	found
grind	ground	ground
wind	wound	wound.

I conjecture that the omission of the termination -*en* may be due to the presence of *n* before the final consonant; and I am inclined to extend the same principle to verbs ending in -*ld* : as,

hold	held	held (*or* holden)
be-hold	be-held	be-held (*or* be-holden).

IRREGULARS.

339. In the following verbs we find an apparent mixture of the two conjugations; the past tense ends in -*ed*, as with verbs of the first, and the perfect participle in -*en* or -*n*, as with verbs of the second conjugation :

grave	graved	graven
hew	hewed	hewn
load (*or* lade)	loaded	laden (*or* loaded)
mow	mowed	mown
rive	rived	riven
saw	sawed	sawn
sew	sewed	sewn
shave	shaved	shaven (*or* shaved)
sow	sowed	sown (*or* sowed)
swell	swelled	swollen (*or* swelled)
wax	waxed	waxen (*or* waxed).

The verb *stand* is conjugated

stand	stood	stood.

Some would say that the letter *n* is dropped in the past tense and perfect participle ; others, perhaps more correctly, that *n* is a strengthening letter in the present.

The verb *dig* exhibits similarity of form in the past tense, and the perfect participle :

dig	dug	dug.

340. *Caution.*—The confusion between *lie* and *lay* should be carefully avoided.

Lie is intransitive, and its past tense is *lay*.

Lay is transitive, and its past tense is *laid*.

Examples of usage :

To-day, I *lay* the book upon the table, and I *lie* down upon the sofa. Yesterday, I *laid* the book upon the table, and I *lay* down upon the sofa.

The old participle perfect of *lie* is *lien*: as, ' Though ye have *lien* among the pots ; ' but the form now commonly used is *lain*. The perfect participle of *lay* is *laid*.

341. Apart from the use of auxiliaries, which we shall consider hereafter, the forms of our verbs are simple, and the inflections are few. We shall take an example of each conjugation.

FIRST CONJUGATION.

INDICATIVE MOOD.

Present Tense.

Singular.	Plural.
1. I love,	1. We love,
2. Thou lovest,	2. You love,
3. He loves.	3. They love.

Past Tense.

Singular.	Plural.
1. I loved,	1. We loved,
2. Thou lovedst,	2. You loved,
3. He loved.	3. They loved.

Future Tense.
[No distinct inflection.]

SUBJUNCTIVE MOOD.

Present Tense.

Singular.	Plural.
1. I love,	1. We love,
2. Thou love,	2. You love,
3. He love.	3. They love.

Past Tense.

Singular.	Plural.
1. I loved,	1. We loved,
2. Thou loved,	2. You loved,
3. He loved.	3. They loved.

Future Tense.
[No distinct inflection.]

IMPERATIVE MOOD.
Love.

Infinitive Mood	[to] love.*
Gerund (or *Infinitive*) in *-ing* . .	loving.
Gerund with *to*	to love.†

PARTICIPLES.

Present	loving.
Perfect	loved.

* The sign *to* is enclosed in brackets [to], in order to show that it may be omitted in certain constructions.
† The Gerundial prefix, *to*, † is never omitted.

SECOND CONJUGATION.

INDICATIVE MOOD.

Present Tense.

Singular.	Plural.
1. I write,	1. We write,
2. Thou writest,	2. You write,
8. He writes.	3. They write.

Past Tense.

Singular.	Plural.
1. I wrote,	1. We wrote,
2. Thou wrotest,	2. You wrote,
8. He wrote.	3. They wrote.

Future Tense.
[No distinct inflection.]

SUBJUNCTIVE MOOD.

Present Tense.

Singular.	Plural.
1. I write,	1. We write,
2. Thou write,	2. You write,
8. He write.	3. They write.

Past Tense.

Singular.	Plural.
1. I wrote,	1. We wrote,
2. Thou wrote,	2. You wrote,
8. He wrote,	3. They wrote.

Future Tense.
[No distinct inflection.]

IMPERATIVE MOOD.

Write.

Infinitive Mood	[to] write.
Gerund (or *Infinitive*) in -*ing* . .	writing.
Gerund with *to*	to write.

PARTICIPLES.

Present	writing.
Perfect	written.

342. The whole number of verbs in the English language has been estimated at upwards of four thousand. Most of them belong to the First Conjugation; those of the Second Conjugation barely amount to one hundred. Even of these, only a certain number exhibit a distinct form in the past tense and the perfect participle; while the general bent of the language is towards the other form, which makes the past tense and the perfect participle the same.

This general tendency of the language has given rise, as Dr. Lowth thinks, to great corruption, and to confusion of the past tense with the perfect participle, in some of these verbs; as 'he *begun*' for 'he *began*;' 'he *run*' for 'he *ran*;' he *drunk*' for 'he *drank*;' the participle being used instead of the past tense. And much more frequently the form of the past tense is found, where we should expect the participle; as, 'I had *wrote*,' 'it was *wrote*,' for 'I had *written*,' 'it was *written*;' 'I have *drank*,' for 'I have *drunk*;' *bid* for *bidden*, *got* for *gotten*, &c.

This confusion, adds the Doctor, prevails in common discourse, and is too much authorised by the example of some of our best writers; as,

> He would have *spoke*.
> > Milton, *Paradise Lost*, x. 517.

> Words *interwove* with sighs found out their way.
> > *Ibid*. i. 621.

> And envious darkness, ere they could return,
> *Had stole* them from me.
> > Id. *Comus*, 195.

(Where the Author's MS. and the first edition read *stolne*.)
> And in triumph *had rode*.
> > Id. *Paradise Regained*, iii. 36.

> I will scarce think you *have swam* in a gondola.
> > *As You Like It*, iv. 1.

> Then finish what you *have began*,
> But scribble faster, if you can.
> > Dryden, *Poems*, vol. ii. p. 172.

> Rapt into future times the bard *begun*
> 'A Virgin shall conceive, a Virgin bear a Son.'
> > Pope, *Messiah*.

> A second deluge learning thus o'er-*run*,
> And the Monks finished what the Goths *begun*.
> > Id. *Essay on Criticism*.

> No civil broils *have* since his death *arose*.
> > Dryden, *on Oliver Cromwell*.

> The sun *has rose*, and gone to bed,
> Just as if Partridge were not dead.
> > Swift.

> Some philosophers *have mistook*.
> > Id. *Tale of a Tub*, § ix.

Why, all the souls that were, were forfeit once ;
And He, that might the 'vantage best *have took,*
Found out the remedy.

Measure for Measure, ii. 2.

Silence
Was took ere she was ware.

Milton, *Comus,* 557.

A fine constitution, when it *has been shook* by the iniquity of former administrations. . . .—Bolingbroke, *Patriot King.* See Lowth, *English Grammar,* pp. 94–96.

To these we may add a stanza from Byron's *Hebrew Melodies*:

And the widows of Ashur are loud in their wail ;
And the idols are *broke* in the temple of Baal ;
And the might of the Gentiles *unsmote* by the sword,
Has melted like snow in the glance of the Lord.

Horne Tooke, opposing the view taken by Dr. Lowth, contends that the Past Participle is the *Past Tense Adjective,* by which he means the past tense used adjectively. He thinks that, just as we use one noun substantive to qualify another noun substantive [*e. g.* 'a *gold* watch'], so we are accustomed to use the Past Tense itself, without any change of termination, instead of the Perfect Participle ; and the Past Tense so used answers the purpose equally with the Participle, and conveys the same meaning.

Dr. Lowth, he adds, who was much better acquainted with Greek and Latin than with English, finds great fault with this our English custom, calls it a very gross corruption, and complains that it is too much authorised by the example of some of our best writers. He then gives instances of this inexcusable barbarism from Shakespeare, Milton, Dryden, Pope, and Bolingbroke. And if he had been pleased to go further back than Shakespeare, he might (in the opinion of Horne Tooke) have given instances of the same from *every* writer in the English tongue. It is, says Horne Tooke, the idiom of the language ; and Dr. Lowth is undoubtedly in error when he says, 'This abuse has been long growing upon us, and is continually making further encroachments.' Horne Tooke thinks, on the contrary, that the custom has greatly decreased ; and as the Greek and Latin languages have become more familiar to Englishmen, our language has proceeded more and more to bend to the rules and customs of those languages.

However, he concludes, we shall be much to blame if we miss the advantage afforded by these very defects ; for they may assist us to discover the nature of human speech, by a comparison of our own language with more cultivated languages. And this is eminently the case in the present instances of the Past Participle and the Noun Adjective. For, since we can and do use our Noun itself unaltered, and our Past Tense unaltered, for the same purpose and the same meaning, as the Greeks and Latins use their Adjective and their Participle ; it is manifest that their Adjective and Participle are merely their Noun and Past Tense *adjectived.*—Horne Tooke, *Diversions of Purley,* vol. ii. pp. 470–474.

343. It is not true that writers older than Shakespeare use the past tense for the perfect participle. No doubt, as the two forms coincide in verbs of the first conjugation, there was a strong tendency to apply the same principle to verbs of the second conjugation. This tendency prevailed, from the time of Shakespeare to the middle of the last century, especially in poetry, where such forms as *took* and *shook* afforded greater facilities of rhyme than *taken* and *shaken*. During the last seventy years, the study of our older literature has made us better acquainted with the original idiom of the language; hence, as Horne Tooke admits, 'the custom has greatly decreased,' though not for the reasons which he assigns. It was not the study of the Greek and Latin languages, but that of Old English, which led us to see the truth.

The case is correctly stated by Dr. Latham. This coincidence of the Past Tense and the Perfect Participle appears to have arisen from the rejection of the participial termination *-en*. The vowel of the participle is often the same as the vowel of the past tense, as *spoke, spoken*; though not always, as *took, taken*. When the vowel is the same, and when the termination *-en* or *-n* is rejected, the Past Tense and the Perfect Participle exhibit the same form as ' I *found*,' ' I have *found*,' ' I was *found*.' In such a case, it seems as if the past tense was used for the participle. But it is only in a few words, and in the most modern forms of our language, that this is really done.—See Latham, *English Grammar*, §§ 3, 14.

VOICE.

344. As there are, in English nouns, no differences of termination to distinguish the objective from the nominative, younger pupils are sometimes perplexed in comparing an active form of verb with the corresponding passive form. Take, for example, the following sentences :—

1. William loves Mary.
2. Mary is loved by William.

Here the same fact is stated in both sentences; but the grammatical construction is very different. In the first case, ' William ' is the subject-nominative, and ' Mary ' is the objective; while, in the second, ' Mary ' is the subject-nominative, and ' William ' is in the objective case, governed by the preposition ' by.'

Those who are familiar with inflected languages, such as Greek and Latin, where the nouns alter their terminations to denote difference of case, may wonder that any perplexity should arise. But the mere English scholar needs assistance to understand this point. Cobbett. states that he was very much puzzled on account of these cases. He says (*Grammar*, § 233), 'I saw, that when "Peter was *smitten*," Peter was in the *nominative case*; but that, when any person or thing " *had smitten* Peter," Peter was in the *objective case*. This puzzled me much. Reflection on the reason for this apparent inconsistency soon taught me, however, that, in the first of these cases, Peter is merely *named*, or *nominated*, as the *receiver* of an action; and that, in the latter instance, Peter is mentioned as the *object* of the action of *some other person* or thing, expressed or understood. I perceived that, in the first instance, "*Peter is smitten*," I had a complete sense. I was informed as to the person who had received an action, and also as to what sort of action he had received. And I perceived that, in the second instance, "*John has smitten Peter*," there was an actor who took possession of the use of the verb, and made Peter the object of it, and that this actor, *John*, now took to the *nominative*, and put Peter in the objective case.

'This puzzle was, however, hardly got over, when another presented itself; for I conceived the notion that Peter was in the nominative *only because no actor was mentioned at all in the sentence*; but I soon discovered this to be an error, for I found that "Peter is smitten *by John*" still left Peter *in the nominative*; and that, if I used the pronoun, I must say " *he* is smitten by John,' and not "*him* is smitten by John."

'At last the little insignificant word *by* attracted my attention. This word, in this place, is a *preposition*. Ah! that is it! prepositions *govern* nouns and pronouns; that is to say, *make them to be in the objective case!* So that John, who had plagued me so much, I found to be in the objective case; and I found that, if I put him out, and put the pronoun in his place, I must say, "Peter is smitten *by him*." '

345. Now let us analyse the examples taken above:

    1. William loves Mary.

        William . . . . *Subject-nominative*
        loves   . . . . *Predicate-verb*
        Mary   . . . . *Objective.*

    2. Mary is loved by William.

According to the method which we have hitherto followed, we analyse

Mary	*Subject-nominative*
is	*Predicate-verb*
loved	*Predicate-nominative*
by William . .	*Adverbial phrase, qualifying the predicate nominative, 'loved.'*

But, in the Latin language 'is loved' would be expressed by a single word *amatur*; hence, in the analysis of Latin sentences, it is proper to call *amatur* a 'predicate-verb.' I am inclined to think that we may do well to introduce the same form of analysis in English sentences : thus,

Mary	*Subject-nominative*
is loved	*Predicate-verb*, compounded of the auxiliary *is*, and the participle *loved*, used as a predicate-nominative.
by William . . .	*Adverbial phrase, qualifying the predicate-verb, 'is loved.'*

346. But here a caution must be observed. We are not to suppose that *is*, or any other part of the verb *be*, is a 'sign of the passive voice.' In the sentence, 'He is *breaking* the windows,' 'is breaking' is transitive; in the sentences 'He is coming,' 'He is come,' *is coming* and *is come* are intransitive.

Every passive voice in English forms its tenses by means of the verb *be*; though every form in which the verb *be* is found is not passive. 'I am writing' is an active form; and 'he is come' is the present-perfect tense of an intransitive verb. Whether, therefore, a verb is in the passive voice, or whether it exhibits the form of a verb transitive or intransitive, is decided not by the presence of the auxiliary, but by the nature of the participle.—See Angus, *Handbook*, § 276.

MOOD.

347. The grammatical term 'Mood' is derived from the French *mode*, signifying 'manner,' and this, in turn, comes from the Latin *modus*.

Our ordinary English word 'mood' has another origin, being derived from the Anglo-Saxon *mód*, which denotes (1) 'mind,' (2) 'mood,' 'disposition,' 'passion.' (Compare the German *muth*, 'courage,' and *ge-múth*, 'mood,' 'disposition.')

The two notions of 'manner' and 'mind' seem to run

together in the definitions proposed by some of our grammarians. For instance, Dr. Lowth says: ' A Mode is a particular form of the Verb, denoting the *manner* in which a thing is, does, or suffers; or expressing an *intention of mind* concerning such being, doing, or suffering.'—Lowth, *English Grammar*, p. 50, *note.* And Sir John Stoddart says: ' The *Mood* of a verb is that *manner* in which its assertive power is exhibited, and which depends on the *state of mind* in which the speaker may be placed with relation to the assertion.'— *Universal Grammar*, p. 50.

We might suspect that English writers were in some way influenced by the twofold derivation of the word ' mood;' but the same remark could not apply to Priscian, who still says: ' Modi sunt diversæ *inclinationes animi*, quas varia consequitur declinatio verbi.' [' Modi sunt diversæ *inclinationes animi* varios ejus affectus demonstrantes.'—Prisc. viii. ed. *Putsch.* p. 819.]

No doubt, the *mode* of the verb, or the manner of expression, will generally correspond with the *mood*, that is, the mind or disposition of the speaker; but it is important to distinguish the original meaning of the terms. Dr. Lowth has retained the grammatical term Mode, and in this he is followed by other writers; but as the term Mood is more common in English grammars, it is hardly worth while to make any change.

Grammarians differ widely as to the number and the names of the Moods. Some make only three; others admit four, five, six, or even more. The names too are various; and some terms have been accepted in the grammar of one language which find no place in the grammar of other languages. For example, in Greek grammar we hear of an ' optative' mood. The ' potential' mood has struggled for a position in some grammars, but with doubtful success; while the ' precative' and ' interrogative' moods have met with still less favour.

If by ' mood' is meant an alteration of form, in any verb, to express variety of assertion, then we have traces of only four moods in English : the Indicative, the Subjunctive, the Imperative, and the Infinitive. But if we admit variations produced by the help of auxiliary verbs, it is difficult to set any limit to the number of moods.

The Four Moods.

348. 1. The Indicative mood is used to make a simple assertion, or declaration: as, 'Light shines,' 'They come,' 'Bread is dear.'

2. The Subjunctive mood is used to make a modified assertion: as, 'If it be,' 'Though he slay me.'

3. The Imperative mood is used to utter commands, entreaties, or exhortations: as, 'Leave me,' 'Spare us,' 'Go forward.'

4. The Infinitive mood is really a Verbal Substantive. It has the force of a substantive, yet it retains some of the powers of a verb. It loses, however, all distinction of person or number.

TENSE.

349. The word *tense* is derived from the French *temps* or *tems*, which itself comes from the Latin *tempus*, 'time.'

But we must carefully distinguish between *tense* and *time.*

Some speculators have maintained that there is no such thing as 'time present;' for each moment is constantly fleeting into 'time past,' and the moment just about to arrive is 'time future.'

But *tense* is the grammatical notion of time; and we are at liberty to consider time under whatever aspects we please; we may regard one day as a thousand years, or a thousand years as one day.

The general division of time is into 'past,' 'present,' and 'future.' Hence, if the time of an event were the only thing to be considered in grammar, we might make three tenses, and three only.

But beside the time of an action, there are three aspects under which an action or event may be viewed.

1. An action may be incomplete, or, as it is usually called, Imperfect.

2. An action may be complete, or Perfect.

3. An action may be regarded as occurring from time to time, or at any time, without any consideration whether it be complete or incomplete: in this case, the term used is Indefinite, or, in Greek grammar, Aorist. The student of Greek grammar should beware of confounding *aorist* with *past.* There might

be a *present-aorist*; and although such a tense has no distinct form in Greek, the aorist, in *Homer*, has often the force of an *indefinite-present*.

We have then :

	Present	*Past*	*Future*
Indefinite	I write	I wrote	I shall write.
Imperfect	I am writing	I was writing	I shall be writing.
Perfect	I have written	I had written	I shall have written.

or, in other words:

Present-Indefinite . . .	I write.
Present-Imperfect . . .	I am writing.
Present-Perfect	I have written.
Past-Indefinite	I wrote.
Past-Imperfect	I was writing.
Past-Perfect	I had written.
Future-Indefinite . . : .	I shall write.
Future-Imperfect . . .	I shall be writing.
Future-Perfect	I shall have written.

350. Younger pupils may be profitably exercised and cross-examined upon a table of this kind, in order to impress upon their minds a correct notion of the tenses. It may be well to explain that the term 'imperfect' denotes something 'continuous,' that is, 'going on.' For example, the 'present imperfect,' *I am writing*, denotes a continuous action, going on at the present time. So the 'past-imperfect,' *I was writing*, denotes a continuous action, going on at some past time. On the other hand, the term 'perfect' means 'complete,' or 'finished:' thus, *I shall have written* means 'I shall have finished the act of writing.'

From this table it appears that *perfect* and *past* are not the same. A tense is past, present, or future, according to the time whereof we speak; not according to the completeness or incompleteness of the action.

Many persons are liable to confound the terms *past* and *perfect*, because they derived their first notions of grammar from the Latin language, where the same form has to do double duty, for the *past-indefinite* and the *present-perfect*. For example, *scripsi* may mean 'I wrote,' or 'I have written.' It is sometimes difficult to make pupils see that 'I have written' implies time present; for they argue that the action is finished. So it is; but it is finished *in time present*, that is, in the time whereof the speaker is now speaking.

If we arrange the Latin tenses in a manner corresponding to the English tenses given above, we at once perceive the deficiency of the Latin language.

	Present	*Past*	*Future*
Indefinite	scribo	scripsi	scribam.
Imperfect	(scribo)	scribebam	(scribam).
Perfect	(scripsi)	scripseram	scripsero.

Here we remark that *scribo* does duty for 'I write' and 'I am writing,' as *scribam* for 'I shall write' and 'I shall be writing.' As, however, these are tenses of the same order, present or future respectively, no serious error is likely to arise. But the case of *scripsi* is very different. That word does duty for tenses of different orders; for the *past* indefinite 'I wrote,' and for the *present* perfect 'I have written.'

It is very important to understand that 'I have written' is a *present* tense; for, although it denotes a 'perfect' or 'completed' action, yet the completion takes place in present time. Thus, for the sake of illustration, we may say:

> *Past.* Yesterday at twelve o'clock, I *had* written my exercise.

> *Present.* To-day, at twelve o'clock, I *have* written my exercise, and the ink is not yet dry.

> *Future.* To-morrow, at twelve o'clock, I *shall have* written my exercise.

It must be clear, that 'I have written' points to time present. And the same tense, the *present-perfect*, is employed in reference to an action, the effects of which continue up to the present time. Thus we may say, 'England has founded a mighty Empire in the East,' because that Empire still continues. But we cannot say, 'Cromwell has founded a dynasty,' because the dynasty exists no longer.—See Mason, *English Grammar*, § 207.

351. Hence, with the present-perfect we should never join adverbs, or other words, which involve a reference to time past. Thus the following passages are incorrect:—

> I *have formerly* talked with you about a military dictionary.—*Johnson.*

Many years after this article was written, *has appeared* the history of English Dramatic Poetry by Mr. Collier. —*D'Israeli.*

On the other hand we should not use the past tense indefinite with an adverb, or other word, which involves time present. In Cork people constantly say, ' I *did* not see him *since*,' ' I *did* not find it *yet*,' for ' I *have* not seen him since,' ' I *have* not found it yet.'

352. The indefinite tenses refer strictly to a point of time, and to single acts without regard to duration : they are, however, used to express repeated acts and habits.

We may observe the following peculiarities :

1. The present indefinite is used to express general truths : as ' Love *is* stronger than death,' ' One fool *makes* many.'

2. Both the present and the past indefinite are used to express habit; as, ' He *writes* a good hand,' ' He *went* to the Hall every day.'

In the Irish language, there are forms called Consuetudinal tenses : as, *bidhim* (pronounced *bee-im*), ' I am usually;' *bhidhim* (pronounced *vee-inn*), ' I used to be.'—See Connellan, *Irish Grammar*, pp. 58, 60.

In the Anglo-Irish, as spoken at Cork, the Consuetudinal present is rendered by the auxiliaries *do* and *be:* as, ' I *do be* thinking.' Those who wish to make it fine, say ' *I'd a be* thinking.' At first I thought this was a contraction for ' I would be thinking;' but I afterwards discovered that this explanation was not correct.

3. In animated narrative, and in poetry, the present is used to describe past events. This is commonly called the *Historic Present.* So :

> He through the armed files
> *Darts* his experienced eye, and soon traverse
> The whole battalion *views*, their order due,
> Their visages and stature as of gods,
> Their number last he *sums.*
>
> Milton, *Paradise Lost*, i. 567.

4. The present indefinite is often used for a future, both for future-indefinite and future-perfect : as,

Indefinite. Duncan *comes* here to-night.
Perfect. When he *arrives*, he will bring the news.

i. e. ' When he shall have arrived.'

353. This is a remnant of the old language. In Anglo-Saxon there was no distinct form for the future; or rather, one form was made to do double duty for the future as well as for the present.

> *Obs.*—In Welsh, on the other hand, there is no distinct form for the present tense, and the future sometimes does duty for the present. More commonly, in Welsh, the present is represented by the verb *bod*, 'be,' joined to a form of the principal verb, with the prefixed particle *yn*. In Hebrew there is no distinctive present tense.

354. From this we may understand the reason why the future tense in English offers so much difficulty. First of all, we must remember, that in modern English there is no *distinct inflection* to represent the future; and that, especially in common conversation, we employ a *present* tense with a *future* signification: as ' I *go* to London to-morrow,' ' He *comes* down next week.' The same usage is very common in accessory clauses: as, ' When he *comes*, he will tell us.' Here other languages would require a form denoting 'when he *shall come*,' or, more strictly, ' when he *shall have come*.' This point should be carefully remembered, when we are translating from English into other languages.

When we wish to employ a distinctive future, we make use of the auxiliaries ' shall' and ' will' followed by the infinitive mood, but without the prefix *to*. For example, in the phrases ' I will *write*,' ' You shall *see*,' the verbs *write* and *see* are grammatically in the infinitive mood, dependent upon the auxiliary verbs ' will' and ' shall.'

In Anglo-Saxon these were independent verbs, with significations of their own : *wilkan*, ' to will, to wish;' *sceolan*, ' to owe.' In modern English *will* retains its independent powers, as ' Man *wills*,' ' What he *wills* must be done.' Hence, because these verbs are not mere signs of futurity, but still retain traces of their original signification, they cannot be used indifferently; but the speaker appropriates as much as he can of the *will*, and puts upon other people as much as possible of the *shall*. It is ' I will' and ' You shall.'

I have often been amused to hear two English children disputing, and to observe how accurately they discriminate the use of the auxiliaries. As, ' I *will not*,' ' But you *shall*;' ' But I *will not*,' ' But, I say, you *shall*;' ' But, I tell you, I *will not*' . . .; and so they have gone on, until little could be heard, but *will* on the one side, and *shall* on the other.

355. On this subject, the older grammars were not only meagre, but likely to mislead the student; for the future was given thus:

Future Tense.

Singular.	Plural.
1. I shall *or* will love,	1. We shall *or* will love,
2. Thou shalt *or* wilt love,	2. You shall *or* will love,
3. He shall *or* will love.	3. They shall *or* will love.

Now the future is not expressed by 'shall *or* will;' but sometimes by 'shall,' and at other times by 'will.' When the one form is to be used, and when the other, is a question which the grammarian ought to answer.

356. We have two future tenses in English; one expressing simple futurity; the other expressing determination of some kind, as command, threat, or promise. I call these, I. the Simple Future; II. the Determinate (or Imperative) Future.

I. *Simple Future.*

Singular.	Plural.
1. I *shall* write,	1. We *shall* write,
2. Thou wilt write,	2. You will write,
3. He will write.	3. They will write.

II. *Determinate Future.*

Singular.	Plural.
1. I will write,	1. We will write,
2. Thou *shalt* write,	2. You *shall* write,
3. He *shall* write.	3. They *shall* write.

These forms are used in indicative sentences. In interrogative sentences the following forms are employed:

357.—I. *Simple Future (Interrogative).*

Singular.	Plural.
1. *Shall* I write?	1. *Shall* we write?
2. *Shalt* thou write?	2. *Shall* you write?
3. Will he write?	3. Will they write?

II. *Determinate Future (Interrogative).*

Singular.	Plural.
1. *Shall* I write?	1. *Shall* we write?
2. *Wilt* thou write?	2. Will you write?
3. *Shall* he write?	3. *Shall* they write?

With interrogatives 'shall' asks permission or advice from

the person addressed. It is, therefore, used with the first and third persons of the Determinate Future Interrogative. In the second person, of the same tense, the inquirer asks the consent of the person addressed, and therefore ' will ' is used, especially in invitations.

Although *shall* is used in the first and second persons of the Simple Future Interrogative, there is a tendency to vary the phrase : as, ' Are you going to write?' 'Am I likely to hear from him?' ' Are they about to sail?'

358. It is a common mistake in Ireland to ask ' *Will* I go?'. and ' *Will* we go?' But the speaker ought to know his own mind, and should never interrogate another person about *his own will.* ' *Will* I?' can never be used, except in the repetition of a question, in a tone of surprise : as, ' Will you go?' ' Will I go? Of course I will.'

On the other hand, the Irish often say ' I shall,' in answer to a question asking for assent: as, ' Will you write to me?' ' I *shall.*' This form occurs in older English, and not uncommonly in Shakespeare :

K. Henry.   Brothers both,
    Commend me to the princes in our camp ;
    Do my good morrow to them ; and, anon,
    Desire them all to my pavilion.
Gloster. We *shall*, my liege.—*Henry V.* iv. 1.

K. Henry.   Good old Knight,
    Collect them all together at my tent ;
    I'll be before thee.
Erpingham. I *shall* do't, my lord.—*Ibid.*

359. But this use of ' shall ' is contrary to present custom. When we expect an assurance of assent, we look for an expression of the *will*—' I will.'

I have observed, in Ireland, that there is an aversion to the use of absolute, imperative language. People seem to avoid the words *ought, must,* and the ' absolute *shall* ' of which Shakespeare speaks :

Licinius.   It is a mind
    That shall remain a poison where it is,
    Nor poison any further.
Coriolanus.   *Shall* remain !
    Hear ye this Triton of the minnows? Mark you
    His absolute ' *shall* ?'—*Coriolanus,* iii. 1.

People in Cork commonly say ' A man *has a right* to pay his debts,' and ' The money *has a right* to be paid,' when they mean that, ' A man *ought* to pay his debts,' and that ' The money *must* or *should* be paid.' Similarly nurses sometimes say to a child, ' Oh ! you *could* not have that,' for ' you *must* not have that.'

In like manner, in Scotland, people often say, ' You *require* to go out,' where there is no requirement at all, in the sense of ' wanting ' or ' wishing ; ' but where the speaker means ' It is your *duty* to go out,' or ' You *must* go out.'

360. The distinction between ' shall ' and ' will ' is one of the great difficulties of the English language, more vexatious to an Irishman or Scotchman than to a foreigner. For the Irishman or Scotchman has to unlearn his own habit of speaking, in addition to acquiring the English idiom. Dr. Lowth, (*English Grammar*, p. 65,) states the rule thus : ' *Will* in the first person singular and plural promises or threatens ; in the second and third persons, only foretels ; *shall*, on the contrary, in the first person, simply foretels ; in the second and third persons, promises, commands, or threatens.' Then he adds in a note : ' This distinction was not observed formerly as to the word *shall*, which was used in the second and third persons to express simply the event. So likewise *should* was used, where now we make use of *would*. See the Vulgar Translation of the Bible.'

He further remarks that this rule must be understood of Explicative, by which, no doubt, he means Indicative sentences ; ' for,' he says, ' when the sentence is interrogative, just the reverse, for the most part, takes place : thus, " I *shall* go ; you *will* go," express event only ; but " *will* you go ? " imports intention ; and " *shall* I go ? " refers to the will of another. But again, " he *shall* go," and " *shall* he go ? " both imply will, expressing or referring to a command. *Would* primarily denotes inclination of will, and *should*, obligation ; but they both vary their import, and are often used to express a simple event.'

Brightland sums up the rule in the following verses :

> In the first person simply *shall* foretells ;
> In *will* a threat, or else a promise dwells.
> *Shall*, in the second and the third, does threat ;
> *Will*, simply, then, foretells the future feat.

This, however, must be understood of Indicative sentences only.

K

361. Sir Edmund W. Head, who has discussed the question at length in a work entitled ' " Shall " and " Will," ' lays down the following rules, pp. 119, 120 :

' WILL.

Will, in the first person, expresses (*a*) a resolution, or (*b*) a promise :

> (*a*) " I *will* not go " = " It is my resolution not to go."
>
> (*b*) " I *will* give it you " = " I promise to give it you."

Will, in the second person, foretells :

> " If you come at twelve o'clock you *will* find me at home."

Will, in the second person, in *questions*, anticipates (*a*) a wish, or (*b*) an intention :

> " *Will* you go to-morrow ? " = " Is it your wish or intention to go to-morrow ? "

Will, in the third person, foretells, generally implying an intention at the same time, when the nominative is a rational creature :

> " He *will* come to-morrow," signifies (*a*) what is to take place, and (*b*) that it is the intention of the person mentioned to come.
>
> " I think it *will* snow to-day," intimates what is, probably, to take place.

Will must never be used in questions with nominative cases of the first person :

> " *Will* we come to-morrow " = " Is it our intention or desire to come to-morrow ? " which is an absurd question.

362. ' WOULD.

Would is subject to the same rules as *will*.

Would, followed by *that*, is frequently used (the nominative being expressed or understood) to express a *wish* :

> " *Would that* he had died before this disgrace befell him " = " I wish that he had died before this disgrace befell him."

Would have, followed by an infinitive, signifies a desire to do or make :

> " I *would have* you think of these things " = " I wish to make you think of these things."

Would is often used to express a custom :

"He *would* often talk about these things " =
"It was his custom to talk of these things."

363. ' SHALL.

Shall, in the first person, foretells, simply expressing
what is to take place :

"I *shall* go to-morrow." *Obs.* No intention or
desire is expressed by *shall*.

Shall, in the first person, *in questions*, asks permission :

"*Shall* I read ? " = "Do you wish me, or will
you permit me, to read ? " [Sometimes *shall*
in the first person marks a simple interrogative, as "*shall* I see him ? "]

Shall, in the second and third persons, expresses (*a*) a
promise, (*b*) a command, or (*c*) a threat.

(*a*) "You *shall* have these books to-morrow "
= "I promise to let you have these books
to-morrow."

(*b*) "Thou *shalt* not steal" = "I command
thee not to steal."

(*a*) (*c*) "He *shall* be punished for this " = "I
threaten or promise to punish him for this
offence."

364. ' SHOULD.

Should is subject to the same rules as *shall*.

Should frequently expresses *duty* :

"You *should* not do so" = "It is your duty
not to do so."

Should often signifies a plan :

"I *should* not do so " = "It would not be my
plan to do so."

Should often expresses a *supposition* :

"*Should* they not agree to the proposals, what
must I do ? " = "Suppose that it happen that
they will not agree to the proposals,' &c."'

365. These practical rules are good, as far as they go. But
then, they have to be modified according to the signification
of other words in a sentence. For instance, if I am leaving
town, to take a journey, a friend says, 'I hope you will write
to me.' I reply, 'Yes, I *will*,' or 'I *will* do so with pleasure.'
But if any word denoting *willingness* is introduced before the

word *write*, the construction is altered. We do not' say, 'I
will be happy to do so,' 'I *will* be very glad to write;' but
'I *shall* be happy to do so,' 'I *shall* be very glad to write.'
And why is this? Because *happiness* implies *willingness*;
and to say 'I *will* be happy' is almost like saying 'I *will* be
willing.'

Hence, it is not enough to study general rules, apart from
the construction of sentences, and the mutual dependence of
words in sentences. The grammatical rules must be supple-
mented by familiarity with the best authors, and by conversation in good society.

We must, however, confess that the same attention has not
been paid to English syntax that has been given to the Greek.
We have nothing in English grammar comparable to the
Greek grammars of Matthiæ, Buttmann, or Kühner (Jelf).
Still, certain points have been discussed. The reader may
consult 'shall and will' in Latham's *English Language*, pp.
618–627, introducing the views of Archdeacon Hare and
Professor De Morgan. See also a correspondence between
H. R. G. and Professor De Morgan, in the *Athenæum*, May 6,
1865.

NUMBER.

366. In modern English there is generally no distinct termination to mark the plural in verbs.

In Anglo-Saxon, the termination of the plural was *-ath* in
the Present Indicative, and *on* in the Past Indicative, and in
the Subjunctive, both Present and Past.

In Old English, and in some provincial dialects to the present day, the termination in *-en* is found; so Chaucer,

> And smale foules *maken* melodie
> That *slepen* all night with open eye.
> > *Canterbury Tales, Prologue*, 9.

> The chambres and the stables *weren* wide,
> And wel we *weren* esed atte beste.
> > *Ibid.* 28.

This termination was in common use down to the sixteenth
century, when all indication of a plural form disappeared.

Ben Jonson says, that ' in former times, till about the reign
of King Henry the Eighth, the persons plural were wont to be
formed by adding *en*: thus,

> *loven, sayen, complainen.*

But now (whatsoever is the cause) it hath quite grown out of use, and that other so generally prevailed, that I dare not presume to set this afoot again : albeit (to tell you my opinion) I am persuaded that the lack hereof well considered will be found a great blemish to our tongue.'—Ben Jonson, *English Grammar*, i. 16.

PERSON.

367. The terminations which mark differences of Person are found in the singular number of the Present and Past tenses Indicative.

1. *First Person Singular.*—The only verb which retains a distinctive termination for the first person singular is *am* (*a-m*), where the letter *m* represents the *-om* of the Anglo-Saxon *e-om*.

2. *Second Person Singular.*—The termination of the second person singular is *-est*, *-st*, or *-t* : as,

> *Present* : call-*est*, can-*st*, ar-*t*.
> *Past* : spake-*est*, called-*st*.

3. *Third Person Singular.*—The termination of the third person is *-eth* or *-th*, which in modern English assumes the form *-es* or *-s*. These terminations appear in the Present Indicative only :

> *Present* : call-*eth*, do-*th*.
> call-*s*, do-*es*, search-*es*.

INFINITIVES AND PARTICIPLES.

Infinitives and Participles are respectively like nouns (substantive) and adjectives. Infinitives resemble nouns, in the fact that they describe acts and states merely as *things* or *notions*; and that the infinitive can be made either the subject or the object of a verb. Participles resemble adjectives in attributing a quality, without *formally asserting it*; and in agreeing with their nouns.

But they differ respectively in the following particulars :— The Infinitive admits no plural form, and rarely a possessive genitive (*i. e.*, the form ending in *-s*); and it can govern an objective case. The Participle active, when formed from a transitive verb, can govern an accusative ; and then it generally stands after its noun. See Angus, *Handbook*, § 286.

In connection with the Infinitive, we must consider the forms called Gerunds,

INFINITIVE AND GERUNDS.

368. In §§ 29—36 we discussed the history of the English infinitive, and we saw that the prefix *to*, its ordinary sign in modern English, belonged originally to the gerundial form of the Anglo-Saxon infinitive. Even in modern English, this prefix is not always necessary; it is generally omitted after some of the auxiliaries, as *may, can*, and after some other verbs, as, *bid, make.*

But in other cases, where *to* signifies 'in order to,' it is a true preposition and marks a gerund. As 'He came to see me,' that is, 'for seeing me,' 'for the purpose of seeing me;' or, as it was expressed at one period, 'for to see me.' We call this the Gerund with *to.*

The form in *-ing* as 'loving,' 'writing,' which must not be confounded with the present participle, is considered by Dr. Adams, whose opinions we followed, a remnant of the old infinitive. But as it has been usual to call this form a Gerund, some may wish to retain that term. If so they should distinguish between the Gerund in *-ing*, and the Gerund with *to.*

369. There is considerable difficulty in determining the forms in *-ing*. The account given by Dr. Adams is the most consistent that I have seen. The following view is taken by Professor Max Müller, *Lectures on the Science of Language*, Second Series, pp. 15–18: " We have not very far to go in order to hear such phrases as ' he is a-going, I am a-coming, &c.' instead of the more usual ' he is going, I am coming.' Now, the fact is that the vulgar or dialectic expression 'he is a-going' is far more correct than ' he is going.' (Archdeacon Hare, *Words corrupted by False Analogy or False Derivation*, p. 65.)"

" *Ing*, in our modern grammars, is called the termination of the participle present, but it does not exist as such in Anglo-Saxon. In Anglo-Saxon the termination of that participle is *ande* or *inde*. This was preserved as late as Gower's and Chaucer's time, though in most cases it had then already been supplanted by the termination *-ing*. For example,

> Pointis and sleves be wel *sittande*
> Full right and straight upon the hande.
> *Romaunt of the Rose*, 2264.

" Now, the termination *-ing* is clearly used in two different senses, even in modern English. If we say a ' loving child,' *loving* is a verbal adjective. If we say ' loving our neighbour is our highest duty,' *loving* is a verbal substantive. Again, there are many substantives in *-ing*, such as *building, wedding, meeting*, where the verbal character of the substantive is almost, if not entirely, lost."

" Now, if we look to Anglo-Saxon, we find the termination *-ing* used,

(1) To form patronymics; for instance, *Godvulfing*, the son of *Godvulf.* In the Anglo-Saxon translation of the Bible, the son of *Elisha* is called *Elising.*

(2). "*Ing* is used to form more general attributive words, such as *æþeling* (atheling), 'a man of rank;' *lyteling*, 'an infant;' *niðing*, 'a bad man.' This -*ing* being frequently preceded by another suffix, the *l*, we arrive at the very common derivative -*ling*, in such words as *darling*, *hireling, yearling, foundling, nestling, worldling, changeling.*

"It has been supposed that the modern English participle was formed by the same derivative; but in Anglo-Saxon, this suffix -*ing* is chiefly attached to nouns and adjectives, not to verbs. There was, however, another derivative in Anglo-Saxon, which was attached to verbs in order to form verbal substantives. This was -*ung*, the German -*ung*. For instance, *clænsung*, 'cleansing;' *beácnung*, 'beaconing,' &c. In early Anglo-Saxon, these abstract nouns in -*ung* are far more numerous than those in -*ing*. *Ing*, however, began soon to encroach on -*ung*, and at present no trace is left in English of substantives derived from verbs by means of -*ung*.

"Although, as I said, it might seem more plausible to look on the modern participle in English as originally an adjective in -*ing*, such popular phrases as *a-going, a-thinking* point rather to the verbal substantive in -*ing* as the source from which the modern English participle was derived. 'I am going' is really a corruption of 'I am a-going,' i.e. 'I am on going,' and the participle present would thus, by a very simple process, be traced back to a locative case of a verbal noun."

PARTICIPLES.

370. Participles are *verbal adjectives*, differing from ordinary adjectives in this, that they retain some of the powers of a verb; for instance, the active participle of a verb transitive can govern an objective case: as, 'He stood there *throwing stones*.'

We have, in English, two participles:—

    (1) The Imperfect or incomplete participle in -*ing*.
    (2) The Perfect or complete participle ending in -*ed*, -*d*,   -*t*, -*en*, or -*n*.

Sometimes the Imperfect participle is called the *present* participle, and the Perfect is called the *past* participle.

The participle in -*ing* has an active force. And as it happens that, in the case of Transitive verbs, the Perfect participle is always *passive*, a confusion has arisen in the minds of some persons, who have not been able to decide whether the form in -*ed* is originally a *past* participle, or a *passive* participle, or whether there be any connection between *past* and *passive*.

The participle in -*ed* is Perfect, that is to say, it denotes an action completed or finished, but it is not necessarily passive: for example, in 'I have *walked*,' there is nothing passive. But in 'I have *written*,' though the whole phrase stands for the perfect tense *active*, yet 'written' is a *passive* participle. The difficulty is thus explained : that 'I have written a letter ' is originally 'I have a letter written,' where 'written' is the passive participle used as an adjective, and agreeing with 'letter.' In Latin, we find such forms as *habeo scriptam epistolam*, which means 'I have (or hold) a letter written,' rather than 'I have written a letter; ' but the construction is near enough to throw light upon our form, and has suggested the explanation.

371. The participle in *-ing* is used with the active form of verbs transitive, or with intransitive verbs : as ' He is *making* progress,' ' He is *travelling*.' Although the auxiliary *be* is commonly used with passive forms, we must be careful not to mistake it for a sign of the passive : ' He is *making* ' is active and transitive.

We should carefully watch the use of the participles with the verb *be*, in the case of intransitive verbs; for instance,—

He is coming	Present-imperfect tense.
He was coming . . .	Past-imperfect tense.
He is come	Present-perfect tense.

In modern English, we more commonly say ' He *has* come; ' but ' he *is* come ' is more common in older English, and is warranted by the German ' er *ist* gekommen.'

372. There is, however, one construction in which, to all appearance, we find an active participle in *-ing*, where we should expect a passive ; as,

> The house is building.
> The temple was forty years building.

In older stages of the language, these sentences were expressed ' The house is *a*-building,' ' The temple was forty years *a*-building; ' and the particle *a* is said to be a contraction of the Anglo-Saxon preposition *an*, ' on,' ' in.'

If so, then the word ' building ' is here not a participle but a Gerund (or Infinitive) in *-ing*. For the participle standing alone could not be governed by a preposition; such government demands an infinitive or a gerund.

373. But in a few instances, wherein this explanation does not seem applicable, we still find the form in *-ing*, where we should expect a passive participle : as,

beholding for *beholden*.
owing for *owed* (*i.e.* ' owe ').
wanting for *wanted*.

I would not be *beholding* to fortune for any part of the victory.—*Sidney*.
I'll teach you what is *owing* to your Queen.—*Dryden*.
We have the means in our hands, and nothing but the application of them is wanting.—*Addison*.

The phrase *a-wanting* is heard in some dialects.

374. On the other hand, we sometimes find the Perfect participle of a transitive verb used, where we expect an active and not a passive sense: as,

mistaken for *mistaking*.

You are too much *mistaken* in this king.—*Hen. V.* ii. 4.

Compare the question addressed by Othello to Cassio:

How comes it, Michael, you *are* thus *forgot?*
i. e. ' that you have so far forgotten yourself.'
Othello, ii. 3.

AUXILIARIES.

375. As the inflections of English verbs are few, we need some assistance to express the various relations of Voice, Mood, and Tense. Hence, we call in the aid of certain verbs, which are termed Auxiliaries or Helpers. We have one auxiliary of Voice; several auxiliaries of Mood; and three auxiliaries of Tense.

I. AUXILIARY OF VOICE.

376. The verb *Be*, joined to the perfect participle of a transitive verb, is used to form the Passive Voice: as,

Active.	Passive.
Present, I love,	*Present*, I am loved.
Past, I loved,	*Past*, I was loved.

The verb *be* is thus conjugated:

INDICATIVE MOOD.

Present Tense.

Singular.	Plural.
1. I am,	1. We are,
2. Thou art,	2. You are,
3. He is,	3. They are.

Past Tense.

Singular.	Plural.
1. I was,	1. We were,
2. Thou wast,	2. You were,
8. He was,	8. They were.

SUBJUNCTIVE MOOD.

Present Tense.

Singular.	Plural.
1. I be,	1. We be,
2. Thou be,	2. You be,
8. He be,	8. They be.

Past Tense.

Singular.	Plural.
1. I were,	1. We were,
2. Thou wert,	2. You were,
8. He were,	8. They were.

IMPERATIVE MOOD.

be.

INFINITIVE MOOD.

[to] be.

Gerund (or Infinitive) in -ing . . . **being.**
Gerund with *to* . . . . **to be.**

PARTICIPLES.

Present . . . being.
Past . . . . been.

The auxiliary verb *be* is not always the sign of the passive voice. With the present participle of transitive verbs, it denotes the present-imperfect tense of the active voice : as ' I am loving,' ' I am striking.'

It is also employed in the present-imperfect tense of intransitive verbs, which are never used in the passive; as, ' I am walking,' ' I am coming,' ' I am going.' These would be rendered in Latin, *ambulo, venio, eo.* See § 846.

II. AUXILIARIES OF MOOD.

377. Several verbs, all more or less defective in their own conjugation, are used as auxiliaries to express the notions of possibility, permission, obligation, or necessity. The most remarkable of these are, *may, can, must, dare, let, ought.* The principal verb, dependent upon them, follows in the infinitive mood; and the particle *to* is generally omitted before the infinitive, but not always.

378. 1. MAY.

INDICATIVE MOOD.

Present Tense.

Singular.	Plural.
1. I may,	1. We may,
2. Thou mayest,	2. You may,
3. He may,	3. They may.

Past Tense.

Singular.	Plural.
1. I might,	1. We might,
2. Thou mightest,	2. You might,
3. He might,	3. They might.

This verb expresses permission: as, 'He *may* go, if he likes.' It is also used to express a prayer, a wish, or a desire; in which case it precedes the subject-nominative: as, 'May he prosper,' 'May they be happy.' The beggars in Cork reverse this order: as, 'The Lord may bless you,' 'The Lord may spare you to your family.'

379. 2. CAN.

INDICATIVE MOOD.

Present Tense.

Singular.	Plural.
1. I can,	1. We can,
2. Thou canst,	2. You can,
3. He can,	3. They can.

Past Tense.

Singular.	Plural.
1. I could,	1. We could,
2. Thou couldst,	2. You could,
3. He could,	3. They could.

This verb denotes power, or capability, and is used to form what some grammarians call the Potential Mood. The verb *can* (A.-S. *cunnan*) originally signifies ' to know,' and then ' to be able ; ' like *savoir* in French, as *je sais le faire*, ' I know how to do it,' that is, ' I can (to) do it.' The past tense of the Anglo-Saxon verb is *cuðe* (*cudhe*), whence the Old English *coud*. The form ' could ' has arisen from false analogy, from a fancied resemblance to *would* and *should*. But in these words *l* is part of the root ; whereas in ' cou*l*d ' it is quite superfluous.

380.   3. Must.

INDICATIVE MOOD.

Singular.	Plural.
1. I must,	1. We must,
2. Thou must,	2. You must,
3. He must,	3. They must.

This verb is used to denote necessity. It has no inflection whatever, and there is some difficulty in determining the question of tense. Dr. Latham says (*English Language*, § 607):— ' I can only say of this form [*must*] that it is common to all persons, numbers, and tenses.' But compare Adams (*Elements of the English Language*, § 366).

For my own part, I have always felt the want of a past tense in this auxiliary. For example, when we wish to translate from German such a phrase as *er musste gehen*, we cannot say ' he must go.' We are obliged to give the sentence a turn : ' he was obliged to go,' ' he was bound to go,' ' he had to go.' We do, indeed, sometimes hear the phrase ' he must needs go ; ' but the past tense of the verb *must* seems confined to that construction.

381. 4. DARE.

INDICATIVE MOOD.

Present Tense.

Singular.	Plural.
1. I dare *or* durst,	1. We dare *or* durst,
2. Thou darest *or* durst,	2. You dare *or* durst,
3. He dares, dare, *or* durst,	3. They dare *or* durst.

Past Tense.

Singular.	Plural.
1. I dared *or* durst,	1. We dared *or* durst,
2. Thou daredst *or* durst,	2. You dared *or* durst,
3. He dared *or* durst,	3. They dared *or* durst.

Dr. Latham says (*English Language,* § 598):—'*Dare, durst.*
—The verb *dare* is both transitive and intransitive. We can
say either *I dare do such a thing,* or *I dare* (challenge) *such a
man to do it.* This, in the present tense, is unequivocally
correct. In the perfect, the double power of the word *dare* is
ambiguous; still it is, to my mind at least, allowable. We
can certainly say, *I dared him to accept my challenge*; and we
can perhaps say, *I dared not venture on the expedition.* In this
last sentence, however, *durst* is preferable. *Durst* is intransitive only. *Dare* can be used only in the present tense, *dared*
in the perfect only. *Durst* can be used in either.'

382. 5. LET.

This verb is derived from the A.-S. *lætan,* past tense *let,*
perfect participle *læten,* which, according to Dr. Bosworth,
bears four significations:

1. To let, suffer, permit, to let be, leave—*sinere.*
2. To let go, release, send, dismiss—*mittere.*
3. To hinder, let, trifle—*impedire.*
4. To admit, think, suppose, pretend—*admittere, putare.*

Mr. Wedgewood, in his *Etymological Dictionary,* endeavours
to account for the two senses of *let,* apparently the reverse of
each other—(1) ' to allow, permit,' or even ' to take measures
for the execution of a purpose,' as when we say, ' *let* me alone,'
' *let* me go,' ' *let* me have a letter to-morrow;' and (2) ' to
hinder,' as ' I was *let* hitherto.'

In his opinion the idea of *slackening* lies at the root of both applications of the term. When we speak of 'letting one go,' 'letting him do something,' we conceive of him as previously restrained by a band, the loosening or slackening of which will permit the execution of the act in question. Thus the Latin *laxare*, 'to slacken,' was used in later times in the sense of its modern derivatives, Italian *lasciare*, French *laisser*, 'to let.' So *modicum laxa stare*, 'let it stand a little while:' Muratori, *Diss.* 24, p. 365.

At other times, Mr. Wedgewood thinks, the slackness is attributed to the agent himself, when *let* acquires the sense of 'be slack in action,' 'delay,' or 'omit doing.'

> And down he goth, no longer would he *let*,
> And with that word his counter door he shet.
>
>   *Chaucer.*

Then in a causative sense to *let* one from doing a thing is 'to *make* him *let* or omit to do it,' 'to hinder his doing it.'

On the other hand, Richardson thinks that in *let* we have two distinct verbs, the same in spelling, but different in meaning :

1. *Let*, 'to give leave,' 'permit,' he connects with Ger. *lassen*, Ital. *lasciare*, Fr. *laisser*, 'to relax,' 'loosen.'
2. *Let*, 'to retard, delay, hinder,' he connects with Goth. *latyan*, and the adjective *læt*, 'late.'

It is in the first of these significations that *let* is an auxiliary in English, commonly used in the first and third persons of the Imperative Mood.

Singular.	Plural.
1. Let me go,	1. Let us go,
3. Let him go,	3. Let them go.

In Cork, the same auxiliary is frequently used with the second person : as, 'let you sit here,' 'let you go away.'

383.   6. OUGHT.

INDICATIVE MOOD.

Present Tense.

Singular.	Plural.
1. I ought,	1. We ought,
2. Thou oughtest,	2. You ought,
3. He ought,	3. They ought.

Ought is properly the past tense of *owe*, which originally meant 'to own, possess:' so Shakespeare,

> I am not worthy of the wealth I *owe*.
>
> *All's Well,* ii. 5.

> Not poppy, nor mandragora,
> Nor all the drowsy syrups of the world,
> Shall ever medicine thee to that sweet sleep
> Which thou *ow'dst* yesterday.
>
> *Othello,* iii. 3.

In the following passage, the verb is used in two senses: 'to be bound to pay' and 'to own:'

> Be pleased then
> To pay that duty, which you truly *owe*,
> To him that *owes* it, namely, this young prince.
>
> *King John,* ii. 1.

Dr. Latham remarks, (*English Language,* § 605,) that we can say, 'I owe money;' but we cannot say, 'I owe to pay some;' while, on the other hand, we cannot say, 'I ought money,' though we can say, 'I ought to pay some.' The effect of this twofold sense has been to separate the words *owe*, and *ought*, by giving to the former the modern præterite *owed*. It has also deprived *ought* of its 'present' form.

The auxiliary *ought* has lost its original force as a past tense, and is used as a present. Hence, when we wish to state that some duty was imperative in time past, we annex the auxiliary *have* to the dependent infinitive: as, 'he *ought* to *have* gone.' This must be remembered in translating into Latin: 'he ought to have gone' is *debuit ire*, literally, 'he *did owe* to go.'

III. AUXILIARIES OF TENSE.

384. These are *have, shall, will.*

1. HAVE.

INDICATIVE MOOD.

Present Tense.

Singular.	Plural.
1. I have,	1. We have,
2. Thou hast,	2. You have,
3. He has,	3. They have.

Past Tense.

Singular.	Plural.
1. I had,	1. We had,
2. Thou hadst,	2. You had,
8. He had,	8. They had.

SUBJUNCTIVE MOOD.

Present Tense.

Singular.	Plural.
1. I have,	1. We have,
2. Thou have,	2. You have,
8. He have,	8. They have.

Past Tense.

Singular.	Plural.
1. I had,	1. We had,
2. Thou had,	2. You had,
8. He had,	8. They had.

IMPERATIVE MOOD.

have.

INFINITIVE MOOD.

[to] have.

GERUND (*or* Infinitive) in *-ing* . . **having.**
GERUND with *to* . . . . **to have.**

PARTICIPLES.

Present . . . . having.
Perfect . . . . had.

This auxiliary is joined with the perfect participle, and forms the perfect tenses : as,

Present-perfect . . . I *have* written.
Past-perfect . . . I *had* written.
Future-perfect . . . I shall *have* written.

Shall and *will* are joined to the infinitive mood of a principal verb, to denote the future.

385. 2. SHALL.

INDICATIVE MOOD.

Present Tense.

Singular.	Plural.
1. I shall,	1. We shall,
2. Thou shalt,	2. You shall,
8. He shall,	8. They shall.

Past Tense.

1. I should,	1. We should,
2. Thou shouldst,	2. You should,
8. He should,	8. They should.

The original meaning of this verb is 'owe' (A.-S. *sceal*). So Chaucer, 'By the faithe I *schal* to God,' i.e., 'I *owe* to God.' And so Robert of Gloucester, 'al that to Rome *sholde* servise,' i.e., '*owed* service.'

Should, when used as an independent verb, means *ought*: as, 'You *should* be careful'—'You *ought* to be careful.'

386. 8. WILL.

INDICATIVE MOOD.

Present Tense.

Singular.	Plural.
1. I will,	1. We will,
2. Thou wilt,	2. You will,
8. He will,	8. They will.

Past Tense.

Singular.	Plural.
1. I would,	1. We would,
2. Thou wouldst,	2. You would,
8. He would,	8. They would.

Will is also used as an independent verb. Hence we find the infinitive [to] *will*, and the participle *willing*.

367. Besides these, we have an auxiliary in constant use, the verb *do*, which is employed in various significations.

Do.

INDICATIVE MOOD.

Present Tense.

Singular.	Plural.
1. I do,	1. We do,
2. Thou dost,	2. You do,
8. He does,	8. They do.

Past Tense.

Singular.	Plural.
1. I did,	1. We did,
2. Thou didst, .	2. You did,
8. He did,	8. They did.

SUBJUNCTIVE MOOD.

Present Tense.

Singular.	Plural.
1. I do,	1. We do,
2. Thou do,	2. You do,
8. He do,	8. They do.

Past Tense.

Singular.	Plural.
1. I did,	1. We did,
2. Thou did,	2. You did,
8. He did,	8. They did.

IMPERATIVE MOOD.

do.

INFINITIVE MOOD.

[to] do.

GERUND (*or* Infinitive) in -*ing* . . . doing.
GERUND with *to* . . . . to do.

PARTICIPLES.

Present . . . . . doing
Past .   . . . . done.

388. This verb is used as an auxiliary,

1. For emphasis: as, 'When they *do* agree, their unanimity is wonderful.'

2. In negations: as, 'I *do* not like it.' As a general rule, the negative stands between *do* and the dependent infinitive: as, 'I do *not* think.' But after *neither* or *nor*, the auxiliary *do* follows immediately, and precedes the subject-nominative: as, 'neither *does* he wish,' 'nor *do* I think.'

3. In questions: as, '*Does* he say so?' '*Do* they not consent?' or '*Do* not they consent?' often contracted '*Do-n't* they consent?'

4. After an adverb, or an adverbial phrase, the auxiliary *do* follows immediately, and precedes the subject-nominative:

Once again
Do I behold those steeps and lofty cliffs.
Wordsworth.

5. In reply to a question with an ellipsis of the dependent infinitive: as,

Portia. Do you confess the bond?
Antonio. I *do*.

Merchant of Venice, iv. 5.

See Adams, *Elements of the English Language*, § 617. Here, when Antonio says 'I do,' he means 'I do confess.'

389. *Caution.* Whenever we employ any part of the verb *do*, in reference to some principal verb in the former part of a sentence, there is risk of error; and, in particular, the reference to an intransitive verb is open to cavil. Take this example:

It is somewhat unfortunate, that this paper did not end, as it might very well have *done*, with the former beautiful period.—Blair, *Rhetoric*, xxiii.

A caviller might ask, 'done what?' Surely not 'done ending.' In such constructions, it is better to repeat the principal verb; 'did not end, as it might very well have *ended*.' Repetition is sometimes disagreeable, and tends to enfeeble a sentence; but it is always preferable to ambiguity. See Cobbett, *Grammar*, § 273.

390. Dr. Latham points out that we have in English two distinct words which assume the form *do*. In the phrase 'this will *do*,' meaning 'this will answer the purpose,' he considers the word *do* wholly different from *do* = act.

1. The word .in common use *do*, meaning ' to act,' is from the A.-S. *dón*, and corresponds to the German *thun*.

2. The word *do*, meaning ' to answer the purpose,' is from the A.-S. *dugan*, and corresponds to the German *taugen*.

He quotes the following passages in illustration of the second meaning. The past tense *deih* occurs in these lines:

Philip of Flaundres fleih, and turned sonne the bak;
And Thebald nouht he *deih*.

Robert of Bourne, 133.

(Philip of Flanders fled, and turned soon the back;
And Thebald *did no good*.)

The king Isaak fleih, his men had no foyson,
All that time he ne *deih*.

Robert of Bourne, 159.

(King Isaac fled, his men had no provisions,
All that time he *prospered* not.)

The present *I dow*, in the sense of *I can*, occurs in Burns:

I'll laugh, an' sing, an' shake my leg
As lang's I *dow*.

See Latham, *English Language*, § 593.

IMPERSONALS.

391. When a verb is used without any apparent subject-nominative it is called an Impersonal Verb.

Some grammarians contend that verbs of this kind are not Impersonal; but that they are used in the third person, and in the third person only. Hence they propose to call such verbs *Unipersonal*.

In English we commonly prefix the neuter pronoun *it* before the so-called Impersonals.

Dr. Lowth says: ' *It* rains; *it* shines; *it* thunders.' From which examples it plainly appears, that there is no such thing in English, nor indeed in any language, as a sort of Verbs which are really impersonal. The agent or person in English is expressed by the neuter pronoun; in some other languages it is omitted, but understood.' Lowth, *English Grammar*, p. 110.

Dr. Latham admits three Impersonals: (1) *methinks*, (2) *meseems*, (3) *me listeth*. The word thinks in 'methinks' is from the Anglo-Saxon *thincan*, 'to seem,' and not from *thencan*, 'to think.' Hence 'methinks' and 'meseems' both signify 'it seems to me;' for *me* is here the old dative. See Latham, *English Grammar*, § 205.

But Dr. Adams, *Elements of the English Language*, § 276, will not allow that even these are Impersonals; for he argues that the subject is expressed in the words that follow or precede the verb. Thus in the sentence,

Methinks the lady doth protest too much,

he would make 'the lady doth protest too much' a subject-nominative (noun-clause) to the verb 'thinks.'

It may be, as Dr. Lowth maintains, that there are no such things as Impersonal Verbs in any language. But the omission of *it* is more common with our older poets, than some of the grammarians seem to imagine:

So Chaucer:

Byfel that in that sesoun on a day
In Southwark at the Tabard as I lay.
Canterbury Tales, Prologue.

and so Spenser:

Seemed in heart some hidden care she had,
And by her in a line, a milk-white lamb she lad. (*i.e.* led.)
Faerie Queene, I. i. 4.

'Now,' saide the ladie, '*draweth* toward night.'
ibid. I. i. 32.

May seeme the wayne was very evil ledd,
When such an one had guiding of the way,
That knew not, whether right he went, or else astray.
ibid. I. iv. 19.

CAUTIONS.

392. In no points of grammar do even good writers more frequently make mistakes than in the use of verbs.

'I intended to have written last week' is a very common phrase; but it is certainly vicious. For how long soever it now is since 'I intended,' still the act of writing was then present to my mind, and must be considered as present when I recall that time, and the thoughts of it. Therefore, we should say, 'I intended *to write* last week.' Take the following examples:—

I cannot excuse the remissness of those whose business it should have been, as it certainly was their interest, *to have interposed* their good offices.—*Swift.*

There were two circumstances, which would have made it necessary for them *to have lost* no time.—*Id.*

History-painters would have found it difficult *to have invented* such a species of beings.—Addison, *Dialogue on Medals.*

In these passages, the infinitives should be *to interpose, to lose, to invent.*

So Goldsmith says:

I called on him, and wished *to have submitted* my manuscript to him.

This should be 'wished to submit.' For the meaning is, 'I wished then and there to submit my manuscript to him.' I wished to do something *there,* and did not *then* wish that *I had done* something before.

So here: 'I did not speak yesterday so well as I wished *to have done.*' The meaning intended is 'so well as I wished to speak.' The use of the auxiliary *do* is not elegant in such constructions; but if used at all, it should stand 'so well as I wished *to do.*'

On the other hand, in this sentence, 'I had not the pleasure of *hearing* his sentiments when I wrote that letter,' we ought to say *having heard* instead of *hearing* if we mean to imply that the hearing did not take place before the writing of the letter. See Lowth, *English Grammar,* p. 124; and Cobbett, *English Grammar,* § 249.

Sequence of Tenses.

393. The sequence of tenses should be carefully observed; so that the tenses in an accessory or subordinate clause may not be inconsistent with those of the principal sentence.

Take this example:

Ye *will* not come unto me, that ye *might* have life.

In two clauses thus connected, when the principal verb is in the present or the future, the verb in the accessory clause cannot be in the past tense. The words, therefore, ought to have been translated 'that ye *may* have life.'

On the contrary, had the principal verb been in the past

tense, the verb in the accessory clause would be correctly put in the past tense also : as,

> Ye *would* not come unto me, that ye *might* have life.

or,

> Ye *did* not come unto me, that ye *might* have life.

but,

> Ye *will* not come unto me, that ye *may* have life.

Dryden writes :

> Some, who the depths of Eloquence *have found,*
> In that unnavigable Stream *were drowned.*
>
> Dryden, *Juvenal*, Satire x.

The event mentioned in the first line is connected with present time by the present-perfect tense *have found.* But the fact stated in the second line is referred to past time, by the past tense *were drowned.* Now the last-mentioned event must be subsequent to the first, and therefore there is an inconsistency between the facts stated and the tenses employed. Therefore, we ought to have either

(1) in the second line, ' *are* or *have been* drowned ' in the present-indefinite or present-perfect, which would be consistent with the present-perfect *have found* in the first line ;

or,

(2) in the first line we ought to read *had found* in the past-perfect tense, which would be consistent with the past-indefinite *were drowned* in the second line.

Pope writes :

> Friend to my life, which *did* you not prolong,
> The world *had wanted* many an idle song.
>
> Pope, *Epistle to Arbuthnot.*

Here the construction is inconsistent. It ought to be, ' *had* you not *prolonged* . . . the world *had wanted*,' or ' *did* you not *prolong* . . . the world *would want.*'

394. Dr. Campbell thinks, that in expressing abstract or universal truths the present tense of the verb ought, according to the idiom of our language, and perhaps of every language, always to be employed. According to this view, the sentence ' He said that there *was* no God ' is incorrect, because God always exists ; and it ought to be, ' He said that there *is* no God.' Yet the Doctor admits that this peculiarity in the present has sometimes been overlooked, even by good authors, who, when speaking of a past event which occasions the mention of some general truth, are led to use the same tense in enunciating the general truth with that which has been employed in the preceding part of the sentence. See Campbell, *Philosophy of Rhetoric*, p. 185.

Dr. Webster, in the preface to his *English Dictionary*, takes the same view, and condemns the following construction :— ' Then Manasseh *knew* that the Lord he *was* God,' 2 Chron. xxxiii. 13. In order to show the impropriety of the past tense *was*, he remarks that the present tense is that which is used to express what exists at all times : thus we say ' God is ' or ' exists ' whenever we speak of his permanent existence. The German version reads, ' Da erkannte Manasse, dass der Herr Gott *ist*,' and this, as far as it goes, corroborates the view taken by Dr. Campbell and Dr. Webster. But their reason does not appear to be quite satisfactory. It is true, that in principal sentences the present is used to express general propositions, or ' what exists at all times.' But it is not quite so clear that the rule applies to the verb in a subordinate or accessory clause. The Latins, in a reported speech, throw the verbs of subordinate sentences into the subjunctive mood ; and though in English we do not vary the mood in a reported speech, I am inclined to think that a variation of tense is agreeable to the idiom of our language. It is confessed that good authors use this construction ; and in conversation most persons would express themselves thus :

He *says*, that there *is* no God.
He *said*, that there *was* no God.

To allege the permanent existence of God is nothing to the purpose, because this is merely a question of grammar, and most persons would expound these sentences in the following way :

1. He *says*, that there *is* no God = He *denies* the existence of God.

2. He *said*, that there *was* no God = He *denied* the existence of God.

No one would interpret the second sentence as signifying a denial of *past* existence, in opposition to present or future existence.

395. In accordance with his theory, Dr. Webster undertakes to correct this passage :

If my readers will turn their thoughts back on their old friends, they will find it difficult to call a single man to remembrance who *appeared* to know that life *was* short [*is* short], till he was about to lose it.

Rambler, No. 71.

396. But beside this, we find the past tense used in accessory clauses where other languages would employ a future indicative, or some tense of the subjunctive mood. Take the following examples, with Dr. Webster's corrections:

It was *declared* by Pompey, that if the commonwealth *was* [should be] violated, he could stamp with his foot and raise an army out of the ground.—*Rambler*, No. 10.

And he said, Nay, father Abraham, but if one *went* [shall (or) should go] to them from the dead, they will repent. And he said unto him, If they hear not Moses and the prophets, neither will they be persuaded, though one *rose* [shall (or) should rise] from the dead.—*Luke* xvi. 30, 31.

Our verbs are very deficient in forms of the subjunctive mood; and were anyone to contend that *went* and *rose* are past tenses *subjunctive*, there is nothing in the form to contradict him. The verb *was* in the extract from *Rambler*, No. 10, is against that explanation; for *was* must be considered indicative. If I made any change at all, in that passage, I would read, 'It was declared by Pompey, that if the commonwealth *were* violated, &c.'

397. I have often thought, that the doctrine of the subjunctive might be used to defend a passage condemned as bad English, by some grammarians. It is this:

I *had* fainted, unless I had believed to see the goodness of the Lord in the land of the living.—*Psalm* xxvii. 13.

We are told, that this ought to be, 'I *should have* fainted.' But if *had* be taken as the past tense subjunctive (German *hätte*), the construction may be defended.

398. In the following sentence, there is an error in the use of mood:

If thou *bring* thy gift to the altar, and there *rememberest* that thy brother hath ought against thee.—*Matt.* v. 23.

The construction of the two verbs *bring* and *rememberest*

L

ought to be the same; yet the one is in the subjunctive mood, and the other in the indicative. We should read,

> If thou *bring* thy gift to the altar, and there *remember*, &c.,

or,

> If thou *bringest* thy gift to the altar, and there *remem-berest*, &c.

The same mood should be employed in both clauses.

399. When two or more auxiliaries are used in reference to one principal verb, care should be taken that the form of the principal verb be applicable to each of the auxiliaries. Take this sentence:

> This dedication may serve for almost any book, that *has*, *is*, or *shall be* published.

The auxiliary *has* makes no sense in connection with *published*. It requires the addition of *been*. We should read:

> This dedication may serve for almost any book, that *has been* or *shall be* published.

The word *is*, adding nothing to the sense, may advantageously be omitted.

So in this passage:

> I shall do all I can to persuade others to *take* the same measures for their cure which I *have*.

Here, we find *have* referred to the verb *take*. Yet it is not the word *take* which the sense demands, but *taken*. The participle, therefore, ought to have been added: ' which I *have taken*.'

See Campbell, *Philosophy of Rhetoric*, p. 186.

POSITION.

400. In Indicative sentences the verb generally follows the subject-nominative; but in Interrogative sentences the subject-nominative follows the principal verb or the auxiliary: as, ' Was he there?' 'Did Alexander conquer?'

In older English, and in poetry, the use of the principal verb, in the first place of an interrogative sentence, is not uncommon:

> Says the king so?
>
> Stands Scotland where it did?—*Macbeth*, iv. 3.

Breathes there the man with soul so dead,
Who never to himself hath said,
This is my own, my native land?
        Scott, *Lay of the Last Minstrel*, vi. 1–3.

401. When several interrogative clauses follow one another, care must be taken to use all the verbs consistently. Take this example:

> *Did* he not *fear* the Lord, and *besought* the Lord, and the Lord *repented* him of the evil, which he had pronounced against him?—*Jeremiah* xxvi. 19.

Here the interrogative and indicative forms are confounded. It ought to be:

> *Did* he not *fear* the Lord, and *beseech* the Lord? and *did* not the Lord *repent* him of the evil?

So in this passage:

> If a man have an hundred sheep, and one of them be gone astray, *doth* he not *leave* the ninety and nine, and *goeth* into the mountains, and *seeketh* that which is gone astray?—*Matt.* xviii. 12.

It ought to be *go* and *seek*; that is, '*doth* he not *go* and *seek* that which is gone astray?'

402. In negative sentences the adverb *not* is placed after the auxiliary, or sometimes after the principal verb itself: as, 'it *did not* touch him,' 'it touched him *not*.'

Older writers frequently place the negative before the principal verb: as,

                    For men
Can counsel and speak comfort to that grief
Which they themselves *not* feel.
           Much Ado about Nothing, v. i.

Iago. Good name, in man and woman, dear my lord,
Is the immediate jewel of their souls:
Who steals my purse, steals trash; 'tis something, nothing;
'Twas mine, 'tis his, and has been slave to thousands;
But he that filches from me my good name,
Robs me of that which *not* enriches him,
And makes me poor indeed.
              Othello, iii. 3.

The merry Greek, tart Aristophanes,
Neat Terence, witty Plautus, now *not* please, .

But antiquated and deserted lie,
As they were not of nature's family.
>   Ben Jonson, *To the Memory of Shakespeare.*

I hope, my lord, said he, I *not* offend.
>   Dryden, *Fables.*

CHAPTER XI.

GENERAL REMARKS ON PARTICLES.

403. Under the term 'Particles,' we include the words commonly called Adverbs, Conjunctions, and Prepositions.

It is not always possible to draw the line between these, as the same word may be at one time a preposition, at another an adverb or a conjunction. Thus *before,* in the phrase ' before sunset,' is a preposition; but in the sentence ' before the sun sets,' it is commonly called a *conjunction.* Dr. Morell terms it a *continuative conjunction.* Mr. Mason thinks that it should rather be classed among the *adverbs.* Professor Bain calls it a *relative adverb,* or a *subordinating conjunction.*

Now, if grammarians would candidly confess that the so-called Parts of Speech cannot always be discriminated, they would save themselves and their followers a world of perplexity. Instead of this, they lay down dogmatic rules, which are not always applicable, and then they try to make their cause good by numerous exceptions and counter-exceptions. It is no wonder that young persons are utterly distracted, or that they consider the study of grammar dull and unprofitable.

But if the inductive method were followed, much of this perplexity would vanish. Pupils should be taught to observe the usage of words in their reading; to compare one phrase with another; to suspend judgment; and gradually to arrive at general principles. In this way they would acquire the habits of observation and comparison; they would learn to think and to reason; and Grammar would form an excellent introduction to Logic.

404. In order to concentrate the difficulties which pervade this part of the subject, we shall devote a separate chapter to

those doubtful words, which are variously termed Conjunctive
Adverbs, Adverbial Conjunctions, Relative Adverbs, Subordinating Conjunctions, Continuative Conjunctions, &c., &c.

Thus, we shall be able to obtain a clearer view of Adverbs
and Conjunctions properly so called; and the student will
perceive wherein the difficult part of the investigation specially
consists.

CHAPTER XII.

ADVERBS.

Omnis pars orationis, quando desinit esse quod est, migrat
in Adverbium.—SERVIUS.

405. The passage quoted from Servius is thus humorously
construed by Horne Tooke:—*Omnis pars orationis,* 'every
word,' *quando desinit esse quod est,* 'when a grammarian
knows not what to make of it,' *migrat in Adverbium,* 'he calls
an Adverb.'

But, according to Sir John Stoddart, the expression of
Servius is literally true: *Omnis pars orationis migrat in Adverbium,* 'Every part of speech is capable of being converted
into an Adverb.'

Servius saw part of the truth; and his remark is capable of
a wider application. The character of a word is determined
by its function or usage in a sentence: hence every part of
speech, when 'it ceases to be what it is,' undergoes a change
of function, and partakes of a new character. There can be
little doubt, as Horne Tooke has shown, that the particle *if*
was originally *gif,* the imperative of the verb *gifan,* 'to give,'
and was used in making a supposition, or asking for an admission, 'grant,' 'suppose.' In course of time its verbal
power was forgotten; its initial *g* was lost; and the word
remained as an introductory particle. But Horne Tooke was
wrong in supposing that because all particles were originally
nouns or verbs, they remain so still, and that their function is
not changed. For he keeps out of sight, as self-evident, the
other premiss, which is absolutely false—namely, that the
meaning and force of a word, now, and for ever, must be that

which it, or its root, originally bore. See Whateley, *Logic*, iii. § 14. Compare §§ 445, 461.

406. The usual definition given of an Adverb is to this effect :

'An Adverb is a word used to qualify verbs, adjectives, or other adverbs.'

But a distinction is set up between two kinds of adverbs :— (1) Simple Adverbs, (2) Relative or Conjunctive Adverbs.

(1) A Simple Adverb qualifies the word with which it is used : ' They came *yesterday*,' ' He is *always* ready.' Here the definition is immediately applicable.

(2) A Relative or Conjunctive Adverb is said to be one which not only qualifies the word with which it is used, but also serves to connect clauses in a sentence : as, ' He comes *when* he likes.'

In the present chapter we shall confine our attention to Simple Adverbs, reserving the second class for consideration in Chapter XIV.

407. A question may arise, how we ought to treat those sentences, where an adverb is used with a verb which merely expresses existence : as, 'he is *well*,' ' he is *asleep*.' It may be asked, for example, whether the word *well* is here an adverb or an adjective. In the English language, this word is so far adverbial, that it cannot be used to qualify a substantive : we cannot say ' a *well* man,' any more than we can say ' an *asleep* man.' Yet these words stand in the place of predicates, and have the force of adjectives. We may allow that they are adverbs used as predicates : see §§ 5, 6. But after all, this is only another proof how difficult it is to draw a sharp line between the various parts of speech.

In Greek, an adverb placed between an article and a noun, or with the article alone, has the force of an adjective. A similar construction is sometimes found in English : as,

Our *then* dictator,
Whom with all praise I point at, saw him fight.
Coriolanus, ii. 2.

Drink no longer water, but use a little wine, for thy stomach's sake, and thine *often* infirmities.—1 *Timothy*, v. 23.

408. Many adverbs are formed from adjectives, nouns, and pronouns.

1. *Adverbs derived from Adjectives.*

We saw, §§ 22, 23, that some adjectives appear to be used adverbially, having lost the final *e*, which in Anglo-Saxon was the distinctive mark of an adverb formed from an adjective. These are chiefly words of Anglo-Saxon origin: as, *clean, fast, hard, ill, late, long, loud, right, sore, soft, thick, wide, wrong.* We shall discuss these severally.

We also saw the origin of the termination -*ly*, which, though originally the mark of an adjective, came to be regarded as an adverbial suffix. In Anglo-Saxon -*lic* was an adjective termination, and -*lice* an adverbial. We have still in English some adjectives ending in -*ly*, as *god-ly, love-ly, lone-ly*; and to these we cannot add another -*ly* to form adverbs. The word 'godly' has an adverbial force in the phrase, 'to live soberly, righteously, and godly.'

409. We shall now consider those words, in which the adjective and adverbial forms coincide, in modern English:

clean. A.-S. *clæn*, adjective; *clæne*, adverb. The adverbial use of *clean*, in the sense of 'entirely,' is found in the authorised version of the Scriptures: as,

Is his mercy *clean* gone for ever, doth his promise fail for evermore?—*Psalm* lxxvii. 8.

The same usage still prevails in some provincial dialects.

fast. A.-S. *fæst*, adjective; *fæste*, adverb. The English *fast* is used as an adjective and an adverb: 'It was *fast*,' 'He ran *fast*.'

hard. A.-S. *heard*, adjective; *hearde*, adverb. In English, *hard* is an adjective, and both *hard* and *hardly* are adverbs, but with a difference of meaning. *Hard* means 'with force or severity,' as, 'He hits *hard*;' but *hardly* means *scarcely*. Some persons, wishing to be accurate, say, 'He hits *hardly*,' meaning 'He hits *hard*.' But 'He hits *hardly*' might mean 'He *scarcely* hits.'

ill or *evil*. A.-S. *yfel*, adjective; *yfele*, adverb. In English, *evil* and *ill* are used as adjectives; and *ill* as an adverb. The form *evilly* is sometimes found, but is not generally approved.

late. A.-S. *læt* or *lat*, adjective; *læte* or *late*, adverb. The English *late* is used as an adjective, and as an adverb: 'He was *late*,' 'He came *late*.' The form *lately* is used in the sense of 'recently.'

long. A.-S. *lang* or *long*, adjective; *lange* or *longe*, adverb. In English the form *longly* is never used.

loud. A.-S. *hlud*, adjective; *hlude*, adverb. The English *loud* is used as an adjective, and as an adverb: as,

> Curses, not *loud*, but deep.—*Macbeth*, v. 3.
> And the singers sang *loud*.—*Nehemiah* xii. 42.

The three forms *loud*, *aloud*, and *loudly*, are used as adverbs:

right. A.-S. *riht*, adjective; *rihte*, adverb. In English, the forms *right*, *aright*, and *rightly* are used as adverbs.

soft. A.-S. *seft* or *soft*, adjective; *sefte* or *softe*, adverb. In poetry, the adverbial use of *soft* is common: as, 'And *soft* he said,' '*Soft* sighed the flute.' In prose, *softly* is more common.

sore. A.-S. *sar*, 'sore, painful,' adjective; *sare*, 'sorely, painfully,' adverb. In older English, *sore* is used adverbially: as, 'He wept *sore*.'

thick. A.-S. *thic*, adjective; *thicce*, adverb. In English, the forms *thick* and *thickly* are used as adverbs.

wide. A.-S. *wid*, adjective; *wide*, adverb. The word is used as an adverb in this passage:

> Is my lord well, that he doth speak so *wide*?—*Much Ado*, iv. 1.

wrong. Horne Tooke derives this word from *wrung*, the participle of the verb *wring*, and explains it '*wrung* or *wrested* from the "right" or "ordered" line of conduct.' See *Diversions of Purley*, ii. 91, 101. Mr. Wedgwood, in his *Dictionary of English Etymology*, gives a similar explanation. He says *wrong* is 'what is *wrung* or turned aside from the right or straight way to the desired end.' He compares the Danish *vrænge*, 'to twist;' *vrang*, 'wrong;' and Old Norse *rangr*, 'wry,' 'crooked,' 'unjust.'

Wrong is used adverbially in the following passages:—

> *Portia.*   You must take your chance;
> And either not attempt to choose at all,

Or swear, before you choose, if you choose *wrong*,
Never to speak to lady afterward
In way of marriage; therefore be advised.
                Merchant of Venice, ii. 1.

           In choosing *wrong*,
I lose your company.   *Ibid.* iii. 2.

2. *Adverbs derived from Nouns.*

410. In many languages, nouns in an oblique case are used as adverbs. For example, the noun *home* is used adverbially, in the literal sense, ' to go *home* ' (aller à la maison), and in a figurative sense, to denote ' thoroughly,' ' entirely ; ' as,

    Cloten.   Where is she, sir ?   Come nearer ;
No further halting ; satisfy me *home*
What is become of her.
                 Cymbeline, iii. 5.

    Imogen.   That confirms it *home* :
This is Pisanio's deed, and Cloten's.
                 Ibid. iv. 2.

It is true that our *home* appears to be the same in form as the nominative *home*. But a reference to the Latin shows the distinction. The nominative in Latin is *domus*, but our *home* answers to the accusative *domum*, and our *at home* to *domi*.

Vossius observes of *domi focique* in Terence, *Eunuchus*, act iv. scene 7, that ' without doubt they are genitives used adverbially.' And Donatus goes further, calling not only these genitives, but accusatives and ablatives, adverbs. He thinks that *Romæ, Romam, Româ,* ignorantly considered nouns, are adverbs of place : ' *Romæ, Romam, Româ,* sunt adverbia loci, quæ imprudentes putant nomina. In loco, ut sum *Romæ*; de loco, ut *Româ* venio ; ad locum, ut *Romam* pergo.'—Sir John Stoddart, *Universal Grammar*, p. 106.

Professor Key thinks, that *domi* is not a genitive, but a ' dative in *i*, with the meaning *at* ;' so also, *humi*, ' on the ground,' *belli*, ' in war,' *ruri*, ' in the country.' He considers that this dative, denoting *place*, [hence termed by some grammarians the ' locative,'] maintained itself in certain words, in spite of the increasing tendency to express this idea by the preposition *in* and an ablative. See *Latin Grammar*, § 114, and compare § 952 of the same Grammar.

411. We seem to have genitive cases in the words *eftsoons* (' soon after '), *outwards, unawares,* and *needs*, in the phrase ' he *needs* must go.' *Sometimes* may be a genitive singular, or plural objective.

The following are possibly genitives :—

else,	old English	*el-es, ell-es, el-s*
once	„	*on-es*
hence	„	*henn-es*
thence	„	*thenn-es*
since	„	*sithen-s.*

The terminations *wise* and *ways* are liable to be confounded. The Anglo-Saxon *wise* is a noun signifying 'manner;' hence *otherwise* means 'in another manner.'

We find *always, noways,* and *nowise.* Dr. Adams, *Elements of the English Language,* § 396, says, that the form *ways* is not connected with the word *way,* 'a road.' But compare the German *alle-wege,* 'all-ways,' with the French *toujours,* 'all-days,' and *tous les jours,* 'all the days.'

412. *Whilom.* A.-S. *hwilum, hwylum, hwilon.* This is considered to be a dative plural from the nouns *hwil, hwile,* 'a while, time,' from which our adverb *a-while,* 'for a time,' is probably derived. According to this view, *whilom* signifies 'at whiles,' 'at times.'

seldom. A.-S. *seld, seldan, seldon.* Whether the termination *-om* in this instance marks a dative, may be doubted. *Seld* is used in composition by Shakespeare :

> *Seld*-shown flamens
> Do press among the popular throngs, and puff
> To win a vulgar station.
>
> *Coriolanus,* ii. 1.

413. *Beside, between,* and *because* are respectively 'by side,' 'by twain,' (i. e. 'near two '), and 'by cause,' also used in the sense of ' by reason.'

The *s* in *besides* is not easy to explain. Dr. Adams considers it as the mark of an old genitive *besid-es.* But this is very doubtful.

8. *Adverbs having the prefix a.*

414. The prefix *a* is of different origin in different adverbs, and demands very close examination.

1. Sometimes it represents the A.-S. preposition *an, in, on,* 'in,' 'on;' not only with substantives, as *a-bed, a-board, a-shore*; but also with adjectives, as *a-broad, a-loud.*

2. Sometimes it represents the preposition *of,* as *a-new,* 'of new,' *de novo* : compare ' of late.'

3. It also represents the A.-S. participial prefix *ge*, Early English *ye*: as *a-drift*.

4. It stands for the indefinite article *a*, as *a-while*, ' for a time.'

415. We shall take examples of each.

1. *a* representing the preposition *an, in, on,* 'in,' 'on.' *Prefixed to nouns.*

> *a-back, a-bed, a-blaze, a-board, a-breast, a-fire, a-foot, a-gape, a-ground, a-head, a-jar, a-loft, a-shore, a-slant, a-sleep, a-stern, a-stride.*

We may remark that several of these are nautical terms, and others might be quoted, as *a-midships, a-thwartships, &c.*

For the sake of illustration, we add the following notes:—

a-back. A.-S. *on bæc*, ' on back.'

> Gang thu *on bæc.*
> Go   thou *on back.*

' Get thee hence.'—*Matt.* iv. 10.

> Gá *on bæc.*
> Go *on back.*

' Get thee behind me.'—*Mark* viii. 33.

a-jar. This is explained as *on char*, ' on the turn,' ' half open,' from A.-S. *cer, cyr*, ' a turn,' verb *ceorran, cerran*, ' to turn.'

The form *on char* is used by Gawain Douglas, in his Translation of Virgil:

> Ane schot wyndo unschet ane litel *on char.*

See Wedgwood, *Dictionary of English Etymology*, ' *ajar*.'

a-loft. ' On loft,' ' up in the air.' German, *in der Luft*; Scottish, *in the lift*; so Burns:

> ' It is the moon, I ken her horn,
>   That's blinking *in the lift* sae hie,
>   She shines sae bright to wyle us hame,
>   But, by my sooth, she'll wait a wee!'

a-live. This word appears in older English as *on lyve, on liue*; as,

> By God, quoth he, that wol I tel as bliue,
> For prouder woman is there none *on liue.*
> Chaucer, Troilus.

Inquire whether *live* is here a noun ' life,' or an adjective as in the phrase ' on loud.'

We find the prefix before adjectives in *a-broad, a-loud, a thwart.*

The use of the preposition *in* or *on* with adjectives is not uncommon in modern English: we have 'in vain,' 'in secret,' 'on high.'

We have authority to prove the form *on broad*: Gawain Douglas (quoted by Sir John Stoddart, *Universal Grammar*, p. 77) has

> His baner quhite as floure
> In sign of battell did *on brede* display.

So too:

> But it ne was so sprede *on brede*,
> That men within might know the sede.
> > *Roman de la Rose.*

We observe *a* prefixed to adverbs in *a-far, a-gain.*

a-gain. A.-S. *on-gean, on-gen, an-gean, a-gean, a-gen.* In Anglo-Saxon *gen* itself is an adverb, signifying 'again,' 'moreover,' 'besides.'

416.—2. *a* representing the preposition *of.*

a-down. In Anglo-Saxon *dun* signifies 'a hill'; whence our North Downs, and South Downs. Then *of-dúne,* 'from hill,' 'downward,' 'down,' appears in the form *a-dúne, adún,* whence our 'a-down,' 'down.' Mr. Wedgwood compares the Old French *à mont,* 'to the hill,' and *à val,* 'to the valley,' used in the sense of 'upwards' and 'downwards' respectively. *Down* is used as a preposition.

a-new. That this word represents *of new,* we may infer from a line of Gawain Douglas:

> The battellis were adjoinit now *of new.*

Compare the Latin *de novo.*

417.—3. The participial force of *a* is seen in *a-drift*; unless the particle in that word is a verbal prefix. For, in Anglo-Saxon, there are two verbs, *drifan,* participle *ge-drifan*; and *a-drifan,* 'drive away,' participle *adrifed.*

The participial *a* may possibly be seen in *a-float, a-miss.*

418. The prefix *a* sometimes has the force of 'from,' 'out,' as, perhaps, in *a-way,* 'out of the way.'

The following words are of doubtful derivation: *a-ghast, a-kimbo, a-loof, a-skance, a-skant, a-skew, a-stray.* The roots of these words may be traced in other languages, but the force of the prefix *a* is not clear.

a-fore is from A.-S. *æt-foran,* 'at-fore.'

4. *Adverbs derived from Pronouns.*

419. Adverbs formed from Pronouns, sometimes termed Pronominal Adverbs, form a large class.

For instance, the words *here* and *there*; *hence* and *thence*, are manifestly derived from demonstrative pronouns; they signify 'at *this* place,' 'at *that* place;' 'from *this* place,' 'from *that* place.' Similarly *where* and *whence* are related to the interrogative and relative pronouns.

It so happens, that the adverbs of place exhibit three varieties, to express 'at a place,' 'from a place,' and 'to a place.' The adverbs of time, manner, and cause are not so completely developed. The following table will show this difference :—

1. Place	*here*	*there*	*where*
	hence	*thence*	*whence*
	hither	*thither*	*whither.*
2. Time		*then*	*when*
3. Manner		*thus*	*how*
4. Cause			*why.*

We observe, that *here, hence, hither,* are related to the pronoun *he*. *There, thence, thither* to *that*; *where, whence, whither* to *who, what.* Similarly *then* and *when* are related to *that* and *what.* *Why* is related to *who*; and *how* may possibly be related to both *he* and *who*.

420. The following table exhibits the same adverbs in another form :—

	Place	*Motion from*	*Motion to*	*Time*	*Manner*	*Cause*
Demonstrative	here	hence	hither	——	how	——
Demonstrative	there	thence	thither	then	thus	——
Interrogative and Relative	where	whence	whither	when	how	why

Compare Adams, *Elements of the English Language,*
§ 268.

421. These adverbs are frequently compounded with prepositions: as *here-of, there-of, where-of, here-in, there-in,
where-in, here-by, there-by, where-by,* and many others.

In the simple forms, *here* and *there* are principally confined to significations of *place*; whereas in the compounds
they may refer to *things*; for example, *here-of* may denote
' of this,' *there-of* may signify ' of that.' In our authorised
version of the Scriptures, we constantly find *thereof* in places
where a modern writer would employ *its*; as 'the candle-
stick and the branches *thereof*.' Shakespeare often uses
thereby and *whereby*, to signify ' with that,' ' upon that,'
' upon which,' ' in reference to which,' 'on which occasion : ' as,

> *Dame Quickly.* Well, *thereby* hangs a tale.
>> *Merry Wives of Windsor,* i. 4.

> *Musician. Whereby* hangs a tale, sir ?
>> *Othello,* iii. 1.

> *Hostess.* Canst thou deny it ? Did not goodwife Keech,
> the butcher's wife, come in then, and call me gossip
> Quickly ? coming in to borrow a mess of vinegar;
> telling us she had a good dish of prawns; *whereby*
> thou didst desire to eat some; *whereby* I told thee
> they were ill for a green wound ?
>> *2nd Hen. IV.* ii. 1.

422. The words *therefore* and *wherefore* mean ' for that,'
' for which,' denoting ' for that cause,' ' for which reason.'
The words *for* (Latin *pro*), and *fore* (Latin *præ*) are sometimes used indifferently. Mr. Wedgwood thinks they are one
and the same word. Sir John Stoddart, *Universal Grammar,*
pp. 80, 81, quotes from a Scottish Act of Parliament 1493,
James IV. ' *Heirfoir,* we, James, be the grace of God, King of
Scottis, &c.,' where *heirfoir* signifies ' for this cause,' ' for this
reason.' He has collected other compounds, from Scottish
Acts of Parliament, as, *heirintill,* ' in this,' ' within this,' *heirof,
heirupone, heirtofoir, heirafter, heiranent.*

NEGATIVE ADVERBS.

423. In Anglo-Saxon the common form of the negative is
ne, which precedes the verb: as,

And.iç hyne *ne* cuðe.

And I him *ne* knew.

'And I knew him not.'—*John* i. 33.

Mín tima *ne* com.

My time *ne* came.

'Mine hour is not yet come.'—*Id.* i. 4.

In Anglo-Saxon and in Early English, two negatives strengthen the negation, instead of destroying it as in modern English : so,

Ne geseah *næfre nan* man God.

Ne saw *never no* man God.

'No man hath seen God at any time.'—*John* i. 18.

He *never* yit *ne* vilonye *ne* sayde
In all his lyf unto. *no* maner wight.

Chaucer, *Canterbury Tales, Prologue,* 70.

i.e. ' Unto no manner of person.'

Ther was *no* man *nowher* so vertuous,
He was the beste begger in al his hous.

Id. 251.

This particle *ne* was commonly incorporated with the following verb : as,

I not,	' I ne wot,'	' I know not.'
I nabbe,	' I ne have,'	' I have not.'
I nolde,	' I ne wolde,'	' I would not.'
It nis,	' It ne is,'	' It is not.'
It nas,	' It ne was,'	' It was not.'

But soth to say I *not* what men him calle.

Chaucer, *Canterbury Tales, Prologue,* 286.

Nowher so besy a man as he ther *nas,*
And yit he semed besier than he was.

Ibid. 323.

424. Our usual negative *not* is a compound word, allied to *naught, nought,* and derived from the Anglo-Saxon *naht, nauht, noht,* which is compounded of the negative *ne* and *aht,* ' aught,' ' anything.' Compare the forms *nawht, na-wiht, na-wuht,* derived from *na,* ' not,' and *wiht,* ' anything.'

The negative *not* when used with the infinitive always precedes it ; with other forms of the verb, it either follows the verb, or stands between the principal verb and the auxiliary.

Grant me, O God, thy voice to know,
And *not* to be afraid.

Hemans.

He blenches *not*, he blenches *not*.

Scott, *Ivanhoe.*

I will *not* sing.

1*st Hen. IV.* iii. 1.

The use of the double negative, with a negative force, was common, down to a late period of our literature: so,

I *never was, nor never* will be, false.

Rich. III. iv. 4.

The man that hath no music in himself,
Nor is *not* moved with concord of sweet sounds,
Is fit for treasons, stratagems, and spoils.

Merchant of Venice, v. i.

This England never did, *nor never* shall
Lie at the proud foot of a conqueror.

King John, v. 7.

425. *Nay (nae),* and *no.*

A.-S. *ná* and *no.*
Ne eom ic *ná* Crist.
Ne am I *no (not)* Christ.
' I am not the Christ.'—*John* i. 20.

No thy læs, ' na-the-less,' ' never the less,' whence in older English we have ' natheless ' and nathless.'

In the Scottish dialect, *nae* and *no* are constantly used for *not*: as, ' This is *no* my ain lassie,' and ' This is *nae* my ain lassie.' I suspect that in the phrase ' whether or *no*,' we have a remnant of the old language; ' It is all the same, whether he comes, or *no*,' that is, ' whether he comes, or comes *not*.'

426. In ordinary English, *nay* and *no* are chiefly used in answers. As a general rule, *nay* is more common in provincial English, than in the language of the metropolis or the universities.

Sir Thomas More asserts a distinction between *nay* and *no*, corresponding to a distinction between *yea* and *yes*; and he censures Tyndal for not observing the difference in his translation of John i. 21 : ' And thei asked him, what then, art thou Helias? And he sayd I am not. Arte thou a prophet? And he aunswered, No.' According to Sir Thomas More, *No* should have been rendered *Nay*. But the reason assigned by Sir Thomas does not support his argument. He says: ' *No* aunswereth the question framed by the affirmative. As, for ensample, if a man should ask Tindall himself: ye an heretike mete to translate holy scripture into englishe? Lo to thys question if he will aunswere trew englishe, he must aunswere *naye* and not *no*. But and if the question be asked hym thus, lo ; Is *not* an heretyque mete to translate holy scripture into Englishe? To thys question lo if he wil aunswere true englishe he must aunswere *no* and not nay.'

According to these examples, the rule should have been stated thus:

Nay answers a question framed in the affirmative: as

Art thou a prophet? *Nay.*

No answers a question framed in the negative: as,

Art thou *not* a prophet? *No.*

See Marsh, *Lectures on the English Language*, xxvi. 582.

427. *No* appears in composition with many words. We say *no-where* and *no-whither*, but not *no-whence* or *no-when*. *No-how* is sometimes employed, but it is not considered elegant.

For *neither, nor*, see § 449.

428. *Never* is compounded of *ne*, 'not,' and *ever*. *Never* and *ever* are often confounded. *Never* is an adverb of time: as, ' Seldom or never has an English word two full accents.' *Ever* is an adverb both of time and of degree: as, ' Ever so rich,' ' Ever so good.' Hence ' charm he *ever* so wisely ' is now preferred to the older form, ' charm he *never* so wisely.'

We may remark that 'seldom *or never*' has the same force as 'seldom *if ever*;' but 'seldom *or ever*' is doubtful. Atterbury says:—

We seldom *or ever* see those forsaken who trust in God.

Here it is better to say 'or never.' See Angus, *Handbook*, § 567.

COMPARISON OF ADVERBS.

429. Some adverbs, expressing degree or quality, admit degrees of comparison: as,

Well,	better,	best.
Ill,	worse,	worst.
Little,	less,	least.
Long,	longer,	longest.
Much,	more,	most.
Soon,	sooner,	soonest.
Often,	oftener,	oftenest.

The use of the terminations *-er* and *-est* in forming the comparative and superlative of adverbs, was formerly much more common than at present: as,

Touching things which generally are received . . . . we

are *hardliest* able to bring such proof of their certainty as may satisfy gainsayers.—Hooker, *Ecclesiastical Polity*, v. 2.

That he may the *stronglier* provide.—Hobbes, *Life of Thucydides.*

The things *highliest* important to the growing age.— Shaftesbury, *Letter to Molesworth.*

The question would not be, who loved himself and who not, but who loved and served himself the *rightest,* and after the truest manner.—Id., *Wit and Humour.*

430. These forms are often found in the poets. So Shakespeare:

> O Melancholy !
> Who ever yet could sound thy bottom ? find
> The ooze, to show what coast thy sluggish crare
> Might *easiliest* harbour in ?
> *Cymbeline,* ir. 2.

where the folios have *easilest.*

> Thrice blessed they that master so their blood,
> To undergo such maiden pilgrimage ;
> But *earthlier* happy is the rose distilled,
> Than that which, withering on the virgin thorn,
> Grows, lives, and dies in single blessedness.
> *Midsummer Night's Dream,* i. 1.

On this passage Dr. Johnson remarks :—' Thus all the copies; yet *earthlier* is so harsh a word, and *earthlier happy,* for *happier earthly,* a mode of speech so unusual, that I wonder none of the editors have proposed *earlier happy.*' Steevens observes, that Pope did propose *earlier.* But the whole force of the passage consists in the contrast between ' earthly happiness ' in the one state, and ' heavenly bliss ' in the other. In this, as in many cases, Shakespeare was wiser than his editors.

And so Milton :

> Scepter and power, thy giving, I assume,
> And *gladlier* shall resign, when in the end
> Thou shalt be all in all, and I in thee
> For ever; and in me all whom thou lov'st.
> *Paradise Lost,* vi. 730–733.

> Which Eve
> Perceiving, where she sat retired in sight,
> With lowliness majestick from her seat,

And grace that won who saw to wish her stay,
Rose, and went forth among her fruits and flowers,
To visit how they prospered, bud and bloom,
Her nursery; they at her coming sprung,
And touched by her fair tendance, *gladlier* grew.
Paradise Lost, viii. 40–47.

To overcome in battle, and subdue
Nations, and bring home spoils, with infinite
Man-slaughter, shall be held the highest pitch
Of human glory, and, for glory done,
Of triumph to be styled great Conquerors,
Patrons of mankind, Gods, and Sons of Gods;
Destroyers *rightlier* called, and plagues of men.
Ibid. xi. 691–697.

Princes, Heaven's ancient Sons, ethereal Thrones,
Demonian spirits now, from the element
Each of his reign allotted, *rightlier* called
Powers of fire, air, water, and earth beneath!
Paradise Regained, ii. 121–124.

Each act is *rightliest* done,
Not when it must, but when it may be best.
Ibid. iv. 475–476.

Adverbs ending in *-ly* are now usually compared by *more*
and *most* : as, *briefly, more briefly, most briefly.*

431.—*rather.* The A.-S. adverb is *raðe, rað, raðe,* 'soon,'
'quickly;' comparative, *raðor, raður;* superlative,
raðost.

Hence 'I would *rather* do so,' means 'I would *more quickly*
do so,' 'I would *sooner* do so.'

He regned fiftene gere, and died all to *rathe.*—*Robert de
Brunne.*

i. e. 'all too soon.'

O dere cosin min, Dan John, she saide,
What aileth you so *rathe* for to arise?
Chaucer, *Shipmannes Tale.*

Some of our later poets use *rathe* as an adjective; so
Milton,

Bring the *rathe* primrose that forsaken dies.
Lycidas, 142.

In a note on this passage, Todd says that, in the West of

England there is an early species of apple called the *rathe-ripe*,
' early-ripe.'

432.—*liefer.* This is a comparative from the A.-S. adjective
leof, ' loved,' ' beloved,' ' dear.'

God saith, As verely as I lyve, I wilnot the death of a
sinner but had *liefer* hem to be converted and lyve.—
Joye, *Exposicion of Daniel.*

Shakespeare uses the positive form *lief*: as,

> But for my single self,
> I had as *lief* not be, as live to be
> In awe of such a thing as I myself.
> *Julius Cæsar,* i. 2.

Speak the speech, I pray you, as I pronounced it to you,
trippingly on the tongue; but if you mouth it, as
many of our players do, I had as *lief* the town-crier
spoke my lines.—*Hamlet,* iii. 2.

POSITION.

433. Adverbs are placed before the adjectives or participles which they qualify: as, ' It was *very* good;' ' a man
greatly beloved.'

So when one adverb qualifies another, the modifying adverb
stands first: as, ' not wisely, but *too* well.'

The qualifying adverb usually follows an intransitive verb:
as, ' He behaved *nobly,*' ' She walks *gracefully.*' When a
transitive verb is used with a following objective, the adverb
generally comes after the objective: as, ' He received them
kindly,' ' He treated his friends *generously.*' The reason is,
that the verb and the objective should be kept as closely together as possible. And if, for rhetorical purposes, it is desirable
to vary the order of the sentence, still the connection of the
verb and the objective should not be broken. We may say,
for example, ' He *kindly* received them;' ' *Generously* he
treated his friends.'

When an auxiliary verb and a participle are used, the
adverb may come between them: as, ' I have *lately* written to
him,' ' They were *kindly* received.' Or the adverb may
follow the participle, or the phrase: as, ' They were received
kindly;' ' I have written to him *lately.*'

When two auxiliaries are employed, their connection should
not be interrupted; the adverb should come between the

second auxiliary and the participle: as, 'They have been *badly* treated;' or it may follow the whole phrase, as, 'They have been treated *badly*.'

434. With regard to position no adverb presents greater difficulties than *only*. There is no absolute rule to determine whether it should precede or follow the word which it qualifies. In common conversation, great latitude is allowed. When we say 'I *only* spake three words,' most people understand 'I spake three words and *no more*;' though strictly the adverb qualifies the verb *spake*. Some critics would alter thus: 'I spake *only* three words;' but even then the position of *only* is ambiguous. Others would say, 'I spake three words *only*'; but that is rather formal, and there can be no doubt that, in ordinary conversation, most persons would say 'I only spake three words.'

In composition, however, greater attention is required; although the best writers are not always free from fault. Dryden says:

> Her body shaded with a slight cymarr,
> Her bosom to the view was *only* bare.
> > *Cymon and Iphigenia.*

But the poet means to say, that 'her bosom *only* . . . was bare.'

Dr. Johnson says:

> For thoughts are *only* criminal, when they are first chosen, and then voluntarily continued.—*Rambler*, No. 8.

As the words stand, they imply that 'thoughts are *nothing else* or *nothing more* than criminal,' in the case supposed; but the doctor meant, 'thoughts are criminal, *only when* they are first chosen, and then voluntarily continued.'

So this passage: 'Think *only* of the past, as its remembrance gives you pleasure,' should be, 'Think of the past, *only* as its remembrance gives you pleasure.'

435. In the following sentence the adverb *only*, from its position, gives a turn to the meaning quite different from that which the author intended:

> He had suffered the woodward *only* to use his discretion in the distant woods. In the groves about his house he allowed no marking-iron but his own.—Gilpin, *Forest Scenery.*

As the words stand, they imply that 'he had suffered the woodward' (or guardian of the wood), and no other person than the woodward, to use his discretion in the distant woods.' But from the context it is clear that 'he had suffered the woodward to use his discretion in the distant woods *only*.' The following arrangement would make the sentence plain:

> It was in the distant woods *only*, that he suffered the woodward to use his discretion. In the groves about his house he allowed no marking-iron but his own.

436. Gibbon writes:

> The province of Gaul seems, and indeed *only* seems, an exception to this universal toleration.—*Decline and Fall of the Roman Empire*, c. ii.

On this, Mr. Harrison remarks (*English Language*, p. 387), as the passage stands, it means that Gaul was in reality no exception at all; but that it *only seemed* an exception, 'whereas Mr. Gibbon means that the sanguinary religious rites of the Gauls, under the Druids, were not tolerated by the Romans, and that the restraint imposed upon the exercise of those rites was the only exception to the toleration which the Roman world freely enjoyed.'

Mr. Harrison has quite mistaken the meaning. Gibbon intends to say that the exception was merely apparent and not real; for the Romans, while abolishing human sacrifices and suppressing the dangerous power of the Druids, allowed the priests themselves, their gods, and their altars, to subsist in peaceful obscurity till the final destruction of Paganism.

The whole passage reads thus:

> The province of Gaul seems, and indeed only seems, an exception to this universal toleration. Under the specious pretext of abolishing human sacrifices, the emperors Tiberius and Claudius suppressed the dangerous power of the Druids; but the priests themselves, their gods and their altars, subsisted in peaceful obscurity till the final destruction of Paganism.

437. Again Gibbon writes:

> Pestilence and famine contributed to fill up the measure of the calamities of Rome. The first could be *only*

. imputed to the just indignation of the gods; but a monopoly of corn, supported by the riches and power of the minister, was considered as the immediate cause of the second.—*Decline and Fall of the Roman Empire*, c. iv.

' According to this form of expression,' says Mr. Harrison, ' the pestilence could be imputed, and *nothing more than imputed*, to the just indignation of the gods; whereas Gibbon means to say that the pestilence could not be attributed to the wicked administration of Commodus, but *solely* and *entirely* to the just indignation of the gods; *only* to the just indignation of the gods.'

Here there is no doubt of the meaning. The writer intends to say, that the pestilence could be imputed to the just indignation of the gods, and to that alone. No one would suppose that *only* is intended to qualify the word *imputed*; and where there is no possibility of mistake or ambiguity, we ought not to be too severe in our criticism.

438. We observe the following errors in the use of *not only*:

Addison writes,

> By greatness I do *not only* mean the bulk of any single object, but the largeness of the whole view.— *Spectator*, No. 412.

Dr. Blair, *Rhetoric*, Lecture xxi., says that the author intended to refer *only* to the ' bulk of a single object; ' and he corrects,

> I do not mean the bulk of any single object *only*, but the largeness of a whole view.

439. The adverbial phrase *at least* is often misplaced. Dr. Blair says,

> To support this weighty argument, he enters into a controversy with A. Gellius, in order to prove that Aristotle's Rhetoric was not published, till after Demosthenes had spoken *at least* his most considerable orations.—*Rhetoric*, Lecture xxvi.

It is evident that the phrase *at least* is intended to qualify the words ' most considerable; ' and it would have been better to say, ' had spoken the most considerable *at least* of his orations.'

440. The inconsistent combination of adverbs should be carefully avoided; for *almost never* it is better to say *scarcely ever*, or *very seldom*.

Dr. Blair writes:

> It produces that slow Alexandrian air, which is finely suited to a close, and for this reason such lines *almost never* occur together, but are used in finishing the couplet.—*Rhetoric*, Lecture xxxviii.

In the following passage we observe an unhappy combination and accumulation of adverbs:

> *How much soever* the reformation of this corrupt and degenerate age is *almost utterly* to be despaired of, we may yet have a more comfortable prospect of future times.—Tillotson, *Preface to Sermon*, 49.

CHAPTER XIII.

CONJUNCTIONS.

441. A Conjunction, from the Latin *con-junctio*, signifies a 'joining together,' and the term is applied to a certain class of 'connective' words. It is agreed that a conjunction joins *sentences* together; but whether a conjunction may be said to join individual *words* together, is a disputed point.

The early grammarians, says Sir John Stoddart (*Universal Grammar*, p. 159), included what we call *conjunctions* and *prepositions* under the general name of *connective* (σύνδεσμος). Subsequent writers, however, thought it would be convenient to separate these two classes of connectives. Hence, they gave to that which shows the relation of word to word the name of *preposition*; and to that which shows the relation of sentence to sentence the name of *conjunction*.

Harris expressly says (*Hermes*, ii. 2), 'the conjunction connects not words, but sentences;' and other grammarians have concluded that 'a preposition connects words; a conjunction connects propositions.'

Horne Tooke objects, that there are cases in which the words, commonly called conjunctions, do not connect sentences, or show any relation between them: as, 'Two *and* two make four.' ' John *and* Jane are a handsome couple.' He asks does *two* make four? Is *John* a couple? See *Diversions of Purley*, i. 209, 210.

442. Again, in this sentence, ' All men are black *or* white,' we cannot say that it is compounded of ' All men are black, *or* all men are white.' The meaning is not that ' all men are of one colour,' but that, ' If a man is not black, he is white; if he is not white, he is black.'

Sir John Stoddart's reply to this objection is not satisfactory. He contends that the conjunction varies the assertion, and does *potentially*, if not *actually*, combine different sentences. For example, in such a sentence as this : ' I bought a book for two *and* sixpence,' he argues that the purchaser did employ two shillings in buying, and he did employ sixpence in buying. So that if the meaning were fully developed, it would be, ' I bought a book for two shillings *and* I bought a book for sixpence.'

This is very far-fetched. Why, ' I bought the book for *half-a-crown*;' and if we choose to call half-a-crown ' two and sixpence,' that does not divide one sentence into two.

But Sir John Stoddart is not quite satisfied with his own theory; for he adds:

' Nevertheless, if any one contend that the word *and* in the above sentences does simply and solely connect together the nouns, then we say it must in such cases be called a *preposition*; but this will in no degree alter its property or character as a conjunction, when it is really employed to connect sentences.' *Universal Grammar*, p. 160.

443. This suggestion, that under certain circumstances *and* must be called a *preposition*, may be contrasted with Mr. Cobbett's notion that *with* has sometimes the force of a *conjunction*. He thinks (*Grammar*, § 246) that when *with* means *along with*, *together with*, *in company with*, it is nearly the same as *and*. Hence he would say, ' He, with his brothers, *are* able to do much.' ' If,' says he, ' the pronoun be used instead of *brothers*, it will be in the objective case : " He, with *them*, are able to do much." But this is no impediment to the including of the noun (represented by *them*) in the nominative. *With*, which is a preposition, takes the objective case after it; but if the persons, or things, represented by the words coming after the preposition, form part of the actors in a sentence, the *understood* nouns make part of the nominatives. " The bag,

M

with the guineas and dollars in it, *were* stolen ; " for if we say
" was stolen," it is *possible* for us to mean that the *bag only*
was stolen.   " Sobriety with great industry and talent, *enable*
a man to perform great deeds," and not *enables* ; for sobriety
alone would not enable a man to do great things.'

444. Here we observe a confusion of form and meaning.
As a general rule, a subject-nominative in the singular must
have a predicate-verb in the singular.   Any number of nouns,
under government of the preposition *with*, cannot discharge
the function of subject-nominatives.   Even if these nouns
represent persons, that makes no difference ; because they are
not formally stated as nominatives.   The use of the objective
in the phrase *with them*, when a pronoun is substituted for the
noun, evidently suggests a doubt to Mr. Cobbett's mind ; but
he has recourse to the artifice of ' understanding,' and he says
that ' the *understood* nouns make part of the nominatives.'
The brothers may have been actors in the work, but to maintain that ' they form part of the actors in the sentence ' is quite
wrong.   He confounds the actors in a work with the subject-
nominatives in a sentence, the meaning with the grammatical
form.   The sentence should be, ' He, with his brothers, *is* able
to do much.'

' The bag with the guineas and dollars in it *was* stolen ' is
equivalent to ' the bag containing guineas and dollars was
stolen.'   To allege that this construction might imply that
' the *bag only* was stolen' is a piece of special pleading.

445. Horne Tooke confounds the origin of conjunctions with their
function in a sentence ; and because all conjunctions may, as he thinks,
be etymologically traced to other kinds of words, he denies them to
be a separate sort of words or Part of Speech.

First of all, he endeavours to show that *if* and *an*, which have been
called *conditional* conjunctions, are merely the original imperatives of
the verbs *gifan* ' to give,' and *annan* ' to grant.'   Then he says that
those words which are called *conditional conjunctions* are to be accounted for in *all* languages, in the same manner as he has accounted
for *if* and *an*.   Not, indeed, that they must all mean precisely *give* and
grant ; but that they have some equivalent meaning, such as, *be it*,
suppose, &c.   Hence he discards all supposed mystery, not only about
these *conditionals*, but about all those words called *conjunctions* of
sentences.   He denies them to be a separate sort of words ; and he
contends, that the peculiar signification of each must be traced
among other parts of speech, by the help of the particular etymology
of each respective language.   ' In short,' he says, ' there is not such a
thing as a *conjunction* in *any* language, which may not, by a skilful
herald, be traced down to its own family and origin.'—*Diversions of
Purley*, pp. 109–126.

This may or may not be the case; but even if true, it is nothing to the purpose, unless we are prepared to admit the principle that Parts of Speech are to be arranged according to signification and not according to function. Sir John Stoddart allows that Horne Tooke has accurately 'traced home' some conjunctions; while, in regard to others, he has been mistaken. But whether right or wrong in the particular instances, his general doctrine can derive no benefit from them. To prove that a word performs one function at one time, does not disprove its performing another function at another time. To which we may add, that the etymology of a word has nothing necessarily to do with its function in a sentence; just as a man's pedigree is not absolutely connected with his occupation as a citizen.—See *Universal Grammar,* p. 159; and compare §§ 405, 461.

446. On the whole, there is no sufficient reason against the doctrine, that conjunctions may join together individual words; and by admitting this principle, we gain an advantage in the analysis of what are termed 'contracted sentences.' Take for example the sentence 'He saw *you and me.*' Now, if conjunctions cannot couple individual words, this sentence must be analysed thus: (1) He saw you, *and* (2) He saw me. Whereas, if we admit that the conjunction *and* couples *you* and *me*, we may take *you and me* as a compound objective dependent upon the verb *saw.*

Nor can there be any great difficulty in distinguishing between conjunctions and prepositions. A preposition can govern nouns, but a conjunction can not. The two words joined by a conjunction are both affected by a common concord or government: as, '*You and I* will accompany *him and them.* A conjunction can join sentences together, which is never the office of a preposition. When, for instance, *before* is used to introduce a subordinate sentence, as, 'He came *before* they left,' it ceases to be a preposition and becomes a conjunction (or conjunctive adverb). Lastly,. a preposition may denote various relations of time and place; while the relations denoted by a conjunction are chiefly three: (1) Addition, as *and*; (2) Alternation, as *or*; (3) Opposition, as *but.*

447. Accordingly we divide conjunctions into three classes: (1) Copulative; (2) Alternative; (3) Adversative. These are also termed Co-ordinating Conjunctions, because they join together co-ordinate sentences, that is, sentences of equal rank. The so-called Subordinating Conjunctions will be considered separately. See Chapter xiv.

1. COPULATIVE CONJUNCTIONS.

and. This is the chief of the class; it unites sentences, where the meaning *adds* something to that which precedes. Horne Tooke derives the word from *an-ad,* which he expounds *da congeriem.* But this is altogether doubtful. It has been doubted whether *anan* meant ' to give,' or ' to grant,' and of the syllable *ad* which he translates ' *congeriem,*' we know nothing.

Mr. Wedgwood, in his *Dictionary of English Etymology,* considers *and* and *an* the same word; but he does not throw any light upon the origin.

both ... and. For the sake of emphasis, sometimes each coordinate sentence has a prefix. The word *both* is frequently used with the first sentence. It is originally *ba-twa,* ' both-two,' also written *bu-twu* and *bu-tu.*

Other forms are employed to join co-ordinate sentences, as ' not only ... but,' ' partly ... partly,' ' first ... then.'

also and *likewise* are enumerated by Professor Bain among co-ordinating conjunctions, *Grammar,* p. 64. On the other hand, Mr. Mason says that these words are not conjunctions, but demonstrative adverbs.—*Grammar,* § 409.

Also is A.-S. *eall-swa,* ' all-so; ' and *likewise* is compounded of *like* and A.-S. *wise,* ' way,' ' manner; ' hence *likewise* signifies ' in like manner.' Professor Bain mentions a play upon the word *wise* in this compound : a remark was made upon the son of a judge who had succeeded to his father's office, but not to his ability, that ' he was a judge *also,* but not *like-wise.*' —*Grammar,* p. 64.

eke. This word, as a conjunction, has become nearly obsolete in modern English, with the exception of a few colloquial phrases, or in ballad poetry : as,

> John Gilpin was a citizen
> Of credit and renown ;
> A train-band captain *eke* was he,
> Of famous London town.
>
> *Cowper.*

But it is from the same root as the verb *eke,* ' to increase,' or, ' to make a thing last out.' The A.-S. *eac,* 'also,' is similarly connected with *eacan*, or *ecan*, ' to increase, add.' Compare the Latin *augeo*, and the Greek αὐξάνω.

> See Horne Tooke, *Diversions of Purley*, i. 134, 171; Sir John Stoddart, *Universal Grammar*, p. 163; and Wedgwood, *Dictionary of English Etymology*, ᴇᴋᴇ.

2. ALTERNATIVE CONJUNCTIONS.

448. The chief word of this class is *or*, which appears to be contracted from the A.-S. pronoun *oðer*, ' other;' though the A.-S. word corresponding in signification to *or* is *oððe*. In older English we find *other* in the sense of the modern *or*: as,

> Ful feole and fille
> Beoth yfounde, in heorte and wille
> That hadde levere a ribaudye
> Than to here of God, *other* of seynte Marie.
> > *Kyng Alisaunder.*

i. e. ' Than to hear of God, *or* of St. Mary.'

It is very important to distinguish between *or* when it is a true alternative, pointing out different things (Latin *aut*); and *or*, where it expresses an equivalent in other terms, and merely indicates a nominal difference (Latin *id est*, or *alias*).

Thus in the phrase ' Christ *or* the Messiah,' the particle introduces merely an alternative name, the person being the same. And the same occurs when we say, ' A Sovereign *or* Supreme Ruler always rules in England.' But when we say, ' A king *or* queen always rules in England,' the difference is real, indicating distinct persons.

> *nor.* This word is formed from the negative *ne* and *or*. The corresponding A.-S. word is *naðor, naðer, nawðer*, forms used sometimes as pronouns, and at other times as conjunctions.

We must remember that in some cases, *nor* has, not an alternative, but a copulative force, equivalent to ' and not : ' as,

> My ventures.are not in one bottom trusted,
> *Nor* to one place ; *nor* is my whole estate
> Upon the fortune of this present year.
> > *Merchant of Venice*, i. 1.

449. In alternative sentences, it frequently happens that each clause has an introductory particle, as *either* . . . *or*; and so in the negative, *neither* . . . *nor*.

either. This is one of the words variously -termed an adjective pronoun, or a pronominal adjective (see § 285). But it is also used as a conjunction. The A.-S. *ægther*, 'either,' is used in a similar manner; and so is the pronominal form *aðor, auðer.*

neither. This word is formed from the negative *ne* and *either.*

Where these particles are used, care should be taken to observe the correct sequence, *either* . . . *or*, *neither* . . . *nor.* Of course, *neither* . . . *or* is quite wrong. Some critics say that *nor* should not be used, unless preceded by *neither.* If this rule is sound, and it needs verification, it must be restricted to the alternative use of *nor.*

In poetry, *or* is frequently substituted for *either*, *nor* for *neither* : as,

> *Or* by the lazy Scheldt, *or* wandering Po.—*Goldsmith.*
> > *Nor* Simois,
> *Nor* rapid Xanthus' celebrated flood.
> > > > *Addison.*

Either, or, neither, nor should be placed next the words to which they refer : as, '*Neither* he, *nor* his friends were present.' ' It *neither* improves the understanding, *nor* delights the heart.'

3. ADVERSATIVE CONJUNCTIONS.

450. The principal conjunction in this class is *but*, originally a preposition, A.-S. *be-utan, butan*, 'by-out,' corresponding in form, and even in signification, to ' with-out.' See § 473.

In older English, the forms *bot* and *but* occur. Horne Tooke attempts to set up a distinction between them, and derives *bot* from the imperative of *botan*, ' to boot,' that is, ' to superadd.' See *Diversions of Purley*, i. 182, 306. This distinction is not considered tenable; but some of Horne Tooke's observations are well worth consulting. He shows that, in older English, *but* and *without* were indifferently used as prepositions and as conjunctions; but that in course of time, *but* ceased to be recognised as a preposition; and *without* ceased to be correctly used as a conjunction, p. 306.

His criticism of Locke's remarks on the word *but*, is given *ibid.* pp. 182–205.

The adversative force of *but* is emphatically marked in this passage :—

Messenger. Madam, madam——
Cleopatra. Antony's dead ?—
If thou say so, villain, thou kill'st thy mistress:
But well and free,
If thou so yield him, there is gold, there
My bluest veins to kiss : a hand, that kings
Have lipped, and trembled kissing.
Messenger. First, madam, he's well.
Cleopatra. Why, there's more gold. *But*, sirrah, mark;
we use
To say the dead are well.——
Messenger. Good madam, hear me.
Cleopatra. Well, go to, I will;
But there's no goodness in thy face.

 .   .   .   .   .   .

Messenger. Madam, he's well.
Cleopatra. Well said.
Messenger. And friends with Cæsar.
Cleopatra. Thou'rt an honest man.
Messenger. Cæsar and he are greater friends than ever.
Cleopatra. Make thee a fortune from me.
Messenger. *But yet*, madam——
Cleopatra.. I do not like *but yet*, it does alloy
The good precedence : fie upon *but yet*.
But yet is as a gaoler to bring forth
Some monstrous malefactor.

Antony and Cleopatra, ii. 5.

451. Professor Bain remarks (*Grammar*, p. 66) :—

It is a loose employment of this forcible word, to bring it in where there is no exception taken, or no arrest put upon a natural inference. 'No man taketh it from me, *but* I lay it down of myself.'

In this passage Professor Bain considers *but* unnecessary. It is also a common mistake to use it in the sense of *now*, as signifying the completion of a case in order to draw an inference. 'Men are mortal; *but* (for ' now ') we are men; therefore we are mortal.'

still. This word appears to be derived from the adjective *still*, and is used in the sense of *yet*. It is even more emphatic than *but*, suggesting a pause to hear what may be said by way of exception or opposition to the previous statements. 'Everything went against him, *still* he persisted.'

however. This word is compounded of *how* (see § 460, p. 253), and the word *ever.* It may be used either at the beginning of a sentence, or in the middle of a clause : as, ' However, this statement was not true ;' or, ' This statement, however, was not true.'

Conjunctions of these three classes are termed Co-ordinating Conjunctions, because they join together co-ordinate clauses, or independent affirmations. For the so-called Subordinating or Continuative Conjunctions see Chapter XIV.

Chapter XIV.

WORDS VARIOUSLY TERMED CONJUNCTIVE ADVERBS, ADVERBIAL CONJUNCTIONS, RELATIVE ADVERBS, SUBORDINATING CONJUNCTIONS, CONTINUATIVE CONJUNCTIONS, &c.

452. This is another case of Border Land. Just as we were unable to draw an exact line between Adjectives and Pronouns, so there is often a difficulty in discriminating between Adverbs and Conjunctions. Words which by some grammarians are termed Relative Adverbs or Conjunctive Adverbs, are termed by others Adverbial Conjunctions, Continuative Conjunctions, or Subordinating Conjunctions.

If we look closely, we shall find that there is some reason for this diversity of opinion ; because classes really have a tendency to run into one another. The great error consists in attempting to draw a hard and fast line, where the nature of things will not admit it.

453. First of all, we shall endeavour to explain what is meant by Relative Adverbs and Continuative Conjunctions. Beside the simple adverbs, which contain a positive meaning in themselves, as *well, truly,* there are others which refer to some adjoining clause for a completion of their meaning, as *when, where,* &c. These are to other adverbs what the pronoun is to the noun ; or rather, what the relative pronoun is to the demonstrative pronoun ; hence they are called *relative* adverbs. They are also called *connective* or *conjunctive* adverbs ; and by some grammarians are reckoned among *conjunctions.*

For example, to take *while*, as a specimen of this class. 'He came while . . . ' is not intelligible. The sense is suspended till some other clause is supplied: 'He came *while I was speaking.*—See Bain, *Grammar*, pp. 39, 40.

454. The term Continuative Conjunction appears to be taken from Harris's *Hermes*. Mr. Harris divides conjunctions into Connexive and Disjunctive; and then he subdivides the Connexives into (1) Copulatives, and (2) Continuatives. Accórding to him, the Copulative does no more than barely couple sentences, and is therefore applicable to all subjects whose natures are not incompatible. Continuatives, on the contrary, by a more intimate connection, consolidate sentences into one continuous whole, and are therefore applicable only to subjects which have an essential coincidence.

For example, it is not improper to say:

Lysippus was a statuary, *and* Priscian was a grammarian.
The sun shineth, *and* the sky is clear.

But it would be absurd to say,

Lysippus was a statuary, *because* Priscian was a grammarian;

though not absurd to say,

The sun shines, *because* the sky is clear.

The reason is that, with respect to the first, the coincidence is merely accidental; with respect to the last, it is essential, and founded in nature.—See Sir John Stoddart, *Universal Grammar*, p. 161; and compare Harris, *Hermes*, ii. 2.

> *Obs.*—These Continuative Conjunctions are otherwise termed Subordinative or Subordinating Conjunctions, as uniting subordinate or dependent clauses to the principal clause of a sentence.

It will be found that similar difficulties affect Relative or Conjunctive Adverbs and Continuative Conjunctions.

We may, indeed, distinguish by the form one class of Relative Adverbs—namely, those which are derived from pronouns: *where, whence, whither, when, how,* and *why.* But this will not lead us very far. Many other particles, of various forms, are referred to the same class.

455. We have further to consider the *function* of these words.

What we have called the Accessory Clause in Correlative Sentences, is termed by Becker and his followers an Adverbial

Clause, and is supposed to qualify some verb, or other word, in the Principal Clause. Mr. Mason says (*Grammar*, § 422): —'An Adverbial Clause is one which, in its relation to the rest of the sentence, is equivalent to an adverb. It stands in the adverbial relation to a verb, an adjective, or another adverb. Thus, in the sentence, 'He was writing a letter *when I arrived*,' the clause *when I arrived* indicates the time at which the action expressed by the verb *was writing* took place. The clause *when I arrived* is therefore in the adverbial relation to the verb *was writing*.'

Mr. Mason considers that the Relative or Conjunctive Adverbs, which introduce adverbial clauses, do double duty; they not only connect the adverbial clause with the principal clause, but themselves qualify the verb of the clause which they introduce. *English Grammar*, § 424. According to this view, in the example just given, *when* connects the adverbial clause *when I arrived* with the principal clause *He was writing a letter*; and also qualifies the verb *arrived* in the clause which it introduces.

Practically, it will be found that this view is encumbered with difficulties. Many of the explanations offered by Mr. Mason, in his examples, are exceedingly far-fetched. To my mind, the Correlative view is much simpler, and far safer. We have seen that these introductory particles are often used in pairs, one corresponding to the other. This is particularly the case in older stages of the language; and in the oldest forms we find two demonstrative particles, where a later stage exhibits a demonstrative and a relative. See § 49.

456. We have arranged these particles as they are used to express the various relations of Time, Place, &c.

	I.	II.
1. Time	*when*	*then.*
2. Place	*where*	*there.*
	whence	*thence.*
	whither	*thither.*
3. Manner	*as*	*so.*
4. Degree (equality)	*as*	*so.*
	the	*the.*
,, inequality	—	*than.*
5. Cause and Effect	*because*	*therefore.*
6. Reason and Conclusion	*because*	*therefore.*
7. Action (or State) and Result	(*so*)	*that.*

	I.	II.
8. Purpose and End	*so*	*that.*
9. Condition and Consequence	*if*	*then.*
10. Concession and Declaration	*though*	*yet.*

457. The following is an alphabetical list of the leading words (excluding compounds), which are employed as introductory particles. The terms assigned to them by Dr. Morell, Mr. Mason, and Professor Bain, respectively, are added. I would only remark, how unreasonable it is to expect schoolboys to distinguish accurately between Adverbs and Conjunctions, when the learned themselves cannot agree.

458. *although.* 'all though.' See 'though.' Compare *albeit, al-so.*

an.

Bottom. I will aggravate my voice so, that I will roar you as gently as any sucking dove; I will roar you *an* 't were any nightingale.

Midsummer Night's Dream, i. 2.

Dame Quickly. 'A made a finer end, and went away, *an* it had been any Christom child.

Henry V. ii. 3.

Prince Henry. What manner of man, *an* it like your majesty?
I. Henry IV. ii. 4.

Horne Tooke derives the word from *an*, the imperative of *anan*, 'to grant;' he compares it with *if*, which he takes from *gif*, the imperative of *gifan* 'to give;' and he thinks that *if* and *an* are words of very much the same meaning.—See *Diversions of Purley*, i. 106, 134, 153.

Mr. Wedgwood thinks that there is no radical distinction between *an* and *and*. He says, that in our older writers, it was not unusual to use *an* for *and*, and *and* in the sense of *an* or *if*.

First *an* for *and* :
He nome with hym of Engelond god knygt mony one,
An myd grete poer and much folc thuderwarde wende anon.

Robert of Gloucester, p. 319.

Secondly, *and* for *if* or *an* :
Me reweth sore I am unto hire teyde,
For *and* I shulde rekene every vice
Which that she hath, ywis I were to nice.

Chaucer, *Squire's Prologue.*

We find *an if, and if,* or simply *an*, in the sense of *if.*
I pray thee, Launce, *an if* thou seest my boy, bid him make haste. *Two Gentlemen of Verona*, iii. 1.

But *and if* that servant shall say in his heart, &c.
Luke xii. 45; compare *Matth.* xxiv. 48.

Nay, *an* thou dalliest, then I am thy foe.
Ben Jonson.

See Wedgwood, *Dictionary of English Etymology*: AN.
The derivation is doubtful. Mr. Wedgwood thinks that both sense and form might well be taken from the English *even*, in the sense of 'continuous,' 'unbroken,' 'level.'

I have sometimes thought, that the original idiom may have exhibited two co-ordinate forms; something like this :

And thou dalliest, *and* I am thy foe.

But this is a mere conjecture. Our wisest course is to reserve a knotty point like this for future investigation.

459. *after.* The same word as the preposition *after.*—See § 472. In older English the usual form of the Connective was *after that*; as, '*after that* I was turned, I repented.'—*Jeremiah* xxxi. 19.

Termed :

Continuative Conjunction.—*Morell.*

Usually called a Conjunction; better an Adverb.—*Mason.*

Relative Adverb, or Subordinating Conjunction.—*Bain.*

as. Horne Tooke thinks that *as* is the same as the German *es*, meaning *it*, *that*, or *which*. Sir John Stoddart approves of this etymology. Mr. Wedgwood, from a comparison of the German dialects, infers that *as* is a contraction from *all-so*, A.-S. *eallswa*, German *also*, *als*, as. Dr. Bosworth, in his Anglo-Saxon Dictionary, gives *swa* an 'adverb' *so, thus*; and *swa* a 'conjunction' *as, so as, as if.* In Anglo-Saxon we constantly find *swa . . . swa* used as correlatives, *swa hit is swa thu segst*, '*so* it is *as* thou sayest.' I have sometimes been tempted to think that *as* and *so* are both derived from *swa*.

Termed :

Continuative Conjunction.—*Morell.*

Conjunctive or Connective Adverb, in some cases; Subordinative Conjunction, in other cases.—*Mason.*

Relative or Conjunctive Adverb; or Subordinating Conjunction.—*Bain.*

because. 'by cause.' This word is not confined to sentences denoting Cause and Effect; but is used to signify 'by reason,' in sentences expressing the connection of Reason and Conclusion.

Termed:
Continuative Conjunction.—*Morell.*
Usually called a Conjunction; better an Adverb.—
Mason.
Relative Adverb or Subordinating Conjunction.—*Bain.*

before. The same word as the preposition *before.* See § 481.
· In older English, the usual form of the Connective
was *before that*: as, '*Before that* certain came from
James, he did eat with the Gentiles.'—*Galatians* ii. 2.
Termed:
Continuative Conjunction.—*Morell.*
Usually called a Conjunction; better an Adverb.—
Mason.
Relative Adverb or Subordinating Conjunction.—*Bain.*

460. *for.* The same word as the preposition *for.* See § 474.
In older English, a common form of the connective is *for
that*: as,

I doubt not but great troops would be ready to run; yet
for that the worst men are most ready to remove, I
would wish them chosen by discretion of wise men.—
Spenser, *State of Ireland.*

We also find the forms *for as much as* and *for why*:

For as much as the thirst is intolerable, the patient may
be indulged the free use of spaw water.—Arbuthnot,
On Diet.

Solyman had three hundred field-pieces, that a camel
might well carry one of them, being taken from the
carriage; *for why* Solyman purposing to draw the
emperor unto battle, had brought no greater pieces of
battery with him.—Knolles, *History of the Turks.*
Termed:
Continuative Conjunction.—*Morell.*
Subordinative Conjunction.—*Mason.*
Subordinating Conjunction.—*Bain.* ·

how. A.-S. *hu*, originally an Interrogative Adverb, 'how?'
'in what manner?'
It is frequently used to introduce indirect questions: as,
'they asked, *how* he was.'
Termed:
Continuative Conjunction.—*Morell.*
Relative Adverb.—*Mason.*

461. *if.* This word plays a very important part in Horne Tooke's argument about the origin of conjunctions. He contends that many of them were originally the imperative mood of verbs, and that *if* was *gif*, 'give,' 'grant:' as,

Forgiff me, Virgil, *gif* I thee offend.

Douglas, Preface, p. 11.

He shows that *be, set,* and many other verbs, are similarly used. See the whole argument, *Diversions of Purley,* i. 103, 134, 149.

To the passages there quoted, we may add the following :—

> *Petruchio.* I will attend her here,
> And woo her with some spirit when she comes.
> *Say* that she rail; why then I'll tell her plain
> She sings as sweetly as a nightingale :
> *Say* that she frown; I'll say she looks as clear
> As morning roses newly washed with dew :
> *Say* she be mute, and will not speak a word;
> Then I'll commend her volubility,
> And say she uttereth piercing eloquence :
> *If* she do bid me pack, I'll give her thanks
> As though she bid me stay by her a week;
> *If* she deny to wed, I'll crave the day
> When I shall ask the banns, and when be married.

Taming of the Shrew, ii. 1.

Sir John Stoddart says that the etymology deriving *if* from *gif*, the imperative of *gifan* 'to give,' was proposed by Skinner and has never been disputed. 'Mr. Tooke therefore is right so far as he follows Skinner, who first showed the connection between *if* and *give*; but he is wrong when, trusting to his own theory, he says, " Our corrupted *if* has always the signification of the English imperative *give* and *no other*." In short he is right where he is not original, and original only where he is not right.'

Some modern grammarians reject Horne Tooke's etymology altogether, because they cannot find traces of the initial *g* in the cognate languages. Mr. Garnett says, that a comparison of the cognate languages proves that *if* is neither an imperative of *give* nor of any other verb; and quotes with approval the remark of Dr. Jamieson, in his *Scottish Dictionary,* that neither the Gothic *jabai,* the Alemannic *ibu, ob, oba,* nor the Icelandic *if* or *ef* can be formed from the verbs denoting to *give* in those languages. See Garnett, *Philological Essays,*

p. 24. Mr. Wedgwood compares the Gothic *iba*, 'whether;' Old High German *ibu, ob*, 'if,' 'whether;' Dutch *of, oft*, 'if,' 'whether,' 'or;' German *ob*, 'whether;' Old Norse *ef*, 'if,' *efa, ifa*, 'to doubt.' He appears to think that the notion of 'doubt' lies at the root of the word. But the argument from analogy is not absolutely decisive. It is possible, that of all the cognate languages, English alone exhibits this derivative. There is a fair amount of probability in favour of this etymology.

> Termed :
> Continuative Conjunction.—*Morell.*
> Subordinative Conjunction.—*Mason.*
> Subordinating Conjunction.—*Bain.*

462. *lest.* The A.-S. adverb *læs*, 'less,' is used with the particles *the* and *thy* in the sense of *lest*: as,

the læs .	.	.	.	lest
the læs the	.	.	.	„
thy læs .	.	.	.	„
thy læs the :	.	.	.	„

In English *lest* is generally used in the sense of *that not*.

> Termed :
> Continuative Conjunction.—*Morell.*
> Subordinative Conjunction.—*Mason.*
> Subordinating Conjunction.—*Bain.*

463. *since.* In Anglo-Saxon we find the adjective *sið*, 'late,' and an adverb of the same form, 'lately.' We also find *siððan*, 'afterwards,' 'after that,' 'then,' 'since,' 'further.' In Old English we meet with the forms *sith, sithen, sithence*, from which *since* appears to be derived.

> And he axide his fadir how long is it *sithe* this hath falle to him ?—Wiclif, *Mark* ix.

> For *sithen* the fadris dieden.—2 *Peter* iii.

From signifying consequence in time, *since* is transferred to consequence in reasoning and causation : as,

> O mighty God, if that it be thy will,
> *Sin* thou art righteous judge, how may it be, &c.
> Chaucer, *Man of Lawe's Tale.*

See Wedgwood, *Dictionary of English Etymology.*

> Termed :
> Continuative Conjunction.—*Morell.*

Since: expressing a reason, Subordinative Conjunction.—*Mason.*

Adverbial clauses relating to Time begin either with the relative adverbs which denote time, or with the so-called conjunctions, *before, after, since*, &c. These words have no adverbial relation to any word in the clause which they introduce.—*Mason*, § 424.

The words *before, since, after, until*, are usually set down as conjunctions; but they are in reality prepositions. The construction really consists of a preposition followed by a substantive clause. *After* [*that*] *I arrived* is tantamount to *after my arrival*.—*Id.* § 289.

[This remark is applicable to *before* and *after*; but there is no evidence to show that *since* was originally a preposition.]

Subordinating Conjunction.—*Bain.*

so. A.-S. *swa*, ' so,' ' thus.'

Termed:

Adverb.—*Mason*, §§ 433, 435.

so, ' by that,' ' to that measure.' Adverb of Comparison.—*Bain*, p. 43.

so, ' therefore.' Co-ordinating Conjunction (Illative). *Id.* p. 67.

464. *than.* Etymologically *than* and *then* are equally derived from A.-S. *thonne* or *thœnne*. In older English we constantly find *then* for *than*. In the following passages the particles are employed in significations precisely the reverse of our present usage :—

> *Than* hadde the douke ich understond,
> A chief steward of alle his lond.
> *Amis and Amiloun.*

> Hire swyre is whittore *then* the swon.
> *Ballad on Alisoun.*

i.e. ' Then had the duke, &c.' ' Her neck is whiter *than* the swan.'

Termed:

Continuative Conjunction.—*Morell.*

' *Than* is commonly set down as a conjunction. This is a mistake. It is a conjunctive adverb.'—*Mason*, § 267, *note*; compare the examples discussed, *Mason*, §§ 545–571.

Relative or Conjunctive Adverb.—*Bain.*

that. The same word as the pronoun *that.* Horne Tooke discourses largely on this word. He endeavours to show that ' the word *that*, call it as you please, either *Article* or *Pronoun* or *Conjunction*, retains always one and the same signification.'—See *Diversions* of Purley, i. 81, 135, 256; ii. 61, 514, 555.

Termed :
Continuative Conjunction.—*Morell.*
Conjunctive or Connective Adverb, in some cases;
Subordinative Conjunction, in other cases.—*Mason.*
Subordinating Conjunction.—*Bain.*

465. *therefore.* 'for that,' 'for that cause,' 'for that reason.'

Termed :
Conjunctive Adverb, or Illative Adverb.—*Morell.*
'Such words as *therefore, consequently,* &c., are not conjunctions, but demonstrative adverbs.'—*Mason,* § 408; compare § 292 and §§ 266, 285.
Adverb, denoting Cause and Effect.—*Bain,* p. 45.
Co-ordinating Conjunction of the Illative Class, expressing effect or consequence.—*Id.* p. 67.

though. A.-S. *theah*; Old English *thah*:
Richard, *thah* thou be ever trichard,
Tricchen shalt thou never mo.
Song on Richard of Cornwall.

Termed :
Continuative Conjunction.—*Morell.*
Subordinative Conjunction.—*Mason.*
Subordinating Conjunction.—*Bain.*

thus. A.-S. *thus,* 'thus,' 'so.' Compare A.-S. *thœs,* 'of this,' 'for this,' 'thus,' probably from *thœs,* the genitive of the pronoun *thœt.*

Termed :
Adverb.—*Morell.*
Co-ordinating Conjunction of the Illative Class.—*Bain.*

466. *unless.* Skinner suggests two derivations of this word: (1) *one-less,* that is, 'one being taken away ;' or rather, (2) from *onlesan,* 'to dismiss,' 'set free,' as though it were *Hoc dimisso.* Horne Tooke accepts the latter derivation, and sees another proof in favour of his theory that conjunctions are often formed from the imperative mood of verbs; here from *onles,* 'dismiss.'
He quotes several passages to prove that the word was written *onlesse* and *onles* : as,
It was not possible for them to make whole

Christes cote without seme, *onlesse* certeyn
great men were brought out of the way.—
Trial of Sir John Oldcastle, anno 1413.

This peticion cannot take effect *onles* man be made
like an aungel.—Lupset, *Treatise of Charitie,*
p. 66.

We have the change of *on* to *un* in *un-to* for *on-to,*
un-til for *on-till.*

Less is the comparative adjective; and in form,
on-less may be compared with *on high*; with *aloud,*
that is ' *on-loud,*' and *below,* that is ' by-low.'

Termed:

    Continuative Conjunction.—*Morell.*
    Subordinative Conjunction.—*Mason.*
    Subordinating Conjunction.—*Bain.*

until. The same word as the preposition *until,* that is,
on-till.

Termed:

    Continuative Conjunction.—*Morell.*
    Subordinative Conjunction.—*Mason.*
    Subordinating Conjunction.—*Bain.*

467. *when.* A.-S. *hwænne, hwenne, hwonne* ' when,' ' at
what time.'

Termed:

    Continuative Conjunction.—*Morell.*
    Conjunctive, Connective, or Relative Adverb.—*Mason.*
    Relative or Conjunctive Adverb; or Subordinating
Conjunction. The Relative-Adverbs introducing clauses
of Time, may be called Subordinating Conjunctions of
Time: ' when,' ' while,' ' as,' ' until,' ' ere,' ' before,'
' after.'—*Bain,* p. 72.

where, whither, whence.

where. A.-S. *hwær,* ' at what place.'

whither. A.-S. *hwæder,* ' to what place.'

whence. A.-S. *hwanan, hwanon.*—Old English *whannes,
whennes,* ' from what place?'

Termed:

    Continuative Conjunctions.—*Morell.*
    Conjunctive, Connective, or Relative Adverbs.—
Mason.

Relative or Conjunctive Adverbs.—*Bain.*

wherefore. ' for which,' ' for which cause,' ' for which reason.'

Termed :
Conjunctive Adverb of the Illative Class.—*Morell.*
Demonstrative Adverb (see *therefore*).—*Mason.*
Adverb denoting Cause and Effect.—*Bain*, p. 45.
Co-ordinating Conjunction of the Illative Class.—
Id. p. 67.

whether. A.-S. *hwæðre,* called by Dr. Bosworth a Conjunctive Adverb ; derived from the pronoun *hwæðer* ' whether ? ' ' which of two ? '

Termed :
Subordinative Conjunction.—*Mason.*
Subordinating Conjunction.—*Bain.*

while. This word is derived from the A.-S. noun *hwil* *hwile,* ' a while, ' time,' ' duration.' In Anglo-Saxon we find the phrase *tha hwile,* ' the while,' and *tha hwile the,* ' the while that.'—*Matth.* v. 25.

Termed :
Continuative Conjunction.—*Morell.*
Conjunctive or Connective Adverb.—*Mason.*
Relative or Conjunctive Adverb ; or Subordinating Conjunction.—*Bain.*

why. A.-S. *hwi,* ' why,' ' wherefore,' ' for what cause,' ' for what reason.'

According to Dr. Bosworth, it is the ablative case of the interrogative pronoun *hwa, hwæt,* ' who ? ' ' what ? '

Termed :
Conjunctive or Connective Adverb.—*Mason.*
Relative or Conjunctive Adverb.—*Bain.*

468. *yet.* A.-S. *gyt.* Horne Tooke would derive this word from *getan* or *gytan,* ' to get ; ' but this is doubtful. Sir John Stoddart calls the word an Adverb, but remarks, ' where *yet* is used for " also," " moreover," or "nevertheless," it is properly to be considered as a Conjunction ; but the distinction between a Conjunction and a Relative Adverb is not always easy to be drawn.'—*Universal Grammar,* p. 87.

Termed :

Continuative Conjunction.—*Morell*, p. 90.
Conjunction or Conjunctive Adverb of the Adversative Class.—*Id.* p. 98.
Co-ordinating Conjunction of the Arrestive Class.—*Bain*, p. 66.

CHAPTER XV.

PREPOSITIONS.

469. Prepositions were originally, and for a long time, classed with conjunctions; and when first separated from them, were only distinguished by the name of Prepositive Conjunctions.

Some of the Greek grammarians, considering that prepositions connect words, as conjunctions connect sentences, ranked both the preposition and the conjunction under the common head of *connective* (σύνδεσμος); and the Stoics called the preposition the ' preposed connective ' (σύνδεσμος προθετικός).

In the Greek and Latin languages, the words thus distinguished were most commonly *placed* immediately *before* the substantives which they governed; and this accidental circumstance was unfortunately selected by some grammarians to give name to the *pre-position*.

If this was their notion, the view was inaccurate; for even in Latin, *tenus* was always placed *after*.the noun which it governed. So Plautus has *mederga* for *erga me*; and *cum* occupies a similar position in the words *mecum, tecum, nobiscum, vobiscum.*

To meet these variations, some grammarians were not ashamed to make a class of *postpositive prepositions*, which is a manifest contradiction of terms; for the same word cannot be at once ' after-placed ' and ' fore-placed.'

There is, however, one aspect of the case, which may account for the origin of the term. In composition with verbs, in Greek and Latin, the preposition generally precedes the verb, and forms one word with it; whereas in English (and this we shall find to be a very important fact), the preposition usually follows the verb, and is written separately.

470. A preposition is a word which is used :

1. To express the relation in which one substantive stands

to another: as, 'The middle *of* the street,' ' The hat *on*
the table,' ' the crumbs *under* the table.'

2. To connect a substantive with a verb : as, ' He went
through the city,' ' They passed *under* the bridge.'

3. To connect a substantive with an adjective: as, ' He
is ready *for* anything.'

4. In composition with verbs; most commonly after the
verb: as, 'carry *off*,' ' run through,' ' take out.' In some
cases, however, the preposition is prefixed, as ' over-
throw,' ' under-go.' It is curious tò observe, that to
' set up ' is to ' establish ; ' but to ' upset ' is to ' over-
turn ; ' and to ' take up ' a cause is to ' undertake ' it.

Certain prepositions correspond to the case-endings of nouns
in Greek and Latin. Thus *of* answers to the genitive case;
to and *for* to the dative; *from*, *by*, and *with* to the ablative.

As English is a mixed language, we shall find it necessary
to consider the English prepositions, strictly so called, and the
Latin prepositions. The necessity of this will fully appear
when we discuss the subject of Composition.

471. The simple original prepositions in English are these :
*a, at, but, by, for, fore, from, in, on, of, over, out, till, to,
through, up, with.*
Down and *since* are employed as prepositions.

472. *a.* The word *a* appears to be a remnant of the Anglo-
Saxon preposition *an*, ' in,' ' on.' It is used before the
gerund (or infinitive) in *-ing*: as, ' a-coming,' ' a-going,'
' a-walking,' ' a-shooting; ' and before nouns, as ' a-bed,'
' a-board,' ' a-shore,' ' a-foot.' Our sailors have preserved many specimens of this, and of other old English
forms.

Dr. Wallis supposes *a* to be the preposition *at*. Dr. Lowth rather
thinks it is the preposition *on*. For *at* has relation chiefly to place;
whereas *on* has a more general relation, and may be applied to action,
as well as to place : ' I was *on* coming, *on* going, &c.' So, likewise, the
phrases above-mentioned, ' a-bed,' &c., exactly answer to ' on bed,' ' on
board,' ' on foot.' Dr. Bentley plainly supposed *a* to be the same with
on, as appears from the following passage :

> He would have a learned University to make barbarisms *a*
> purpose.—*Dissertation on Phalaris*, p. 223.

See Lowth, *English Grammar*, p. 95.

at. A.-S. *æt.*

after. A.-S. *æfter.*

The root is *af*: Gothic *afar*, 'after,' 'behind : ' A.-S. *æft*, *æftan*, *æfter*. According to Grimm, the final *tar* is the comparative termination, and the root *af* is the equivalent of the Greek ἀπό, Latin *ab*.

473. *but*. This is a true preposition, and is originally *be-out*, 'by-out;' A.-S. *be-utan*, *butan*, 'without,' 'except,' 'besides.' It is curious that *but* (be-out) has almost lost its power as a preposition, and remains in force as a conjunction ; while *with-out* is used as a preposition, and not, in modern English, as a conjunction.

In the Scottish dialect we find *ben*, from A.-S. *binnan*, 'within,' the precise correlative of *but*, ' without;' ' *but* and *ben*,' 'without (the house) and within.' Then the terms ' but and ben' are applied to the outer and inner rooms of a house consisting of two apartments. See Wedgwood, *Dictionary of English Etymology*.

Horne Tooke quotes several passages from Gawin Douglas, where the word is used as a preposition. He tries to distinguish between *but*, ' be out,' and *bot*, ' moreover,' ' to boot;' but the distinction is now considered untenable. Among the passages quoted from Gawin Douglas we read,

> *Bot* thy werke shall endure in laude and glorie,
> *But* spot or falt condigne eterne memorie.
> *Preface to Translation of Virgil*, p. 3.

i.e. ' without spot or fault.'

> *Bot* sen that Virgil standis *but* compare.
> *Prologue to Booke* IX. p. 272.

i.e. ' without comparison.'

We add a passage from Dunbar :

> For warld's wrak *but* welfare nought avails.

i.e. ' without welfare.'

Although *but* is no longer used as a preposition before nouns, we have instances of its usage with pronouns: as, ' There was no one present *but me*,' 'They all went away *but him*.' So entirely has the prepositional use of *but* been forgotten, that many grammarians regard the word as a conjunction only. Hence they consider the phrases ' but me' and 'but him' violations of grammar. They regard *but* as a conjunction in all cases ; and they condemn such sentences as these:

> There was no one present but *me*.
> They all went away but *him*.

They correct thus :

> There was no one present but I.
> They all went away but he.

i.e. ' but I [was present],' ' but he [went not].' See § 193. Compare § 550.

by. A.-S. *be*, *bi*, *big*, ' near,' ' beside.'

down. See *adown*, § 416.

474. *for.* A.-S. *for,* ' on account of,' ' because of.'
fore. A.-S. *foran,* ' before.'

W.edgwood, in his *Dictionary of English Etymology,* classes *for* and
fore together. He compares the Gothic *faur, faura,* and the Old Norse
fyrir, ' before,' ' fore, ' for,' with the German *vor,* ' for,' and *für,* ' for.' He
thinks the radical meaning in both cases is ' in front of.' Like the Latin
præ and *pro,* the particles *for* and *fore* may be connected etymologically;
indeed, they may originally have been the same word. But their
difference in usage must be observed; and, in composition, both must
be carefully distinguished from the inseparable prefix *for,* as in *for-*
give, *for*-get, *for*-lorn.

from. A.-S. *fram.*

475. *in.* }
on. } A.-S. *on, in, an.*

In English the preposition *in* is used much more widely than in
Anglo-Saxon. I have remarked that the people of Cork retain many
old uses of the form *on,* as, ' He lives *on* the South Mall,' ' I saw that
report *on* the " Constitution" (newspaper).' So in Italian, ' Si legge *sui*
giornali.'

476. *of.* A.-S. *of,* ' of,' ' from,' ' out of,' ' concerning.'

Of is used to denote what is called the genitive case in Greek and
Latin. It expresses a variety of relations.
(1) Sometimes it has a *partitive* meaning, that is, it denotes the
relation of a part or parts to the whole, as ' the wing *of* an eagle,' ' the
walls *of* the town.'
(2) Sometimes it is used in connection with the properties or qualities
of an object: as, ' the length *of* the room,' ' the strength *of* a lion,' ' the
sweetness *of* honey,' ' the height *of* the mountain.'
(3) Sometimes it has an *objective* force: as, ' the love *of* our neighbour,' meaning, ' love *towards* our neighbour.'

> *Obs.*—There may be an ambiguity in the use of this preposition.
> For example, ' the love *of* God' may signify either
> ' the love exhibited by God towards man,' or ' the love
> felt by man towards God.' The former may be other-
> wise rendered ' God's love,' but not the latter.

(4) *Of* has sometimes an *adjective* meaning: as, ' a crown *of* gold,'
for ' a golden crown ;' ' an act *of* grace,' for ' a gracious act.'
(5) *Of* is sometimes used to connect nouns in apposition: as, ' the
city *of* London,' ' the city *of* Rome (*urbs Roma*). See § 143; and
compare Bain, *English Grammar,* p. 48.
This preposition is sometimes contracted to *o'*: as, ' one *o'*clock,' for
' one *of* the clock.'

over. A.-S. *ofer,* ' over,' ' above,' ' upon,' ' beside,' ' beyond.'
Dutch, *over.* German, *über.*

out. A.-S. *ut, ute,* ' out,' ' without.'
This preposition is constantly used in composition : as,

'turn out,' 'send out.' But it is not found alone before nouns; though 'out of' and 'out from' are usual.

477. *since.*

In Anglo-Saxon we find the adjective *siδ*, 'late,' and an adverb of the same form, 'lately.' We also find *siδδan* 'afterwards,' 'after that,' 'then,' 'since,' 'further.' In Old English we meet with the forms *sith*, *sithen*, *sin* (Scottish *syne*), *sithence*; and from the last our English *since* appears to have come. The old forms were never used as prepositions; but the English *since*, though commonly used as a conjunction, has a true prepositional force in such sentences as these: 'I have not seen him *since* Tuesday,' 'I have not heard of them *since* last Christmas.' See § 463.

through. A.-S. *thurh*, 'through,' 'by.'

478. *till.* A.-S. *til.*

The English *till* is not used with words denoting motion to a place; we cannot say, with the Scots, 'he's ganging *till* Montrose.' Its use in English is chiefly confined to relations of time. *Until* appears to be compounded of 'on-till,' and used to be written 'untill.'

'Dr. Grimm remarks that the English *until*, "donec," "usque," though Old English (and not Anglo-Saxon, which uses *oδ*), appears to be a real Danish form.'—Bosworth, *Anglo-Saxon Dictionary.*

to. A.-S. *to*, 'to,' 'towards,' 'for.'

under. A.-S. *under*; German *unter.*

up. A.-S. *up*; German *auf.*

with. A.-S. *wiδ.*

The Anglo-Saxon *wiδ* has several meanings: (1) 'against,' 'opposite;' (2) 'near,' 'about,' 'by,' 'before;' (3) 'towards,' 'with,' 'for,' 'through.'

The usual signification in English is 'together with,' denoting companionship: as,

> *Shylock.* I will buy *with* you, sell *with* you, talk *with* you, walk *with* you, and so following; but I will not eat *with* you, drink *with* you, nor pray *with* you.
>
> *Merchant of Venice,* i. 3.

It is also employed to denote agency or instrumentality: as, 'fed *with* the same food,' 'hurt *with* the same weapons.' More commonly *by* is used to denote agency, *with* to express instrumentality: as, 'the field was dug *by* the labourer, *with* his spade.'

Other prepositions are formed by combining two simple prepositions together; as *in-to*, *un-to* (i.e. on-to), *un-til* (i.e. on-till), *up-on*, *with-in*, *with-out*, *through-out*, *out of*, *out from.*

479. Some prepositions exhibit a derivative form, especially those which are made by help of the prefixes *a* ('on,' 'in,') and *be* ('by'). These are found in composition with prepositions, nouns, and even adjectives, something like our phrases ' in vain,' ' in secret.'

We have: *a-baft*, *a-bout*, *a-bove*, *a-gainst*, *a-long*, *a-mid*, *a-mong*, *a-round*, *a-thwart* ; *be-fore*, *be-hind*, *be-low*, *be-neath*, *be-side*, *be-tween*, *be-twixt*, *be-yond*.

480. *a-baft*. A.-S. *æftan*, *be-æftan*, *bæftan*, ' after,' ' be-hind.' Hence *on-bæftan*,' ' abaft,' literally ' on-by-aft.'
Every man shewid his connyng tofore the ship and *baft*.
Chaucer.

a-bout. A.-S. *abutan*. From A.-S. *utan* we find *be-utan* (' by-out') and *butan* ; *on-butan* (' on-by-out') and *a-butan*.

above. A.-S. *a-bufan*. From A.-S. *ufan* we find *be-ufan* (' by-up '), *bufan*, and *a-bufan*.

against. From *a-gain*, Old English *a-gen*. From A.-S. simpler forms *gean* and *gegen*, ' opposite,' we find *on-gean*, *on-gegen*. In modern English *a-gain* has lost its prepositional force, remaining in use as an adverb.

a-long. There are two words of this form :

(1) *a-long*, A.-S. *and-lang*, German, *ent-langen*. Here *lang* is originally an adjective agreeing with the noun, which is governed by the preposition *and*, ' through ;' as *and langne dæg*, ' through the long day,' ' through the length of the day.' The adjective has been absorbed by the preposition. Compare *a-mid*.

(2) *a-long*, from A.-S. *ge-lang*, ' owing to,' as in the phrase ' it is along of you.' So Shakespeare,
All this coil is long of you.
Midsummer Night's Dream, iii. 2.

a-mid. There is another instance in which an adjective has been absorbed, or attracted, by a preposition. A.-S. *midd* is an adjective, ' middle :' thus,
On middre nihte, ' at mid night.'
On midne dæg, ' at mid day.'
On midre sæ, ' in mid sea,' ' in the middle of the sea.'
On middan thære ea, ' in middle the water,' ' in the middle of the water,' ' *amid* the water.'

In this last sentence observe the position of the article *thære* between the adjective and the noun. Compare the remarks on ' many *a* youth,' §§ 296–303.

a-mong. Dr. Bosworth gives the following forms of the A.-S. preposition: *ge-mang, ge-mong, a-mang, on-mang.* There is a noun *ge-mang,* ' mixture,' and a verb *mengan,* ' to mingle, mix.' It is possible that *a-mong* originally signified ' in the mixed multitude;' but the word requires further investigation.

a-round, ' on round.' Here we have a preposition with an adjective ; compare the phrases ' in vain,' ' in secret.' So Lydgate, speaking of his youthful days :

Lik a young colt that ran withowte brydil,
Made my freendys ther good to spend *in ydil.*

' In idle' means ' in vain,' ' to no purpose.' The adjective ' round' is from the French *rond,* Latin *rotundus.* I do not think that ' around' is derived from A.-S. *rand, rond,* ' rim,' ' border.' The sense would hardly favour that derivation ; and we may remark that the A.-S. preposition used in this signification was *ymb,* German *um.*

a-thwart. This appears to be another case of a preposition and an adjective. The A.-S. adjective *thweor, thweorh, thwir, thwyr, thwer, thwur, thwurh,* signifies ' crooked,' ' cross,' ' wicked,' ' thwart;' and Dr. Bosworth gives the phrase *on thweorh sprecan* ' perversely speak,' that is, ' speak athwart.' Mr. Wedgwood compares the Old Norse *um thvert,* ' across,' ' athwart.'

481. We have now to consider prepositions exhibiting the prefix *be-,* ' by.' This prefix is the Anglo-Saxon preposition *be, bi, big,* ' by, near to, to, at, upon, about, with.' We find it prefixed to a preposition, as ' be-*fore*;' to a noun, as ' be-*side* ;' to an adjective, as ' be-*low.*'

be-fore. A.-S. *be-foran,* ' by-fore.'

be-hind. A.-S. *be-hindan,* ' by-hind.'

be-low, ' by-low :' compare ' on high.'

be-neath. A.-S. *be-neoð, be-neoðan, be-nyðan,* ' by-neath ;' *neoðan* signifies ' down,' ' downwards.'

be-side, ' by side.'

be-tween, ' by twain,' that is ' near two.' The notion is, that if a thing is between two others, it is near both.

be-twixt. A.-S. *be-twuh, be-twy, be-twih, be-twyh, be-tweoh, be-tweohs, be-tweox, be-twux, be-twuxt.* In Anglo-

Saxon, *h* appears to have had a guttural sound; hence, *hs* are equivalent to *x*.

Mr. Wedgwood says, 'The A.-S. has *tweoh*, a different form of *twa*, "two;" and thence *twegen*, "twain." From the former of these are A.-S. *betwuh*, *betweoh*, *betweohs*, *betwcox*, *betwuxt*, "by two," "in the middle of two;" which may be compared, as to form, with *amid*, A.-S. *amiddes*, *amidst*, or with *again*, *against*. In like manner from *twain* is formed *between*, "in the middle of twain."

> 'The Ile of Man that me clepeth
> By twene us and Irlonde.'
>> *Robert of Gloucester.*

> 'The Isle of Man that man calleth
> By twain us and Ireland.'

See Wedgwood, *Dictionary of English Etymology*, 'between.'

be-yond. A.-S. *be-geond*, *be-geondan*, *be-iundan*, 'by-yond,' 'by-yonder.' *Geond*, as a preposition, signifies 'through, over, after, beyond;' and as an adverb, 'yond, yonder, thither, beyond.'

482. The following words are used as prepositions. They are derived from verbs, either from the imperative mood, or from the form in -*ing*.

From the imperative : *except, save.*
From the form in -*ing*: *bating, concerning, during, excepting, pending, respecting, regarding, notwithstanding.*

It is difficult to say whether the form in -*ing*, here used, is participial or gerundial; or whether some of these words are used in one construction, others in another. We might consider *during* and *pending* to be participial, and to have arisen from an absolute construction : 'pending the battle' (*pendente prœlio*), 'while the battle was hanging in doubt;' so 'during the fight,' that is, 'while the fight lasted.'

But this explanation would not suit 'concerning,' 'excepting,' 'regarding.' Wickliffe, who uses 'out-take' for except, employs the passive participle in an absolute construction : 'out-taken women and little children,' that is, 'excepted women and little children.'

I incline to think that we have borrowed this use of the active participle from the Norman French. We have for example 'in passing,' *en passant*, a construction which furnishes grammatical difficulty both in French and English.

POSITION.

483. The noun or pronoun governed generally follows the preposition which governs it.

But the preposition is often separated from the relative pronoun which it governs, and is thrown to the end of the clause or sentence : as,

> Horace is an author, *whom* I am much delighted *with*.

> The world is too well bred to shock authors with a truth, *which* generally their booksellers are the first that inform them *of.*—Pope, *Preface to his Poems.*

'This is an idiom,' says Dr. Lowth, 'which our language is strongly inclined to ; it prevails in common conversation, and suits very well with the familiar style in writing ; but the placing of the preposition before the relative is more graceful, as well as more perspicuous ; and agrees much better with the solemn and elevated style.'—Lowth, *English Grammar*, p. 137.

Lindley Murray quotes this remark word for word, and has the credit of having laid down a law upon the subject. But the old idiom of throwing a preposition to the end of a sentence was beginning to be thought inelegant in the time of Dryden. In his *Defence of the Epilogue*, he criticises some passages in Ben Jonson's *Catiline* ; and upon these lines,

> The waves, and dens of beasts, could not receive
> The bodies that those souls were frighted *from,*

he remarks, 'The preposition in the end of a sentence : a common fault with him, and which I have but lately observed in my own writings.'—Dryden, *Prose Works* (ed. Malone), ii. 237. Accordingly Dryden altered this construction in every sentence where it occurred in his *Essay on Dramatic Poesy*. The first edition of that work appeared in 1668 ; the second in 1684. Malone has printed the second edition, collated *verbatim* with the first edition, and he adds the various readings at the close of the essay. Thus : 'I cannot think so contemptibly of the age *I live in,*' is exchanged for 'the age *in which* I live.' 'A deeper expression of belief than all the actor can *persuade us to*' is altered, 'can insinuate *into us.*'—Dryden, *Prose Works*, ii. 136–142.

484. Hallam, quoting this passage (*Literary History*, iii. 556), observes, 'though the old form continued in use long after the time of Dryden, it has of late years been reckoned

inelegant, and proscribed in all cases, perhaps with an unnecessary fastidiousness, to which I have not uniformly
deferred; since our language is of a Teutonic structure, and
the rules of Latin or French grammar are not always to bind
us.' In a note Hallam quotes an interrogatory sentence from
Hooker:—' Shall there be a God to swear *by*, and none to
pray *to*?' as an instance of the force which this arrangement,
so eminently emphatic, sometimes gives. Hallam's view of
the question is this:—' The form is, in my opinion, sometimes
emphatic and spirited, though its frequent use appears
slovenly. . . . In the passive voice, I think it better than in
the active; nor can it always be dispensed with, unless we
choose rather the feeble encumbering pronoun *which*.'

We must not forget that Dryden represented the classical
school in our literature; hence he wished to make our language conform to the Latin idiom. Since German studies
have become fashionable, we have seen that the practice of
throwing the preposition to the end of the sentence is a Germanic, and therefore presumptively an old English idiom. The
perusal of our older authors has strengthened this impression.
See § 256, and compare Bain, *English Grammar*, p. 189.

485. Professor Bain (*English Grammar*, p. 190) quotes the
following examples from Massinger's *Grand Duke of Florence*,
to show the usage of the Elizabethan writers:—

> For I must use the freedom *I was born with.*
> In that dumb rhetoric which you *make use of.*
> ———the name of friend,
> Which you are pleased to *grace me with.*
> ———a copious theme,
> Which would, discoursed at large *of*, make a volume.

And so Shakespeare:

> But that the dread of something after death,
> The undiscovered country, from whose bourn
> No traveller returns, puzzles the will;
> And makes us rather bear those ills we have,
> Than fly to others *that we know not of.*
> *Hamlet*, iii. 1.

> To have no screen between this part he played,
> And him he *played it for*, he needs will be
> Absolute Milan. *Tempest*, i. 2.
> These nine in buckram *that I told thee of.*
> *1st Henry IV*. ii. 4.

486. *Caution.*—Where a relative pronoun is dependent upon a preposition, and the preposition is thrown to the end of the sentence, errors are sometimes found, and the nominative is often improperly used for the objective. In the following passages *who* ought to be *whom* :—

> *Who* servest thou *under* ?
> > *Henry V.* iv. 7.

> *Who* do you speak *to* ?
> > *As you Like It,* v. ii.

> I'll tell you *who* time ambles *withal, who* time trots *withal, who* time gallops *withal,* and *who* he stands still *withal.*—*Ibid.* iii. 2.

> We are still much at a loss *who* civil power belongs *to.*—*Locke.*

487. Some writers separate the preposition from the noun which it governs, in order to connect different prepositions with the same noun; as,

> To suppose the zodiac and the planets to be efficient *of,* and antecedent *to,* themselves.—Bentley, *Sermon* 6.

This, adds Dr. Lowth, whether in the familiar or the solemn style, is always inelegant; and should never be admitted but in forms of law, or in documents where accuracy of expression must take place of every other consideration.—See Lowth, *English Grammar,* p. 137, *Note.*

ENGLISH PREPOSITIONS IN COMPOSITION WITH VERBS.

488. Some few of our prepositions are prefixed to verbs, and coalesce with them : these are *fore, over, out, with, under, up,* and the inseparable preposition *for-,* corresponding to the German *ver-.*

fore. As in *fore-tell* (sometimes written *fore-tel*), *fore-bode, fore-know.*

over. As in *over-turn, over-whelm,* and sometimes with the signification of ' excess,' as in *over-do, over-work.*

out. With the sense of ' surpassing,' as in *out-do, out-run.*

with. Not in the sense of ' along with,' but signifying ' against,' ' away,' as in *with-stand, with-hold, with-draw.*

under. As in *under-lay, under-mine, under-write.* Sometimes it bears the signification of ' defect,' as in *under-praise*, *under-value*. At other times we observe an entire modification of meaning : for example, *under-stand* does not mean ' stand under,' but ' comprehend.' Compare the German *ver-stehen*. In *under-go* and *under-take*, the notion of ' under' is borrowed from ' going under,' or 'supporting' a burden.

up. As in *up-hold*, *up-heave*, *up-lift*. Observe that *up-set* means ' over-turn,' but ' set up' means ' establish.'

489. *for.* The particle *for-* may or may not be the same as our preposition *for*. At all events, it seems akin to the German *ver-* and the Latin *per-*. Compare the Old English *for-do*, ' ruin,' ' destroy,' with the German *ver-thun*, ' use up,' ' consume,' and with the Latin *per-do*, ' destroy.' Compare also *for-swear* with the German *ver-schworen*, and the Latin *per-juro*. With a verb of good meaning, it has a contradictory effect, turning good into bad ; but with a verb of bad meaning, it appears to have an intensive force.

for-do. Sometimes written *fore-do*, ' ruin, weary, destroy.' Compare German *ver-thun*, Latin *per-do*.

for-feit. From the French noun *for-fait*, derived from *for-faire*, ' do wrong,' ' transgress.' Hence *forfeit* means ' to lose by misdeed ;' the term being transferred from the act to the consequences. In Low Latin *for-faire* is rendered *foris-facere*.

for-go. Sometimes written *fore-go*, ' go without.'

for-get. ' Lose hold of.'

for-give. ' Give away.' In old time he who pardoned an injury *gave up* his claim to the *wer-gild* or ' compensation.'

for-sake. Properly ' put away the subject of dispute,' ' renounce,' ' deny ;' then simply ' desert.' Old English *sake*, ' dispute,' ' strife.' A.-S. *sacan*, *sacian*, ' contend,' ' strive.'

Mr. Wedgwood, in his *Dictionary of English Etymology*, discusses *for-* under the words ' for,' ' fore,' and says: ' *For*, in composition, answers to G. *ver*, Goth. *fair*, Fr. *for*, and has the meaning of G. *fort*, Dan. *bort*, "forth," "away ;" Latin, *foris*, "without ;" Fr. *fors*, "out," "without." Thus *forbid* is to "bid a thing away ;" to *forget*, to "away-get," to lose from memory ; to *forgo*, "to go without ;" to *forfend*, "to ward off." In other instances the prefix *for*, in the sense of *out* or *utterly*, implies that the action has been carried to its utmost limits : *forwearied* is "wearied out." '

Similarly in Piers Ploughman we read:

> I was wery *for-wandred*,
> And went me to reste
> Under a brood bank
> By a bournes syde.

490. But more commonly, in English, the preposition is placed after the verb, and separated from it. And thus several words may come between the verb and the preposition : as, ' he *took* them all *in*,' ' he *turned* every one *out*.'

It is a very useful exercise to take an English-French Dictionary, as that of Spiers, and to look out an English verb. The prepositions used in composition with that verb are added, with French translations of the compound verbs; and the exercise consists in making a list of the compounds, affixing to each the corresponding Latin-English derivative. The verb *take* will furnish us with an example :

Take away	*Abstract, remove*
Take about	*Conduct, convey.*
Take after	*Imitate.*
Take along	*Convey.*
Take down	(1) *Demolish, deject,*
	(2) *Degrade, humiliate.*
Take from	*Subtract.*
Take in	(1) *Receive* (with hospitality).
	(2) *Deceive.*
Take off	(1) *Destroy.*
	(2) *Ridicule.*
Take on	*Assume.*
Take to	*Adopt.*
Take under	*Subduct.*
Take up	*Raise, elevate.*
Take upon	*Arrogate.*
Take with	*Convoy, escort.*

491. It is also very necessary to observe, that many intransitive verbs become *transitive*, when compounded with prepositions. For example, *run* is intransitive ; but *run through* is transitive.

In the following list, we mark the transitive verbs * :—

Run away	*Abscond.*
* Run away with	(1) *Abduct.*
	(2) *Imagine.*
* Run down	(1) *Catch, overwhelm,*
	(2) *Decry, depreciate.*
Run from	*Eschew, avoid.*
* Run through	(1) *Transfix, pierce.*
	(2) *Squander.*
Run off	*Escape.*
* Run up	*Incur* (a debt).

LATIN PREPOSITIONS IN COMPOSITION WITH VERBS.

492. The Latin element enters largely into the English language; and it is absolutely necessary to have some knowledge of Latin prepositions, as they appear in composition with verbs. For fuller information, on this part of the subject, the student may consult Professor Key's *Latin Grammar,* §§ 808–838, and §§ 1303–1397. It will be sufficient to remark here, that when a Latin preposition ends in a consonant, the final consonant is liable to change, if the verb, with which it is compounded, begins with a consonant. This is called *assimilation,* or a 'making like,' because the final consonant of the preposition is *made like* to the initial consonant of the verb. For example, from *ad* and *rogo* we have, not *ad-rogate,* but *ar-rogate.* In like manner, we have, not *ad-similation,* but *as-similation.*

To the prepositions, in the following list, we annex the changes to which they are liable; for instance, we give,

ad (ac, af, ag, al, an, ap, ar, as, at).

This means, that the preposition *ad* sometimes appears in composition as *ac, af, ag,* &c., according to the initial consonant of the verb.

Latin Prepositions.

493. *a, ab, abs,* 'from,' 'away.'

a-vert	'turn from.'
ab-solve	'loosen away.'
abs-tract	'draw away.'

Prof. Key, *Latin Grammar,* § 1304, translates *ab-use,* 'use up,' *ab-sorb,* 'suck down.'

ad (ac, af, ag, al, an, ap, ar, as, at,) 'to,' 'at,' 'on.'

ad-here	'stick to.'
ac-cede	'step to.'
af-fix	'fix on.'
ag-glomerate	'heap on.'
al-locate	'place to.'
an-nex	'join on.'
ap-preciate	'put value on,' 'set price upon.'
ar-rive	'come to.'
as-similate	'liken to.'
at-tend	'stretch to.'

ante, 'before.'
ante-date	'fore-date,' 'date before.'
ante-cede	'go before.'

494. *circum,* 'round.'
circum-vent	'come round' (i. e. deceive).
circum-navigate	'sail round.'
circum-scribe	'draw a line round.'

com (*col, con, cor, co*), 'with,' 'together,' 'up.'
com-pose	'place together.'
col-lect	'gather together,' 'gather up.'
cor-roborate	'strengthen up.'
cor-rode	'eat up.'
co-operate	'work together.'

> *Obs.*—This preposition is *con* before consonants and *co* before vowels: *con-form, con-sider, con-sist*; but *co-equal, co-eternal.* Many persons write '*co*-temporary' for '*con*-temporary;' but Richard Bentley said that 'he could not *co*-gratulate such persons on the *co*-position of their words.'

contra, 'against.'
contra-dict, 'speak against,' 'gain-say,' where *gain-* contains the root of *a-gain, a-gainst.*
contra-vene, 'come against.'

contro, 'against.'
contro-vert, 'turn against.'

495. *de,* 'down,' 'forth,' 'out,' 'at.'
de-scend	'climb down,' 'come down.'
de-ject	'cast down.'
de-monstrate	'show forth,' 'point out.'
de-ride	'laugh at.'
de-spise	'look down upon.'

dis- (*dif, di*), 'in different directions,' 'apart,' 'away,' 'from.'
dis-solve	'loosen away.'
dis-join	'separate.'
dis-arm	'take weapon away.'
dif-fuse	'scatter apart.'
dif-fer	'carry in different directions.'
di-verge	'turn aside.'

ex (*ef, e*), 'out of,' 'forth.'
ex-port	'carry out.'

ex-pose	' set forth.'
e-merge	' come forth.'
e-nuntiate	' tell out.'
e-migrate	' wander forth.'

496. *in* (*im, il, in,* and in French derivatives *em, en*), ' in,' ' into,' ' upon.'

in-volve	' roll in.'
in-duct	' lead in.'
in-spire	' breathe into.'
il-lude	' play upon.'
il-lustrate	' throw light upon.'
im-pel	' urge on.'
im-pose	' put upon.'
im-port	' carry into.'
ir-radiate	' shine into.'
ir-rigate	' pour water upon.'
em-brace	' put arms round.'
en-vy	' look upon' (i. e. with an evil eye.)

inter (*intel*), ' between,' ' among.'

inter-cede	' pass between,' ' mediate.'
inter-cept	' come between.'
inter-change	' change among.'

This preposition conveys the idea of opposition or obstruction in the words *inter-cept, inter-dict* (' for-bid '), *inter-fere*.

In French derivatives it takes the form *enter*, as *enter-prise* an ' undertaking.'

intro, ' into,' ' in.'

    introduce, ' lead in.'

497. *ob* (*oc, of, op*), ' against,' ' up,' ' upon,' ' towards.'

ob-ject	' cast against,' ' urge against.'
ob-struct	' block up.'
oc-cur	' run towards.'
of-fend	' strike against.'
of-fer	' bring towards.'
op-pose	' put against.'
op-press	' press upon.'
op-pugn	' fight against.'

498. *per*, ' through.'

| *per-mit* | ' let go through.' |
| *per-vade* | ' pass through.' |

Obs.—The particle *per* in composition has sometimes a meaning akin to that of our *for-*, German *ver-*, as in the Latin *per-do*, 'for-do,' i.e. 'destroy;' so too, Latin *per-juro*, 'for-swear;' so, perhaps, *per-vert*, 'turn away from (the right).'

post, ' after,' ' off.'

post-date	' after-date,' 'date-after.'
post-pone	' put off.'

præ (*pre*), ' before.'

pre-cede,	' go before,' not ' fore-go,' which is more strictly 'for-go,' ' go without.'
pre-clude	' shut out beforehand.'
pre-dict	' fore-tell.'
pre-fer	' put before.'
pre-tend	' stretch forward' (for the purpose of concealment).

pro (*por*), ' for,' ' forth,' ' before.'

pro-ject	' cast forward.'
por-tend	' fore-stretch,' ' fore-token.'

This preposition appears in French as *pour*, whence we have *pour-tray*, now written *por-tray*, ' draw forth,' ' draw in outline ;' *pur-pose* of the same meaning as *pro-pose*, ' set forth' (as an object), ' design.'

499. *re* (*red*), ' back,' ' again.'

re-cur	' run back.'
re-ject	' throw back.'
re-move	' move back,' ' take away.'
red-eem	' buy back,' ' buy again.'

retro, ' back,' ' backward.'

retro-grade	' step backward.'

se, ' apart.'

se-cede	' go apart,' ' withdraw.'
se-parate	' put apart.'

500. *sub* (*suc, suf, sug, sup, sur, sus, su[s]*), ' under,' ' up,' ' over,' ' after.'

sub-due	' bring under.'
sub-ject	' cast under.'
sub-mit	' put under.'
suc-ceed	' come up,' ' prosper.'
suc-cour	' run up,' ' help.'
suf-fix	' fix under,' ' put after.'
suf-fuse	' spread over.'

sug-gest	' carry up.'
sup-port	' bear up.'
sup-pose	' lay under,' ' lay down.'
sur-render	' deliver up.'
sus-pend	' hang up.'
sus-tain	' hold up.'
su(s)-spect	' look under.'

super, ' over,' ' on.'

super-add	' add on.'
super-scribe	' write over.'
super-vene	' come on,' ' come in addition.'

The French *sur* is derived from *super*, and appears in

sur-prise	' take suddenly.'
sur-vene	' come in addition.'
sur-vey	' oversee.'
sur-vive	' live after.'

trans (tra), ' over,' ' across.'

trans-mit	' send over.'
trans-mute	' change over.'
tra-duce	' lead over,' ' bring before the public,' ' expose to ridicule,' ' calumniate.'

501. It sometimes happens, that while a verb is compounded with a Latin preposition, an English preposition follows the verb. As a general rule, the two prepositions should agree in meaning; the Latin derivative should be followed by a preposition corresponding to that which is used in composition: as ' *ad*-apt to,' ' *af*-fix *to*,' ' *di*-vert *from*,' ' *ex*-pel *from* (or *out of*).'

But sometimes the meaning of the compound verb overrides the original force of the preposition. Take the verb *differ*. When we say ' *dif*-fer *from*,' the agreement between *dis* (*dif*) ' in various directions ' and *from* is sufficiently close. But we also say ' *dif*-fer *with* ' where the prepositions do not agree. The explanation is this: ' *dif*-fer *from* ' is equivalent to ' contend *with*;' and so, by extension of meaning, we say ' differ *with*.' In this case, the meaning of the verb ' differ ' overrides the force of the prefix *dif*, and custom prevails against etymology.

502. But the misuse of prepositions is not confined to those which follow compound verbs. Dr. Lowth (*English Grammar*,

p. 138) has collected the following examples of improper usage:—

> Your character, which I or any other writer may now value ourselves *by* drawing. [*upon.*]—Swift, *Letter on the English Tongue.*
>
> You have bestowed your favours *to* the most deserving persons. [*upon.*]—*Ibid.*
>
> Upon such occasions as fell *into* their cognisance. [*under.*] —*Id. Contest and Dissensions*, &c., c. iii.
>
> That variety of factions *into* which we are still engaged. [*in.*]—*Ibid.* c. v.
>
> To restore myself *into* the good graces of my fair critics. [*to.*]—Dryden, *Preface to Aurungzebe.*
>
> Accused the ministers *for* betraying the Dutch. [*of.*]— Swift, *Four Last Years of the Queen.*
>
> [It is possible to defend this sentence, thus: ' Accused the ministers, *on account of* their having betrayed the Dutch.']
>
> Ovid, whom you accuse *for* luxuriancy of verse. [*of.*]— Dryden, *On Dramatic Poesy.*
>
> Something like this has been reproached *to* Tacitus. —Bolingbroke, *On History*, vol. i. p. 136.
>
> [It would be necessary to give this sentence a complete turn: ' Tacitus has been reproached *with* something like this.']
>
> He was made much *on* at Argos. [*of.*]
>
> He is so resolved *of* going to the Persian court. [*on.*] —Bentley, *Dissertation on Themistocles's Epistles*, sect. iii.
>
> Neither the one nor the other shall make me swerve *out of* the path, which I have traced to myself. [*from.*]— Bolingbroke, *Letter to Wyndham*, p. 242.
>
> If poesy can prevail *upon* force. [*over.*]—Addison, *Travels*, p. 62.
>
> [We prevail *upon* persons, but *over* physical forces.]
>
> I do likewise dissent *with* the examiner.—*Id. Whig Examiner, No.* 1.
>
> [We ' differ *with* ' but ' dissent *from.*']
>
> Ye blind guides, which strain *at* a gnat, and swallow a camel.—*Matthew* xxiii. 24.

[The original has διϋλίζοντες, i.e. 'straining *out* a gnat,' 'taking a gnat *out* of liquor by straining.']

It was perfectly in compliance *to* some persons, for whose opinion I have great deference. [*with.*]—Swift, *Preface to Temple's Memoirs.*

The wisest Princes need not think it any diminution *to* their greatness, or derogation *to* their sufficiency, to rely upon counsel. [*of*] [*from.*]—Bacon, *Essay* xx.

503. In the use of prepositions after verbs, much depends on usage :

We 'go *beyond*,' and 'rise *above.*'

We 'except *from* censure,' and state 'exceptions *to* a course.'

We 'inquire *of* a person,' and '*at* a place.'

We are 'dependent *on*' and 'independent *of.*'

See Angus, *Handbook of the English Tongue,* § 590, where the student will find a list of verbs followed by the prepositions commonly used after them.

EXAMPLES.

'The ordering of exercises is matter of great consequence
to hurt or help; for, as is well observed by Cicero,
men in exercising their faculties, if they be not well
advised, do exercise their faults and get ill habits as
well as good.'—*Bacon.*

In all studies, much depends upon judicious exercise; for,
however useful theory may be in its proper place, the main
thing is practice.

In grammar, the chief end is accuracy; and slovenly exercises do more harm than good. Scrupulous attention should
be paid to the handwriting, and the spelling. Boys are apt
to despise these things as trifles; but they have to learn, that
attention to trifles often makes all the difference between a
man who succeeds in life, and a man who fails.

In the present day, there is too much hurry; and even boys
are ready to account for their negligence by saying 'that they
had not time.' This is an idle excuse. No portion of their
time can be so well spent as that which is occupied in acquiring habits of neatness, and accuracy.

In grammatical analysis, two methods may be adopted.
The first is the method of construing; that is, to begin by
selecting the principal words in a sentence, as, the 'subject-
nominative' and the 'predicate-verb;' then to subjoin the
qualifications of each; and then, to add the dependent words
of the sentence. For example:

Him the Almighty Power
Hurled flaming.

Subject-nominative	.	.	.	.	Power
Predicate-verb	.	.	.	.	hurled
Qualifications of the ⎱		.	.	.	the
Subject-nominative ⎰		.	.	.	Almighty
Objective	.	.	.	.	him
Qualification of the Objective		.	.	.	flaming.

The second method is to take the words as they stand, and
to explain each in its order: as,

Him	.	.	.	.	*Objective.*
the	.	.	.	.	*Qualification of the Sub-*
					ject-nominative 'Power.'

Almighty . . .	*Qualification of the Subject-nominative 'Power.'*
Power	*Subject-nominative.*
hurled	*Predicate-verb.*
flaming	*Qualification of the Objective 'him.'*

In oral instruction both methods may be employed. But in written analysis, I incline to the second method. For this reason, that the mind is less liable to be distracted by moving from one part of the sentence to another; and there is less danger of omitting any word. In this way, we begin at the beginning, and go on steadily to the end. However, on this point, there may be difference of opinion; some may prefer the one way, and some the other.

For a while, I hesitated whether to use abbreviations, as, *subj. nom., pred. verb,* or to discard them. At first, there is a temptation to save time and trouble. But in looking over an exercise, the analysis written in full is much more pleasing to the eye, than one in which abbreviations are used. And as there is an artistic pleasure in beholding a well-written exercise, I conclude that it is better to discard abbreviations.

In selecting examples, I have introduced several of those given by Dr. Morell and Mr. Mason, in order to exhibit the difference of the systems. The reader may compare the analysis here proposed with that of the writers mentioned: Morell, *Grammar of the English Language,* pp. 80–103; Mason, *English Grammar,* pp. 122–143.

I. EXAMPLES OF SENTENCES.

1. The curfew tolls the knell of parting day.

The	*Definite article,* qualifying the subject-nominative 'curfew.'
curfew	*Noun,* Subject-nominative.
tolls	Predicate-verb.
the	*Definite article,* qualifying the Objective 'knell.'
knell	*Noun,* Objective.
of parting day.	*Prepositional phrase,* qualifying the Objective 'knell: consisting of a *preposition* 'of,' a *participle* 'parting,' a *noun* 'day.'

2. The sun from the western horizon extended his golden wand o'er the landscape.

The	*Definite article*, qualifying the subject-nominative 'sun.'
sun	*Noun*, Subject-nominative.
from the western horizon	*Adverbial phrase*, qualifying the predicate-verb 'extended,' and denoting the place *whence*.
extended	Predicate-verb.
his	*Pronoun possessive* (or in the *possessive case*), qualifying the Objective 'wand.'
golden	*Adjective*, qualifying the Objective 'wand.'
wand	*Noun*, Objective.
o'er the land-scape.	*Adverbial phrase*, qualifying the predicate-verb 'extended,' and denoting the place *where*.

> *Obs.*—The phrase 'of parting day' is called a *prepositional phrase*; whereas 'from the western horizon' and 'o'er the landscape' are termed *adverbial phrases*. In one sense they are all prepositional phrases; but as the first qualifies a noun, while the second and third qualify a verb, it is better to distinguish the latter as *adverbial phrases*.

3. The doctor prescribed his patient a receipt.

The	*Definite article*, qualifying the subject-nominative 'doctor.'
doctor	*Noun*, Subject-nominative.
prescribed	Predicate-verb.
his	*Pronoun in the possessive case*, qualifying the Secondary Objective 'patient.'
patient	*Noun*, Secondary Objective [*to* or *for* his patient].
a	*Indefinite article*, qualifying the Primary Objective 'receipt.'
receipt.	*Noun*, Primary Objective (immediately dependent upon the predicate-verb 'prescribed').

4. He gave him a letter to read.

He	*Pronoun*, Subject-nominative.
gave	Predicate-verb.
him	*Pronoun*, Secondary Objective.
a	*Indefinite article*, qualifying the Primary Objective 'letter.'
letter	*Noun*, Primary Objective.

to read.	*Gerund,* qualifying the predicate-verb 'gave.' Here *to* is a true preposition signifying 'in order to:' i. e. 'for reading,' or in older English, 'for to read.'

5. I saw a man with a sword.

I	*Pronoun,* Subject-nominative.
saw	Predicate-verb.
a	*Indefinite article,* qualifying the Objective 'man.'
man	*Noun.* Objective.
with a sword.	*Prepositional phrase,* qualifying the Objective 'man.'

6. He killed a man with a sword.

He	*Pronoun,* Subject-nominative.
killed	*Predicate*-verb.
a	*Indefinite article,* qualifying the Objective 'man.'
man	*Noun,* Objective.
with a sword.	*Adverbial phrase,* qualifying the predicate-verb 'killed,' and denoting the instrument *whereby.*

Obs.—In Example 5, 'with a sword' is a prepositional phrase, qualifying the noun 'man;' but in Example 6, 'with a sword' is an adverbial phrase, qualifying the verb 'killed.'

7. Having abandoned their fortifications, the troops of the Emperor began a disastrous retreat.

Having abandoned	*Participle,* qualifying the predicate-verb 'began.'
their	*Pronoun possessive,* or in the *possessive case,* qualifying the Objective 'fortifications.'
fortifications	*Noun,* objective dependent upon the participle 'having abandoned.'
the	*Definite article,* qualifying the subject-nominative 'troops.'
troops	*Noun,* Subject-nominative.
of the Emperor	*Prepositional phrase,* qualifying the Subject-nominative 'troops.'
began	Predicate-verb.
a	*Indefinite article,* qualifying the Objective 'retreat.'

disastrous	*Adjective*, qualifying the Objective 'retreat.'
retreat	*Noun*, Objective.

> *Obs.* 1.—Mr. Mason considers 'having abandoned their fortifi-
> cations' a participial phrase qualifying the subject-
> nominative 'troops,' or, as he terms it, an 'attributive
> adjunct of the subject.' I believe that Dr. Morell
> would agree with Mr. Mason.
>
> No doubt in point of concord, the participle 'having
> abandoned' agrees with the noun 'troops;' but in
> point of signification, the participle qualifies the pre-
> dicate-verb 'began.' For the meaning is that the
> troops, when they had abandoned the fortifications,
> began a retreat. In other words, the troops aban-
> doned the fortifications, *and then* began a retreat.
> The qualification affects the act, and not the troops
> themselves. Therefore I am disposed to think that
> the participle must be held to qualify the verb.
>
> *Obs.* 2.—We may take *their* as a possessive pronoun, or as the
> possessive (genitive) case of the personal.

8. The enraged officer struck the unfortunate man dead
on the spot with a single blow of his sword.

The	*Definite article*, qualifying the Subject-nomi-native 'officer.'
enraged	*Participle* or *Adjective*, qualifying the Subject-nominative 'officer.'
officer	*Noun*, Subject-nominative.
struck	Predicate-verb.
the	*Definite article*, qualifying the Primary Objective 'man.'
unfortunate	*Adjective*, qualifying the Primary Objective 'man.'
man	*Noun*, Primary Objective.
dead	*Participle* or *Adjective*, Complement-objective.
on the spot	*Adverbial phrase*, qualifying the Predicate-verb 'struck,' and denoting the place *where*.
with a single blow of his sword	*Adverbial phrase*, qualifying the Predicate-verb 'struck,' and denoting the means or instrument *whereby*.

9. A man of weak health is incapable of the thorough
enjoyment of life.

A	*Indefinite article*, qualifying the Subject-nominative 'man.'

man	*Noun*, Substantive-nominative.
of weak health	*Prepositional phrase*, qualifying the Subject-nominative 'man.'
is	Predicate-verb.
incapable `	*Adjective*, Predicate-nominative.
of the thorough enjoyment of life	*Prepositional phrase*, dependent upon the adjective 'incapable.' Or perhaps this might be taken as an *Adverbial phrase*, qualifying the Predicate-nominative 'incapable.'—See Mason, *English Grammar*, § 512.

10. Now the bright morning star, day's harbinger,
Comes dancing from the East.

Now	*Adverb*, qualifying the Predicate-verb 'comes.'
the	*Definite article*, qualifying the Subject-nominative 'star.'
bright	*Adjective*, qualifying the Subject-nominative 'star.'
morning	*Noun*, used adjectively, qualifying the Subject-nominative 'star.'
star	*Noun*, Subject-nominative.
day's	*Noun in the possessive case*, qualifying the noun in apposition 'harbinger.'
harbinger	*Noun in apposition*, qualifying the Subject-nominative 'star.'
comes	Predicate verb.
dancing	*Participle*, Predicate-nominative.
from the East.	*Adverbial phrase*, qualifying the Predicate-verb 'comes,' and denoting the place *whence*.

11.   Him the Almighty Power
Hurled headlong flaming from the ethereal sky
With hideous ruin and combustion, down
To bottomless perdition.

Him	*Pronoun*, Objective.
the	*Definite article*, qualifying the Subject-nominative 'Power.'
Almighty	*Adjective*, qualifying the Subject-nominative 'Power.'
Power	*Noun*, Subject-nominative.
hurled	Predicate-verb.

headlong	*Adjective*, qualifying the Objective ' him.'
flaming	*Participle*, qualifying the Objective ' him.'
from the ethereal sky	*Adverbial phrase*, qualifying the Predicate-verb ' hurled,' and denoting the place *whence.*
with hideous ruin and combustion	*Adverbial phrase*, qualifying the Predicate-verb ' hurled,' and denoting the attendant circumstances.
down	*Adverb*, qualifying the Predicate-verb ' hurled,' and denoting the direction *whither.* [Or, *down* may be taken as a *preposition* entering into composition with the verb ' hurled:' ' hurled down' = Latin *de-jecit.*
to bottomless perdition.	*Adverbial phrase*, qualifying the Predicate-verb ' hurled,' and denoting the place *whither*, or the condition *to which.*

Cases of difficulty are constantly arising in analysis; and in some instances, grammarians of equal ability might entertain different opinions. Hence, we should guard against hasty conclusions; we should proceed with caution, and learn to suspend judgment, when a case is not clear. It follows, also, that if a boy has done his best, and yet fails to understand the construction of a sentence, he ought not to be discouraged. On the contrary, if he has discovered a real difficulty, that is a sign of growing intelligence.

Let us consider a few doubtful cases.

12. The moon threw its silvery light upon the lake.

The words ' upon the lake' might be taken as an adverbial phrase qualifying the predicate-verb ' threw;' or, possibly, ' the lake' might be taken as a secondary objective dependent upon the compound verb 'threw upon.'

13. He recommended him to use great moderation in his diet.

We might consider ' to use' as an infinitive employed substantively, and as the Primary Objective dependent upon the Predicate-verb ' recommended.' In that case ' him' must be the Secondary Objective, because the use was recommended ' to him.' But it is just possible that ' him' may be the subject-accusative before the infinitive ' to use,' equivalent to ' He recommended that he should use.' In any case, ' moderation' is an objective dependent upon the verb ' to use.'

14. He found all his wants supplied by the care of his friends.

Mr. Mason (*English Grammar*, § 511) would make ' wants' the Objective, and ' supplied' the Complement-Objective. But let us consider : he did not find his *wants*, but the *supply* of his wants. He found, that his wants were supplied. The word ' wants' seems to stand in the position of a subject-accusative : but then no infinitive is expressed. If we might read, ' He found all his wants *to be* supplied,' there would be no further difficulty. Perhaps we may consider ' supplied' as a participle used instead of the infinitive. This idiom is very common in Greek.

Again,

He seems to fly.

According to the old grammar rule, this sentence presents no difficulty. One verb governs another in the infinitive mood, and there is an end of the matter. But if we regard an infinitive as a verbal substantive, we expect some government analogous to the government of a noun. After transitive verbs, the case is clear. In the sentence ' He loves to ride,' the infinitive ' to ride' stands in the place of an Objective governed by the verb ' loves.' But how shall we explain the dependence of an infinitive ' to fly' upon an intransitive verb ' seems?'

The Greeks frequently use a participle in such constructions : as, φαίνεται πετόμενος, ' he seems (or appears) flying;' when the participle is a predicate-nominative. But then the Greeks also employ the infinitive construction, φαίνεται πέτεσθαι; and the Greek grammarians draw a distinction between the use of the infinitive and that of the participle.

If we turn both the verbs into nouns, we find that the second appears in the genitive case. ' He seems to fly' is equivalent to ' He has the semblance of flight.' I offer the conjecture, that the dependence of an infinitive upon an intransitive verb is analogous to the dependence of a noun, in the genitive case, upon another noun.

The provincial idiom ' He seems a flying' is easily explained. ' He seems on flying,' that is, ' in the act of flight.'

II. EXAMPLES OF COMPOUND SENTENCES.

I. CO-ORDINATE SENTENCES.

1. *Sentences standing side by side, without any connecting particle.*

15. The way was long, the wind was cold.

The way was long : *First Co-ordinate Sentence.*
The wind was cold : *Second Co-ordinate Sentence.*
Analysis of the First Co-ordinate.

The   *Definite article,* qualifying the Subject-nominative 'way.'
way   *Noun,* Subject-nominative.
was   Predicate-verb.
long   *Adjective,* Predicate-nominative.
     Analysis of the Second Co-ordinate.
The   *Definite Article,* qualifying the Subject-nominative 'wind.'
wind   *Noun,* Subject-nominative.
was   Predicate-verb.
cold   *Adjective,* Predicate-nominative.

2. *Copulative.*

16. The army advanced, and the enemy fled.

The army advanced   *First Co-ordinate Sentence.*
and   *Conjunction Copulative,* introducing the Second Co-ordinate Sentence.
the enemy fled   *Second Co-ordinate Sentence.*
     Analysis of the First Co-ordinate.
the   *Definite Article,* qualifying the Subject-nominative 'army.'
army   *Noun,* Subject-nominative.
advanced,   Predicate-verb.
     Analysis of the Second Co-ordinate.
the   *Definite Article,* qualifying the Subject-nominative 'enemy.'
enemy   *Noun,* Subject-nominative.
fled.   Predicate-verb.

3. *Alternative.*

17. Either he comes, or you go.

Either	*Conjunction alternative,* introducing the First Co-ordinate Sentence.
he comes,	*First Co-ordinate Sentence.*
or	*Conjunction alternative,* introducing the Second Co-ordinate Sentence.
you go.	Second Co-ordinate Sentence.

Analysis of the First Co-ordinate.

he	*Pronoun,* Subject-nominative.
comes,	Predicate-verb.

Analysis of the Second Co-ordinate.

you	*Pronoun,* Subject-nominative.
go.	Predicate-verb.

4. *Adversative.*

18. The virtuous man dies, but virtue is eternal.

The virtuous man dies,	*First Co-ordinate Sentence.*
but	*Conjunction adversative,* introducing the Second Co-ordinate Sentence.
virtue is eternal.	*Second Co-ordinate Sentence.*

Analysis of the First Co-ordinate.

The	*Definite Article,* qualifying the Subject-nominative 'man.'
virtuous	*Adjective,* qualifying the Subject-nominative 'man.'
man	*Noun,* Subject-nominative.
dies,	Predicate-verb.

Analysis of the Second Co-ordinate.

virtue	*Noun,* Subject-nominative.
is	Predicate-verb.
eternal.	*Adjective,* Predicate-nominative.

II. COMPOUND SENTENCES CONTAINING CORRELATIVE CLAUSES.

19. Where thou dwellest, I will dwell.

Where thou dwellest	*Accessory Clause.*
I will dwell.	*Principal clause.*

Analysis of the Accessory Clause.

Where	*Connective Particle* (variously termed ' Conjunctive Adverb,' ' Adverbial Conjunction, &c.') introducing the sentence, ' thou dwellest.'
thou	*Pronoun*, Subject-nominative.
dwellest.	Predicate-verb.

Analysis of the Principal Clause.

I	*Pronoun*, Subject-nominative.
will dwell.	Predicate-verb, compounded of the auxiliary ' will,' and the infinitive ' dwell.'

20. He spoke loud, that I might hear him.

He spoke loud	*Principal Clause.*
that I might hear him.	*Accessory Clause.*

Analysis of the Principal Clause.

He	*Pronoun*, Subject-nominative.
spoke	Predicate-verb.
loud	*Adverb*, qualifying the Predicate-verb ' spoke.'

Analysis of the Accessory Clause.

that	*Connective Particle*, introducing the sentence ' I might hear him.'*
I	*Pronoun*, Subject-nominative.

---

* In these constructions *that* is usually termed a *conjunction* ; but Mr. Mason prefers to call it a *conjunctional adverb.* See Mason, *English Grammar*, § 534, *Note.*

| might hear | Predicate-verb, compounded of the auxiliary 'might,' and the infinitive 'hear.' |
| him. | Pronoun, Objective. |

21. He spoke loud, in order that I might hear him.

| He spoke loud | Principal Clause. |
| in order that I might hear him. | Accessory Clause. |

Analysis of the Principal Clause.

He	Pronoun, Subject-nominative.
spoke	Predicate-verb.
loud	Adverb, qualifying the Predicate-verb 'spoke.'

Analysis of the Accessory Clause.

in order that	Conjunctional phrase, introducing the sentence 'I might hear him.'
I	Pronoun, Subject-nominative.
might hear	Predicate-verb, compounded of the auxiliary 'might,' and the infinitive 'hear.'
him.	Pronoun, Objective.

22. He ran so fast, that he was quite weary.

| He ran so fast | Principal Clause. |
| that he was quite weary. | Accessory Clause. |

Analysis of the Principal Clause.

He	Pronoun, Subject-nominative.
ran	Predicate-verb.
so	Adverb, qualifying the Adverb 'fast.'
fast	Adverb, qualifying the Predicate-verb 'ran.'

Analysis of the Accessory Clause.

that	Connective Particle, introducing the sentence 'he was quite weary.'
he	Pronoun, Subject-nominative.
was	Predicate-verb.

quite   *Adverb*, qualifying the adjective ' weary.'
weary   *Adjective*, Predicate-nominative.
  But compare the suggestion offered in § 68.

   23. If you write, they will come.

If you write *Accessory Clause.*
they will *Principal Clause.*
 come.

    Analysis of the Accessory Clause.

if   *Connective Particle*, introducing the sentence
      ' you write.'
you   *Pronoun*, Subject-nominative.
write   Predicate-verb.

    Analysis of the Principal Clause.

they   *Pronoun*, Subject-nominative.
will come. Predicate-verb, compounded of the auxiliary
      ' will ' and the infinitive ' come.'

III. COMPOUND SENTENCES CONTAINING SUBORDINATE CLAUSES.

1. *The Noun-clause.*

   24. The opinion of the judge was that the prisoner was
   guilty.

The   *Definite Article*, qualifying the Subject-nomi-
      native ' opinion.'
opinion   *Noun*, Subject-nominative.
of the judge *Prepositional phrase*, qualifying the Subject-
      nominative ' opinion.'
was   Predicate-verb.
that the pri- *Noun-clause*, Predicate-nominative.
 soner was
 guilty.

    Analysis of the Noun-clause.

that   *Connective Particle*, introducing the sentence
      ' the prisoner was guilty.'
the   *Definite Article*, qualifying the Subject-nomi-
      native ' prisoner.'

prisoner	*Noun*, Subject-nominative.
was	Predicate-verb.
guilty.	*Adjective*, Predicate-nominative.

25. That he came is certain.

That he came	*Noun-clause*, Subject-nominative.
is	Predicate-verb.
certain.	*Adjective*, Predicate-nominative.

Analysis of the Noun-clause.

that	*Connective Particle*, introducing the sentence 'he came.'
he	*Pronoun*, Subject-nominative.
came.	Predicate-verb.

26. He informed me yesterday that he had arrived.

He	*Pronoun*, Subject-nominative.
informed	Predicate-verb.
me	*Pronoun*, Primary Objective, immediately dependent upon the Predicate-verb 'informed.'
yesterday	*Adverb*, qualifying the Predicate-verb 'informed.'
that he had arrived.	*Noun-clause*, Secondary Objective, dependent upon the Predicate-verb 'informed.'

[The clause 'that he had arrived' is equivalent to 'concerning his arrival,' or 'of his arrival.']

Analysis of the Noun-clause.

that	*Connective Particle*, introducing the sentence 'he had arrived.'
he	*Pronoun*, Subject-nominative.
had arrived.	Predicate-verb, compounded of the auxiliary 'had,' and the participle 'arrived.'

27. I told him that this would happen.

I	*Pronoun*, Subject-nominative.
told	Predicate-verb.
him	*Pronoun*, Secondary Objective, dependent upon the Predicate-verb 'told.'
that this would happen.	*Noun-clause*, Primary Objective, immediately dependent upon the Predicate-verb 'told.'

Analysis of the Noun-clause.

that	*Connective Particle*, introducing the sentence 'this would happen.'
this	*Pronoun*, Subject-nominative.
would happen.	Predicate-verb, compounded of the auxiliary 'would,' and the infinitive 'happen.'

28. I convinced him that he was mistaken.

I	*Pronoun*, Subject-nominative.
convinced	Predicate-verb.
him	*Pronoun*, Primary Objective.
that he was mistaken.	*Noun-clause*, Secondary Objective, dependent upon the Predicate-verb 'convinced.'

[The clause 'that he was mistaken' is equivalent to the phrase 'of his mistake.']

Analysis of the Noun-clause.

that	*Connective-Particle*, introducing the sentence 'he was mistaken.'
he	*Pronoun*, Subject-nominative.
was	Predicate-verb.
mistaken.	*Participle*, Predicate-nominative.

Noun-clauses involving an Indirect Question.

29. I know who did this.

I	*Pronoun*, Subject-nominative.
know	Predicate-verb.
who did this.	*Noun-clause*, Objective, dependent upon the Predicate-verb 'know.'

Analysis of the Noun-clause.

who	*Pronoun*, introducing sentence 'who did this;' and serving as Subject-nominative of the sentence.
did	Predicate-verb.
this.	*Pronoun*, Objective.

30. He would not say where he lived.

He	*Pronoun*, Subject-nominative.
would ... say	Predicate-verb, compounded of the auxiliary 'would,' and the infinitive 'say.'

not	*Negative Adverb*, qualifying the Predicate-verb ' would . . . say.'
where he lived.	*Noun-clause*, Objective, dependent upon the Predicate-verb ' would . . . say.'

Analysis of the Noun-clause.

where	*Connective Particle*, introducing the sentence ' where he lived,' and qualifying the Predicate-verb ' lived.'
he	*Pronoun*, Subject-nominative.
lived.	Predicate-verb.

31. I wish to know, who you are.

I	*Pronoun*, Subject-nominative.
wish	Predicate-verb.
to know	*Infinitive used substantively*, Objective, dependent upon the Predicate-verb ' wish.'
who you are.	*Noun-clause*, Objective, dependent upon the verb ' to know.'

Analysis of the Noun-clause.

who	*Pronoun*, introducing the sentence ' who you are,' and serving as Predicate-nominative in the sentence.
you	*Pronoun*, Subject-nominative.
are.	Predicate-verb.

2. The Adjective-Clause.

32. The cohort, which had already crossed the river, quickly came to blows with the enemy.

The	*Definite Article*, qualifying the subject-nominative ' cohort.'
cohort,	*Noun*, Subject-nominative.
which had already crossed the river,	*Adjective Clause*, qualifying the Subject-nominative ' cohort.'
quickly	*Adverb*, qualifying the Predicate-verb ' came.'
came	Predicate-verb.
to blows	*Adverbial phrase*, qualifying the Predicate-verb ' came.'
with the enemy.	*Adverbial phrase*, qualifying the Predicate-verb ' came.'

Analysis of the Adjective-clause.

which — *Pronoun*, introducing the Adjective-clause, and serving as Subject-nominative.

had ... crossed — Predicate-verb, compounded of the auxiliary 'had,' and the participle 'crossed.'

already — *Adverb*, qualifying the Predicate-verb 'had ... crossed.'

the — *Definite Article*, qualifying the Objective ' river.'

river. — *Noun*, Objective.

33. I saw the house in which he was born.

I — *Pronoun*, Subject-nominative.

saw — Predicate-verb.

the — *Definite Article*, qualifying the Objective 'house.'

house — *Noun*, Objective.

in which he was born. — *Adjective-clause*, qualifying the Objective ' house.'

Analysis of the Adjective-clause.

in which — *Adverbial phrase*, qualifying the Predicate-verb ' was born.'

he — *Pronoun*, Subject-nominative.

was born. — *Predicate-verb*, compounded of the auxiliary ' was,' and the participle ' born.'

34. I know the man to whom he gave the money.

I — *Pronoun*, Subject-nominative.

know — Predicate-verb.

the — *Definite Article*, qualifying the Objective ' man.'

to whom he gave the — *Adjective-clause*, qualifying the Objective ' man.'

Analysis of the Adjective-clause.

to whom — *Prepositional phrase*, compounded of a preposition and a pronoun, and used as a Secondary Objective.

he — *Pronoun*, Subject-nominative.

gave — Predicate-verb.

the — *Definite Article*, qualifying the Objective ' money.'

money. — *Noun*, Objective (primary).

35. He bought a horse with the money which he had saved.

He — *Pronoun*, Subject-nominative.

bought — Predicate-verb.

a   *Indefinite Article,* qualifying the Objective 'horse.'

horse   *Noun,* Objective.

with the money *Adverbial phrase,* qualifying the Predicate-verb 'bought.'

which he had saved.   *Adjective-clause,* qualifying the noun 'money' in the Adverbial phrase 'with the money.'

Analysis of the Adjective-clause.

which   *Pronoun,* introducing the Adjective-clause, and used as Objective.

he   *Pronoun,* Subject-nominative.

had saved.   Predicate-verb, compounded of the auxiliary 'had,' and the participle 'saved.'

For Contracted and Elliptical Sentences, see Chapter IV.

Long sentences frequently present combinations of the constructions which we have discussed. The student will examine these in his reading. In this place we shall take two examples, given by Dr. Morell, *Grammar,* pp. 91 and 99.

Example I.

A reader unacquainted with the real nature of a classical education will probably undervalue it, when he sees that so large a portion of time is devoted to the study of a few ancient authors, whose works seem to have no direct bearing on the studies and duties of our own generation.

First of all we observe that this Compound Sentence exhibits Correlative clauses:

A reader unacquainted with the real nature of a classical education will probably undervalue it :   *Principal Clause.*

when he sees that so large a portion of time is devoted to the study of a few ancient authors, whose works seem to have no direct bearing on the studies and duties of our own generation.   *Accessory Clause.*

Analysis of the Principal Clause.

A	*Indefinite article,* qualifying the Subject-nominative 'reader.'
reader	*Noun,* Subject-nominative.
unacquainted	*Adjective,* qualifying the Subject-nominative 'reader.'
with the real nature	*Adverbial phrase,* qualifying the Adjective 'unacquainted.'
of a classical education	*Prepositional phrase,* qualifying the Noun 'nature.'
will . . . undervalue	*Predicate-verb,* compounded of the auxiliary 'will,' and the infinitive 'undervalue.'
probably	*Adverb,* qualifying the Predicate-verb 'will undervalue.'
it	*Pronoun,* Objective.

Analysis of the Accessory Clause.

when	*Connective Particle,* introducing the sentence 'he sees,' &c.
he	*Pronoun,* Subject-nominative.
sees	Predicate-verb.
that so large a portion of time is devoted to the study of a few authors.	*Noun-clause,* Objective, dependent upon the Predicate-verb 'sees.'
whose works seem to have no direct bearing on the studies and duties of our own generation.	*Adjective-clause,* qualifying the Noun 'authors.'

Analysis of the Noun-clause.

that	*Connective Particle,* introducing the sentence 'so large a portion,' &c.
so	*Adverb,* qualifying the Adjective 'large.'

large	*Adjective,* qualifying the Subject-nominative ' portion.'
a	*Indefinite Article,* qualifying the Subject-nominative ' portion.'
portion	*Noun,* Subject-nominative.
of time	*Prepositional phrase,* qualifying the Subject-nominative ' portion.'
is devoted	*Predicate-verb,* compounded of the auxiliary ' is,' and the Participle ' devoted.'
to the study	*Adverbial phrase,* qualifying the Predicate-verb ' is devoted.'
of a few authors	*Prepositional phrase,* qualifying the Noun ' study.'

Analysis of the Adjective-clause.

whose	*Pronoun,* introducing the Adjective-clause, and qualifying the Subject-nominative ' works.'
works	*Noun,* Subject-nominative.
seem	Predicate-verb.
to have	*Infinitive,* dependent upon the Predicate-verb ' seem.'
no	*Adjective,* qualifying the Objective ' bearing.'
direct	*Adjective,* qualifying the Objective ' bearing.'
bearing	*Verbal-noun* (or rather, *Infinitive used substantively*), Objective, dependent upon the Infinitive ' to have.'
on the studies and duties	*Prepositional phrase,* dependent upon the Verbal Noun ' bearing ; ' (or, *Adverbial phrase,* dependent upon the Infinitive ' bearing.') *Obs.* The nouns ' studies ' and ' duties ' are coupled by the Conjunction ' and.'
of our own generation.	*Prepositional phrase,* qualifying the Nouns ' studies ' and ' duties.'

Example II.

Bourdaloue is indeed a great reasoner, and inculcates his doctrines with much zeal, piety, and earnestness ; but his style is verbose, he is disagreeably full of quotations from the Fathers, and he wants imagination.

The whole sentence is divided into two sections, separated by the adversative *but.* On the one side, we have a con-

tracted sentence; on the other side, we have three co-
ordinates.

Bourdaloue is indeed a great reasoner, and inculcates his doctrines with much zeal, piety, and earnestness :	*Contracted Sentence.*
(1) his style is verbose,	*Three Co-ordinates.*
(2) he is dis- agreeably full of quotations from the Fathers,	
(3) he wants imagination.	

The third Co-ordinate is joined to the other two, by the
Conjunction *and*.

Analysis of the Contracted Sentence.

By supplying *he* in the second clause, we obtain two co-
ordinate sentences, connected by the Copulative *and* :

    1. Bourdaloue is indeed a great reasoner.
    2. [He] inculcates his doctrines with much zeal, piety,
        and earnestness.

1. Bourdaloue	*Noun,* Subject-nominative.
is	Predicate-verb.
indeed	*Adverb,* qualifying the Predicate-verb ' is.'
a	*Indefinite Article,* qualifying the Predicate-nominative ' reasoner.'
great	*Adjective,* qualifying the Predicate-nominative ' reasoner.'
reasoner.	*Noun,* Predicate-nominative.
2. [He]	*Pronoun,* Subject-nominative.
inculcates	Predicate-verb.
his	*Pronoun in the possessive case,* qualifying the Objective ' doctrines.'
doctrines	*Noun,* Objective.
with much zeal, piety, and earnest- ness :	*Adverbial phrase,* qualifying the Predicate-verb ' inculcates,' and denoting the manner *how.*

Analysis of the Three Co-ordinates.

1. his — *Pronoun in the possessive case*, qualifying the Subject-nominative 'style.'
   style — *Noun*, Subject-nominative.
   is — Predicate-verb.
   verbose, — *Adjective*, Predicate-nominative.
2. he — *Pronoun*, Subject-nominative.
   is — Predicate-verb.
   disagreeably — *Adverb*, qualifying the Predicate-nominative 'full.'
   full — *Adjective*, Predicate-nominative.
   of quotations from the Fathers, — *Prepositional phrase*, dependent upon the Adjective 'full.'
3. he — *Pronoun*, Subject-nominative.
   wants — Predicate-verb.
   imagination. — *Noun*, Objective.

EXERCISES FOR ANALYSIS.

I. SIMPLE SENTENCES.

Subject-Nominative and Predicate-Verb.

1.

1. Time flies.
2. Christmas comes.
3. Winds blow.
4. Snow falls.
5. Ice appears.
6. Boys slide.
7. Men skate.
8. Children sing.
9. Bells ring.
10. Fire burns.
11. Light shines.
12. Joy prevails.

2.

1. Spring returns.
2. Earth smiles.
3. Birds sing.
4. Grass grows.
5. Flowers bloom.
6. Corn springs.
7. Fishes swim.
8. Horses neigh.
9. Boys run.
10. Girls play.
11. Men work.
12. Women sew.

Subject-Nominative, Predicate-Verb, and Predicate-Nominative.

3.

1. Life is short.
2. Art is long.
3. Genius is rare.
4. Vast is art.
5. Narrow is wit.
6. Music is charming.
7. Eloquence is delightful.
8. Extremes are dangerous.
9. Great is truth.
10. Men are fallible.
11. Knowledge is power.
12. Business is business.

4.

1. Virtue is bold.
2. Unbelief is blind.
3. Light is sweet.
4. Trial comes unsought.
5. Harry seems wise.
6. Mary grows tall.
7. Thoughts lie deep.
8. Flowers look pretty.
9. Roses appear fair.
10. Knowledge is good.
11. Boys become idle.
12. Tasks seem heavy.

Qualifications of the Subject-Nominative.

N.B. The Articles *a* and *the* are considered qualifications.

5.

1. The climate is good.
2. Fertile is the island.
3. The proper study of mankind is man.
4. Sweet are the uses of adversity.
5. The road was bad.
6. The storm was boisterous.
7. True hope is swift.
8. His life was gentle.
9. Musical is Apollo's lute.

6.

1. Sweet is the breath of morn.
2. Pleasant is the sun.
3. The better part of valour is discretion.
4. Charming is divine philosophy.
5. Hard are the ways of truth.
6. The air, a chartered libertine, is free.
7. The virtue of prosperity is temperance.
8. The virtue of adversity is fortitude.

Qualifications of the Predicate-Nominative.

7.

1. Order is Heaven's first law.
2. Expression is the dress of thought.
3. Music is the food of love.
4. Full of shapes is fancy.
5. Beauty is a flower.
6. Procrastination is the thief of time.
7. Lowliness is young ambition's ladder.
8. Sufferance is the badge of all our tribe.
9. Mercy is an attribute to God himself.
10. Brutus is an honourable man.

8.

1. Brevity is the soul of wit.
2. God is the spring of good.
3. Love is the star to every wandering bark.

4. Service is no heritage.
5. Fortune is no goddess.
6. Pride is the vice of fools.
7. Prosperity is the blessing of the Old Testament.
8. He was in logic a great critic.
9. Fraud is the ready minister of injustice.
10. She was a maid of grace.
11. They are the faction.

Miscellaneous.

9.

1. A little learning is a dangerous thing.
2. True wit is nature to advantage dressed.
3. All nature is but art.
4. The art itself is nature.
5. Virtue alone is happiness below.
6. All the world is a stage.
7. The fairest flowers of the season are our carnations.
8. The happy only are the truly great.
9. Good sense is the gift of Heaven.
10. The child is father of the man.
11. A double blessing is a double grace.

Qualifications of the Predicate-Verb.

10.

1. A merry heart goes all the day.
2. Cowards die many times before their deaths.
3. There eternal summer dwells.
4.   The Muses in a ring
Aye round about Jove's altar sing.
5. Hard by a cottage chimney smokes.
6. Now fades the glimmering landscape on the sight.
7. So sinks the day-star in the ocean bed.
8. In gallant trim the gilded vessel goes.
9. The lowing herd winds slowly o'er the lea.
10. The river glideth at his own sweet will.

11.

1. The third day comes a frost.
2.   My high-blown pride
At length broke under me.
3. Joy delights in joy.

4. This wine tastes sour.
5. The speech reads well.
6. The rose smells sweet.
7. The violet smells sweetly.
8. A light heart lives long.
9. The merchant from the exchange returns in peace.
10. True ease in writing comes from art.

Miscellaneous.

12.

1. Grace was in all her steps.
2. The time is out of joint.
3. Slow rises worth by poverty depressed.
4. Hope springs eternal in the human breast.
5. Men, at some time, are masters of their fates.
6. Such harmony is in immortal souls.
7.   His former name
Is heard no more in Heaven.
8. All looks yellow to the jaundiced eye.
9. An old man is twice a child.
10. All colours agree in the dark.

The Objective, with or without Qualifications.

13.

1. Eloquence charms the soul.
2. Song charms the sense.
3. Crafty men contemn studies.
4. Gentle dulness ever loves a joke.
5. Children bring cares.
6. Love rules the court.
7. Full many a gem, of purest ray serene,
The dark unfathomed caves of ocean bear.
8. Some natural tears they dropped.
9. Not always actions show the man.
10. The childhood shows the man.
11. The apparel oft proclaims the man.

14.

1. There entertain him all the saints above.
2. Bacchus from out the purple grape
Crushed the sweet poison of misused wine.

3.   Now the herald lark
    Left his ground-nest.
4. Children gather pebbles on the shore.
5. The ruling passion conquers reason still.
6. Virtue itself escapes not calumny.
7. The widow in distress he graciously relieved.
8. Time hath a wallet at his back.
9. His eye begets occasion for his wit.
10. Roses have thorns.
11. On her white breast a sparkling cross she wore.
12. Her lively looks a sprightly mind disclose.

15.

1. Charms strike the sight.
2. Merit wins the soul.
3. Here Britain's statesmen oft the fall foredoom
    Of foreign tyrants.
4. They speak the glory of the British Queen.
5. Wise Peter sees the world's respect for gold.
6. Nature hath framed strange fellows in her time.
7. Education forms the common mind.
8. The power of music all our hearts allow.
9. Every shepherd tells his tale,
    Under the hawthorn, in the dale.
10. Cassius from bondage will deliver Cassius.
11. Honest plain words best pierce the ear of grief.

The Complement-Objective.

16.

1. One touch of nature makes the whole world kin.
2. Perseverance keeps honour bright.
3. They make themselves the measure of mankind.
4. God calleth preaching folly.
5. Histories make men wise.
6. I will make assurance doubly sure.
7. Your wit makes wise things foolish.

The Complement-Nominative.

17.

1. Some are born great.
2. Lowly feigning is called compliment.
3. Now is the winter of our discontent
    Made glorious summer by this sun of York.

4. The prisoner was declared innocent.
5. Henry, his son, is chosen king.
6. Louis of France was elected chief of the expedition.
7. He was appointed ruler over the people.

The Secondary Objective.

18.

1. A subtle happiness thou to thyself proposest.
2. Nature to all things fixed the limits fit.
3. Some to conceit alone their taste confine.
4.   His silver hairs
   Will purchase us a good opinion.
5. The valiant never taste of death but once.
6.   This isle
   He quarters to his blue-haired deities.
7.   A sable cloud
   Turns forth her silver lining on the night.
8. Misery acquaints a man with strange bedfellows.
9. A golden mind stoops not to shows of dross.
10. All my engagements I will construe to thee.
11. To whom our fathers would not obey.

The Subject-Accusative.

19.

1. I know that virtue to be in you, Brutus.
2. All men think all men mortal, but themselves.
3. At thirty, man suspects himself a fool.
4. He thought content the good to be enjoyed.
5. We think our fathers fools.
6. He soon perceived me to be unfit for his service.
7. We found her in her answers to have an eloquent tongue.

The Infinitive used Substantively.

20.

1. All our knowledge is ourselves to know.
2. Not to know some trifles is a praise.
3. Every man desireth to live long.
4. To spend too much time in studies is sloth.
5. To be dull is construed to be good.
6. To gild refined gold is wasteful excess.
7. It is cruelty to beat a cripple with his own crutches.

8. To seek philosophy in Scripture is to seek the dead
   among the living.
9. To seek religion in Nature is to seek the living among
   the dead.

21.

1. Not to know me argues yourselves unknown.
2. To teach a teacher ill beseemeth me.
3. 'Tis phrase absurd to call a villain great.
4. Our humbler province is to tend the fair.
5. That same prayer doth teach us all to render the deeds
   of mercy.
6. 'Tis not in mortals to command success.
7. It is not for your health thus to commit
   Your weak condition to the raw cold morning.
8. To err is human.
9. To forgive is divine.

Forms in -ing.
A. *Infinitives* or *Gerunds*, and
Verbal Substantives.

22.

1. All friendship is feigning.
2. All loving is mere folly.
3. Borrowing dulls the edge of husbandry.
4. The falling out of faithful friends
   Renewing is of love.
5. Well doing is wealth.
6. Of making many books there is no end.
7. I blame you not for praising Cæsar so.
8. Knowing him is enough.
9. You have condemned Lucius for taking bribes of the
   Sardians.
10. Reading maketh a full man.
11. Writing maketh an exact man.
12. Teaching is the best way of learning.
13. Wiving goes by destiny.

B. *Participles in -ing.*

23.

1. The rolling stone gathers no moss.
2. The poet's eye, in a fine frenzy rolling,
   Doth glance from heaven to earth.

3. Life is but a walking shadow.
4. Poetry is a speaking picture.
5. Envy is that dark shadow ever waiting upon a shining merit.
6.   Wandering o'er the earth,
By falsities and lies the greatest part
Of mankind they corrupted.

Gerund with 'to.'

24.

1. Under leave of Brutus
Come I to speak in Cæsar's funeral.
2. Hither the heroes resort
To taste awhile the pleasures of a court.
3. I have spoke thus much
To mitigate the justice of thy plea.
4. A pious man was duly brought
To shrieve the dying.
5.   Here comes in embassy
The French king's daughter with yourself to speak.
6. That is enough to satisfy the senate.
7. I come not to steal away your hearts.
8. I must be cruel, only to be kind.

Miscellaneous.

25.

1. A thing of beauty is a joy for ever.
2. The quality of mercy is not strained.
3. Thou art a monument without a tomb.
4. There is a tide in the affairs of men.
5. I will talk a word with this same learned Theban.
6. Solitude is sometimes the best society.
7. Want of decency is want of sense.
8. Thy wish was father to that thought.

26.

1. This was the noblest Roman of them all.
2. Idleness is not real pleasure.
3. Agreeable occupation is real pleasure.
4. Men are but children of a larger growth.
5. Fair ladies masked are roses in their bud.
6. Tyrants seldom want pretexts.
7. The world is still deceived with ornament.
8. His sceptre shows the force of temporal power.

COMPOUND SENTENCES.

I. CO-ORDINATE SENTENCES.

1. *Co-ordinate Sentences, standing side by side, without any Connecting Particle.*

27.

1. E'en from the tomb the voice of nature cries,
   E'en in our ashes live their wonted fires.
2. Small herbs have grace,
   Ill weeds do thrive apace.
3. Through tattered clothes small vices do appear,
   Robes hide all.
4. The cause is in my will; I will not come.
5. To be contents his natural desire,
   He asks no angel's wing.
6. Self-love, the spring of motion, acts the soul;
   Reason's comparing balance rules the whole.
7. Great Nature spoke; observant man obeyed;
   Cities were formed; societies were made.
8. Antiquity is the young state of the world; the present time is the real antiquity.
9. No work is a disgrace; the true disgrace is idleness.

2. *Copulative.*

28.

1. The vine still clings to the mouldering wall,
   And at every gust the dead leaves fall.
2. Thus to relieve the wretched was his pride,
   And e'en his failings leaned to virtue's side.
3. Jason the Thessalian proposed the plan, Agesilaus the Spartan, attempted its execution, and Alexander the Macedonian finally achieved the conquest.
4. The people are like the sea; and orators are like the wind.
5. Of all virtues, goodness is the greatest; and without it man is a busy, mischievous, wretched thing.
6. A friend loveth at all times; and a brother is born for adversity.

7. A fool's mouth is his destruction; and his lips are the
snare of his soul.

8.   His face
Deep scars of thunder had intrenched; and care
Sat on his faded cheek.

3. *Alternative.*

29.

1. Either there is a civil strife in heaven,
Or else the world, too saucy with the gods,
Incenses them to send destruction.
2. Either he is innocent, or he is the most crafty rogue in
the country.
3. Either your brethren have miserably deceived us, or power
confers virtue.
4. He will either come himself, or he will send a representative.
5. The king must win, or he must forfeit his crown for
ever.
6. He arrived in time, or I should have been lost.
7. Cæsar was an able commander, or Gaul would not have
been conquered.

Adversative.

30.

1. Every subject's duty is the king's; but every subject's soul
is his own.
2. It is an honour for a man to cease from strife; but every
fool will be meddling.
3. The demonstrations of logic are common to all mankind;
but the persuasion of rhetoric must be varied according
to the audience.
4. A fool speaks all his mind; but a wise man reserves something for hereafter.
5. Counsel in the heart of a man is like deep water; but a
wise man will draw it out.
6. Knowledge puffeth up; but charity buildeth up.
7. The wise man's eyes are in his head; but the fool walketh
in darkness.
8. A superficial tincture of philosophy may incline the mind
to atheism; yet a farther knowledge brings it back to
religion.

9. Learning makes the mind gentle; whereas ignorance renders it churlish.
10. We are commanded to forgive our enemies; but we are nowhere commanded to forgive our friends.

II. COMPOUND SENTENCES EXHIBITING CORRELATIVE CLAUSES.

31.

1. But when he once attains the upmost round,
   He then unto the ladder turns his back.
2. Licence they mean when they cry liberty.
3.   To the noble mind
   Rich gifts wax poor, when givers prove unkind.
4. He had a fever, when he was in Spain.
5. Since Cassius first did whet me against Cæsar,
   I have not slept.
6. When beggars die, there are no comets seen.
7. When I spoke that, I was ill-tempered too.
8. From lowest place, when virtuous things proceed,
   The place is dignified by the doer's deed.

32.

1. Fools rush in, where angels fear to tread.
2. He lay still, where he fell.
3. The tongues of mocking damsels are as keen
   As is the razor's edge.
4. Because I love you, I will let you know.
5. Since you can cog, I will play no more with you.
6. If we lose this battle, then is this
   The very last time we shall speak together.
7. If this were true, then should I know this secret.
8. If I live, I will be good to thee.
9. Thou canst not die by traitors
   Unless thou bringest them with thee.

33.

1. I must not give you the book, for it is not mine.
2. As the tree falls, so it will lie.
3.   He cannot thrive
   Unless her prayers reprieve him from the wrath
   Of greatest justice.

4.   If he were honester
He were much goodlier.

5. If I be not deceived, you are an Athenian.

6. He were no lion, were not Romans hinds.

7. The mountain is so high, that there is always snow on the top of it.

8. If it were so, it was a grievous fault.

9. For the strait gate would be made straiter yet,
Were none admitted there but men of wit.

34.

1. As the sun breaks through the darkest clouds,
So honour peereth in the meanest habit.

2. Freely we serve, because we freely love.

3. Thy tooth is not so keen,
Because thou art not seen.

4. Murder, though it hath no tongue, will speak
With most miraculous organ.

5. The people perished so fast, that it was impossible for the survivors to perform the rites of sepulture.

6. Although we seldom followed advice, we were all ready enough to ask it.

7. Wherever they marched, their route was marked with blood.

35.

1. Unless a critic is well acquainted with the sciences, his diligence will be attended with danger.

2. Clothes cannot be made to fit, unless measure of the body be first taken.

3. The nature of the mind would be unruffled, if the affections did not disturb it.

4. If too great a burden be laid upon a middling genius, it blunts the cheerful spirit of hope.

5. If the tasks are too light, a great loss is sustained, in the amount of progress.

6. If Cæsar had been conquered, he would have become more odious than Catiline.

7. If we begin with certainties, we shall end in doubts.

8. If we begin with doubts, we shall end in certainties.

9. If I were not Alexander, I would be Diogenes.

P

III. COMPOUND SENTENCES, COMPRISING SUBORDINATE CLAUSES.

1. *The Noun-clause.*

36.

1. That you have wronged me, appears in this.
2. The congregated college have concluded
   That labouring art can never ransom nature.
3. No man can wade deep in learning, without discovering
   that he knows nothing thoroughly.
4. The opinion of all men was, that the undertaking was
   doubtful.
5. Yet some maintain that to this day she is a living
   child.
6.   Consider this,   ·
   That, in the course of justice, none of us
   Should see salvation.
7. He showed how fields were won.
8. The heart distrusting asks, if this be joy.

37.

1. That a historian should not record trifles is perfectly
   true.
2. That we cannot is pretended; that we will not is the
   true reason.
3. It occasionally happened that his wit obtained the
   mastery over his other faculties.
4. He asked that he might be restored to his former state.
5. He wished to know, where I was.
6. They asked, whether he would come.
7. The good woman saw at once, that her son was a poet.

2. *The Adjective-clause.*

38.

1. Ill blows the wind that profits nobody.
2. He jests at scars that never felt a wound.
3. They also serve, who only wait.
4. Fame is no plant that grows on mortal soil.
5. He talks to me, that never had a son.

6. Uneasy lies the head that wears a crown.
7. All that glitters is not gold.
8. He is well paid that is well satisfied.

39.

1. Thrice is he armed that hath his quarrel just.
2.   The play is the thing,
Wherein I'll catch the conscience of the king.
3.   Yon gray lines,
That fret the clouds, are messengers of day.
4. The evil that men do lives after them.
5. I, that denied the gold, will give my heart.
6. Thou art the ruins of the noblest man
That ever lived in the tide of times.
7. He that is down need fear no fall.
8. Ill fares the land, to hastening ills a prey,
Where wealth accumulates.

CONTRACTED SENTENCES.

40.

1. Cæsar and Pompey fought for victory.
2. William and Mary are a happy couple.
3. The Gauls crossed the Alps, and invaded Italy.
4. Cæsar crossed the Rubicon, and marched to Rome.
5. He must sail, or sell.
6. I come to bury Cæsar, not to praise him.
7. Neither John nor his brother was present.
8. He is a good writer, but a bad speaker.
9. Good nature and good sense must ever join ;
To err is human, to forgive divine.

41.

1. For we will shake him, or worse days endure.
2. Some guide the course of wandering orbs on high,
Or roll the planets through the boundless sky.
3. Men may be read, as well as books, too much.
4. Nor stony tower, nor walls of beaten brass,
Nor airless dungeon, nor strong links of iron,
Can be retentive to the strength of spirit.
5. Stone walls do not a prison make,
Nor iron bars a cage.

6. Princes and lords may flourish, or may fade ;
   A breath can make them, as a breath has made.
7. He tried each art, reproved each dull delay,
   Allured to brighter worlds, and led the way.

ELLIPTICAL SENTENCES.

42.

1. He is as tall as I.
2. They love him, more than I.
3. They love him, more than me.
4. This is the man I saw.
5. There's not a joy the world can give,
   Like that it takes away.
6. Who reasons wisely is not therefore wise.
7. Who steals my purse, steals trash.
8. To me more dear, congenial to my heart,
   One native charm, than all the gloss of art.

43.

1. That is the book I gave you.
2. This is the house we live in.
3. This is the way they came.
4. He left the day I arrived.
5. He arrived the day that I left.
6. Thomas is the same as ever.
7. Henry did as he was bidden.

LONDON: PRINTED BY
SPOTTISWOODE AND CO., NEW-STREET SQUARE
AND PARLIAMENT STREET